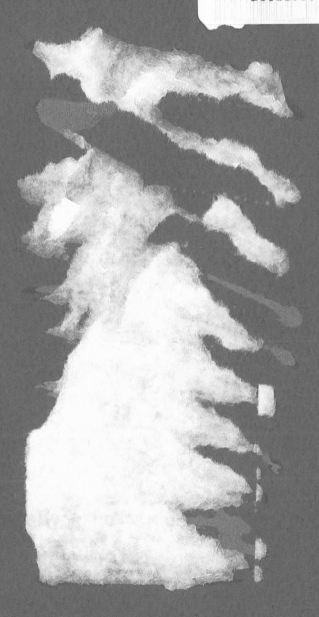

Solzhenitsyn
and
Dostoevsky

VLADISLAV KRASNOV

Solzhenitsyn

and

Dostoevsky

A Study in the Polyphonic Novel

54694

THE
UNIVERSITY OF GEORGIA PRESS
ATHENS

Copyright © 1980 by The University of Georgia Press
Athens 30602

All rights reserved

Set in 11 on 13 point Times Roman type
Printed in the United States of America

Library of Congress Cataloging in Publication Data

Krasnov, Vladislav.
    Solzhenitsyn and Dostoevsky.
    Bibliography.
    Includes index.
    1. Solzhenitsyn, Aleksandr Isaevich, 1918– —Crit-
icism and interpretation. 2. Dostoevskiĭ, Fedor Mi-
khaĭlovich, 1821–1881—Influence. I. Title.
PG3488.04Z725   891.7′3′44   79-70
                ISBN 0-8203-0472-7

TO THE MEMORY OF
MIKHAIL BAKHTIN
(1895–1975)

Contents

Preface	ix
Introduction: The Concept of Polyphony	1
I: Voices from the Inferno	13
II: Stalin, or the Epigone of the Grand Inquisitor	24
III: Rubin, or Ivan in the Hands of the Grand Inquisitor	35
IV: Sologdin, or the Way of a Superman	43
V: Nerzhin, or the Way of a Saintly Hero	53
VI: Innokenty Volodin's Crime and Punishment	69
VII: "No Main Hero," or a Galaxy of Stars	79
VIII: Duality of Setting: Authenticity and Symbolism	96
IX: Structure: A Cathedral, an Ark, a Vicious Circle	108
X: A Language of Dialogue and a Dialogue of Languages	123
XI: The Question of Genre: *The First Circle* as a Menippean Novel	138
XII: Polyphony of *Cancer Ward*	143
XIII: The Unperceived Signal, or *August 1914* as an Anti-Tolstoyan Poem	173
Conclusion: Spiritual Realism, or Solzhenitsyn as a Synthesizer	198
Notes	203
Bibliography	219
Index	223

So perhaps the old triunity of Truth, Goodness, and Beauty is not simply the decorous and antiquated formula it seemed to us at the time of our self-confident materialistic youth. If the tops of these trees do converge, as thinkers used to claim, and if the all too obvious and the overly straight sprouts of Truth and Goodness have been crushed, cut down, or not permitted to grow, then perhaps the whimsical, unpredictable, and ever surprising shoots of Beauty will force their way through and soar up to *that very spot*, thereby fulfilling the task of all three?

And then no slip of the tongue but a prophecy would be contained in Dostoevsky's words: "Beauty will save the world." For it was given to *him* to see many things; he had astonishing flashes of insight.

Aleksandr Solzhenitsyn

The emergence of Aleksandr Solzhenitsyn is the greatest miracle in the art of letters in a long time . . . [his] work is a watershed, a milestone in the history of the novelistic art. His books constitute the authoritative verdict on the post-modern era in which we live. These books present a challenge to that indulgence in form, that crypticism, that lascivious snobbery and exaggerated stylization which mark a great deal of the most admired literature of recent years.

Ruth Halldén

Preface

IT WAS IN the summer of 1967 that I first noted an affinity between Solzhenitsyn and Dostoevsky. A year later, when I was reading *The First Circle*, the major thesis of this book was conceived. Solzhenitsyn's subsequent works have affirmed my conviction and have thus given increased point to my endeavor. Having defended my doctoral thesis on the polyphony of *The First Circle* in 1974, it was only a matter of time before my work expanded to *Cancer Ward* and *August 1914*.

Since most of the criticism on the subject is not to be found in Russian, I determined at the outset to write this book in English rather than my native tongue. Russian names are spelled according to the most common English translations. This includes my own name, in spite of its legal spelling with the Ws for Vs. Russian words and expressions are spelled according to the Library of Congress transliteration.

Acknowledgments are due to George Ivask of the University of Massachusetts for introducing me to the works of the late Mikhail Bakhtin; E. Harold Swayze and Willis Konick of the University of Washington for constructive criticism of my doctoral thesis; Sidney Monas of the University of Texas for taking time to read the first rough chapters and offering a frank opinion; Marcie Shapiro for typing several difficult chapters; Alice Chaffee and Dorothy James for editing the first draft; Yefim Etkind of the University of Paris for reading the first version, accepting its basic thesis and encouraging me to submit it to a university press; Melvin Bradford and his American literature students for their unwavering admiration of Solzhenitsyn and an earnest interest in the progress of my work; Larry Allums for taking time out of his thesis to help with mine;

Serge Zenkovsky of Vanderbilt University, Ludmila Koehler of the University of Pittsburgh, Edward E. Ericson, Jr., of Calvin College, and Jeremy R. Azrael of the University of Chicago for encouraging responses after reading the manuscript; Michael Holquist of the University of Texas for sharing his unpublished materials on Bakhtin; to Mary Suarez and Lauran Lofgren of Southern Methodist University for typing the final draft on short notice; and to Richard Evidon for performing the difficult chore of minimizing the non-native qualities of my English. The index and the final preparation of the text were done with the aid of a grant from the Earhart Foundation.

I am also indebted to my wife Hiroko for graciously subordinating our family life to my work.

Special thanks go to Solzhenitsyn himself for challenging the world with his books impenetrable to bookworms.

Solzhenitsyn
and
Dostoevsky

The Concept of Polyphony

IN THEIR ATTEMPTS to determine Solzhenitsyn's place in Russian literature most critics link him with Lev Tolstoy, finding him similar both stylistically and as a thinker.[1] His similarities with Dostoevsky, on the other hand, are usually considered accidental or superficial. However, Solzhenitsyn himself indicated that his similarity with Dostoevsky, the founder of polyphony in the novel, may be more profound than is usually assumed when he called his own favorite genre and method polyphonic. Ever since then, the term has been used by certain critics in reference to his novels. Gustaw Herling-Grudziński accepted it without question in his review of *The First Circle*. Ludmila Koehler used it to describe the artistic method of *Cancer Ward*. Dorothy Atkinson called both *Cancer Ward* and *The First Circle* polyphonic because in them "we are auditors of the inner voices of numerous characters." Edward Brown admitted that "the novels are polyphonic in the sense that there are frequent shifts from one dominant viewpoint to another; they are structured from many competing centers of attention." Leonid Rzhevsky spoke of *The First Circle*'s polyphonic structure as representing the novel's two choirs, the one of victims and that of their captors. Abraham Rothberg, writing on the same novel in his book *Aleksandr Solzhenitsyn: The Major Novels*, referred to "a polyphonic arrangement" of the characters. David Burg and George Feifer in their book *Solzhenitsyn* directly identified the writer's "theory of the novel" with polyphony, saying that "his revival of the difficult and seldom-used method was largely responsible

for the great sweep and universality of his work." Henning
Falkenstein treated both *The First Circle* and *Cancer Ward*
in a chapter titled "Der polyphone Roman." And finally,
Christopher Moody, in his assessment of the structure of *August 1914*, also seems to accept Solzhenitsyn's utterance about
polyphony.[2]

Yet, despite the fact that many critics have endorsed Solzhenitsyn's opinion, virtually no one has tried to assess its full
significance or paid attention to its wider implications or attempted to examine his work in the light of this definition. The
whole issue of polyphony in his work remains neglected, however benignly.[3] Above all, the question of his affinity with
Dostoevsky, so clearly evoked by this statement, remains unanswered. While recognizing that an author's pronouncements
about his own work should generally not be considered in any
degree binding for his critics, I think that this one deserves
more attention and should be taken into account before any
critical judgment of Solzhenitsyn's art can be made.

The statement's relative neglect by the critics can be partly
explained by their lack of familiarity with it or with the cultural climate in which it was made or with the notion of polyphony.[4] Solzhenitsyn's interview with the Slovak journalist
Pavel Ličko, in which the remarks were made, was not widely
publicized. It originally appeared in the Bratislava newspaper
Kultúrny život on 31 March 1967. Although in that year the
complete interview was also published both in Polish and in a
Russian émigré newspaper, only excerpts from it appeared
in English, and the statement on polyphony was not among
them.[5]

Here is the portion of the interview which contains the remarks in question, translated into English from the Slovak:

> Which genre do I consider the most interesting? A polyphonic
> novel strictly defined in time and space. A novel without a
> main hero. If a novel has a main hero the author inevitably
> pays more attention and devotes more space to him. How do I

understand polyphony? Each person becomes the main hero as soon as the action reverts to him. Then the author feels responsible for as many as thirty-five heroes. He does not accord preferential treatment to any one. He must understand every character and motivate his actions. In any case he should not lose the ground under his feet. I employed this method in writing two books and I intend to use it in writing a third one.[6]

It is clear that Solzhenitsyn identified both his favorite genre and preferred artistic method as polyphony, thus attaching to the notion a singular importance for the understanding of his art. At the time he had just finished *Cancer Ward*, and *The First Circle* had been completed in 1964; these are the two novels which in retrospect he calls polyphonic. The third novel referred to must be the cycle on revolution, the first part of which has appeared under the title *August 1914*. Although Solzhenitsyn mentions neither Dostoevsky nor Bakhtin, it is quite clear from his explanation of polyphony that the notion was not his own—he merely availed himself of one that had been in rather wide circulation among Soviet literary scholars ever since Bakhtin's pioneering research on Dostoevsky's poetics was "rehabilitated" in 1963.

Mikhail Mikhailovich Bakhtin (1895–1975) was born at Orel into an old noble family, prominent in the Russian cultural life of the last century. He graduated from the Gymnasium in Odessa, and in 1913 enrolled in the history and philology department of Odessa University, soon transferring to Petersburg University, where his teachers included D. K. Petrov, a distinguished Hispanicist and follower of Baudouin de Courtenay, A. N. Veselovsky, a founder of the modern study of comparative literature, and the great classicist F. F. Zelinsky. During his student years Bakhtin acquired a vast knowledge of the works of classical and modern, especially German, philosophers. He graduated from Petersburg University in 1918, after the Bolsheviks had taken over. During the Civil War he found himself in Vitebsk, which became a refuge for

a number of prominent cultural personalities of the time.
There he soon formed a circle a friends which would come to
be known as the "Bakhtin School"; among his disciples were
P. N. Medvedev, V. N. Voloshinov, and I. I. Sollertinsky.
Although Bakhtin moved to Leningrad in 1924, the school
proved productive through the publication of *Freidizm* (Freudianism) and *Marksizm i filosofiia iazyka* (Marxism and the
philosophy of language), which appeared under the name of
Voloshinov, and *Formal'nyi metod v literaturovedenii* (The
formal method in the study of literature), which was published
under the name of Medvedev. Under his own name Bakhtin
published *Problemy tvorchestva Dostoevskogo* (Problems of
Dostoevsky's art) in 1929;[7] shortly after the publication he
was arrested, imprisoned and exiled for several years, and persecuted until Stalin's death in 1953. His book on Dostoevsky
was "rehabilitated" only in 1963 and his dissertation on
Rabelais, for which he was denied a doctorate in 1946, was
not published until 1965. In 1957 he was put in charge of the
literature department of the Mordovian University in Saransk,
but was forced to retire in 1961 because of declining health.
He died in 1975.[8]

The notion of polyphony was first introduced by Bakhtin in
his 1929 book on Dostoevsky. In spite of a favorable review
by no less than Anatoly Lunacharsky,[9] a former commissar of
education and highly influential in the cultural politics of the
time, the book soon came under attack by literary dogmatists.
Labeled "formalist," it was fated to vanish from the literary
scene for over three decades.

The book's main thesis may be summed up as follows:
Dostoevsky's principal achievement as an artist lies in the creation of a new type of novel called *polyphonic* in contradistinction to the *homophonic* novels of such writers as Lev
Tolstoy, Turgenev, and Goncharov. (Bakhtin also uses the
terms *dialogical* versus *monological*.) The polyphonic novel
is distinguished by the strong presence of consciousnesses and

voices other than the author's. Characters in such a novel are no longer objects manipulated by the author, as Bakhtin claims they are in a homophonic novel, but subjects coexisting as autonomous worlds with the world of the author and contending with him for the reader's attention. The author expresses himself, then, not so much through one character or another, but chiefly through the structure of the novel. According to Bakhtin this polyphonic technique, rooted in Dostoevsky's vision of the world, permeates all elements of his novels, including their language, and provides the key for their understanding.[10]

Bakhtin's book was remarkable not only for its daring attempt to single out Dostoevsky from his Russian contemporaries on purely artistic grounds, but also for the method of literary criticism used in it. In the preface Bakhtin describes his methodological ideal as a combination of synchronic (theoretical) and diachronic (historical) approaches, insisting that the two are interdependent aspects of a unified process of critical evaluation. Admitting that, for technical reasons, his study of Dostoevsky is mainly synchronic, Bakhtin assures his readers that all his findings have been examined in the context of the history of genres. The preface makes clear that the source of his methodological inspiration was the same as that of the formalists. In his book *Russian Formalism* Victor Erlich observes, for instance:

> Not unlike Structuralist linguistics, with which it had so much in common, Formalist criticism sought to bridge the gap between what Ferdinand de Saussure had called the "synchronic" and "diachronic" approaches to language, i.e., between descriptive and historical studies.[11]

It would be wrong, however, to equate Bakhtin's approach with that of his fellow Soviet formalists. For one thing, his conviction that "every literary work is inherently, immanently sociologic" was certainly not shared by most of them.[12] He particularly rejected the "narrow formalistic" approach which

does not go "beyond the periphery of the form" in respect to
Dostoevsky's work. On the other hand, he also rejected the
then prevailing "narrow ideological" approach to Dostoevsky, for it was totally preoccupied with the author's ideological
pronouncements, often confused with those of his characters,
and paid no attention to that ideology "which determined the
artistic form" of his novels. Bakhtin differs from the "narrow
Formalists" in going far "beyond the periphery of the form."

Although the purpose of Bakhtin's study was purely stylistic, the book abounds in philosophical and sociohistorical remarks of a more general nature. If these remarks do not appear
irrelevant to the book's intentions, it is because they shed light
on the relationship between Dostoevsky's metaphysics and his
artistic strategy. More precisely, Bakhtin considers Dostoevsky's polyphonic technique a function of his "form-determining ideology." Defining the latter as an essentially Christian
world view, Bakhtin suggests that its cornerstones should be
sought in the ideas of personalism, pluralism, coexistence, and
interaction.[13] A measure of his intellectual integrity is evinced
by the fact that he uses the first two notions in defiance of the
official Soviet ban on them as being "antiscientific" and "reactionary," while the latter two clearly imply a challenge to
the perennial Soviet objection to an ideological coexistence.[14]
As to the ideology underlying the homophonic form of art,
Bakhtin defines it as "ideological monologism," which he
considers to have been a determining influence on all aspects
of the cultural life of modern times. Having learned the essen-
tials of formalist criticism, Bakhtin appears to have reached
beyond most formalists.

By singling out Dostoevsky from his contemporaries as the
founder of the polyphonic novel and the polyphonic conception of literature, Bakhtin not only suggested that a reevalua-
tion of the whole heritage of the Russian classical novel was
necessary, but also raised the inevitable question of the direction in which Soviet literature was to go. His answer was un-

equivocal: the most promising direction would be taken by following in the footsteps of Dostoevsky's polyphony rather than in the "homophonic" tradition of Lev Tolstoy, Turgenev, and Goncharov. However, though he insisted that polyphony is most in tune with the twentieth-century world, Bakhtin was far from denying the viability of "monological" art, and envisioned a coexistence of the two. Unfortunately, even as he wrote that Dostoevsky was the most influential model among writers in Russia and abroad, the trend of Russian literature was clearly toward what later became known as socialist realism. Not only was socialist realism the most monological form of art, but it was later to establish, with the help of extraliterary means, an exclusive monopoly on Soviet art, one which to a great extent still exists. Its proponents would tolerate neither polyphony nor even any monologism other than their own. Keenly aware of this problem, Bakhtin concluded his book in 1929 with a warning addressed to those who would oppose polyphony in literature and suppress it in life:

> Any attempt to render this world as completed, in the usual monological sense of this word, as subdued to one idea and one voice, is inevitably doomed to defeat.[15]

The warning proved justified: the country as well as its literature were indeed soon totally "subdued to one idea and one voice." As a result, Bakhtin's book on Dostoevsky was suppressed, its author persecuted for decades,[16] and Dostoevsky's writings relegated to a virtually underground existence. But the warning also proved prophetic: in the wake of de-Stalinization Bakhtin's book was not only rehabilitated but also published in a revised and enlarged edition under a new title, *Problemy poètiki Dostoevskogo* (Problems of Dostoevsky's poetics).[17]

In the new edition Bakhtin did not change his basic views; nor did he change his methodology. In fact, by adding to the synchronic study of 1929 an extensive diachronic excursus

into the history of genres, he came closer to his stated methodological ideal. This excursus constitutes perhaps the most important addition to his original book. Noting that Dostoevsky's
novels belong to a different "genre type" (*zhanrovyi tip*) than
those of Lev Tolstoy, Turgenev, and Goncharov, he proceeded
to establish their genetic link with the seriocomic genres of
antiquity, most notably, the Socratic dialogues and Menippean
satire. In the process he launched his theory of the "carnival world view" (*karnalval' noe mirooshchushchenie*) and the
"carnivalization of literature" as an important source for the
development of certain genre peculiarities of Dostoevsky's
novels. He came to the conclusion that although Dostoevsky
was a true founder of polyphony, the outward form of his polyphonic novels was essentially prepared by the long tradition of
"carnivalized literature" stretching from ancient Greece and
Rome through early Christian literature, and then through
Dante, Cervantes, and Shakespeare to Balzac, Poe, Pushkin,
and Gogol.

While concentrating on Dostoevsky's poetics, the 1963 edition is particularly emphatic about the general cultural significance of polyphony. In Bakhtin's view Dostoevsky's artistic
innovation is not an isolated matter of stylistics, but concerns
"prime principles of European aesthetics." In fact, he goes so
far as to proclaim Dostoevsky the originator of a "completely
new type of artistic thinking" (which for want of a better word
he also called polyphonic) and the creator of a "new artistic
model of the world." Discussing Dostoevsky's "form-determining ideology" he not only continues to operate with the
"reactionary" notions of personalism and pluralism, but dares
to oppose "polyphonic artistic thinking" to the "monological
principle" which he considers the trademark of modern times:

> In modern times European rationalism with its cult of unified
> and sole reason, and particularly the Enlightenment, during
> which the basic genres of European prose were formed, con-
> tributed to the strengthening of the monological principle and

to its penetration into all spheres of ideological life. All European utopism is also founded on this monological principle.
And so is Utopian socialism with its belief in the omnipotence
of persuasion.[18]

Here Bakhtin clearly echoes Dostoevsky's negative attitude to
European rationalism, the Enlightenment, and socialism. Although he does not single out the Marxist, "scientific" kind
of socialism, the passage may be seen as a challenge to one
of the holiest premises of the Soviet experiment, the belief in
the "omnipotence of persuasion."

Despite the fact that the rehabilitation of his book was largely due to Lunacharsky's favorable review, Bakhtin repudiates
his intimations that polyphony is time-bound to capitalism. He
insists that at this very moment there is an acute need for polyphony which, in his view, is unique in its capability for up-
dating the artistic consciousness of modern man in accordance
with the reality of "the Einsteinian world with its plurality of
systems of measurement." [19]

The rehabilitation of Bakhtin's scholarly study did not pass
unnoticed in the USSR. In fact, it stirred up a more than
scholarly controversy, of which Mihajlo Mihajlov gives the
following account in his book *Moscow Summer* (1964):

Bakhtin's rehabilitation followed his recent publication in
Italy. Since every rehabilitation provokes a contrary reaction,
his book was soon attacked by the veteran "official arbiter"
Dymshits in *Literaturnaya Gazeta* (*Literary Newspaper*). Significantly, this time Dymshits was countered by almost all of
the most eminent Soviet critics: Asmus, Pertsov, Shklovsky,
Khrapchenko, Vasilevskaya and Myasnikov (also in *Literaturnaya Gazeta*). Even V. Ermilov, the ill-reputed theoretician
of strict Socialist Realism, defended Bakhtin. This shows that
the strength of the Russian renaissance has grown to such an
extent that even the most stubborn Socialist Realists have
started to go over to the opposite camp.[20]

Despite the fact that, on the surface, the controversy was centered around Bakhtin's alleged formalism, the real point at is-

sue was not formalism but socialist realism. Bakhtin's book challenged some of the unquestioned assumptions of social-ist realist critics about nineteenth-century Russian literature. Dymshits was aghast to discover that Bakhtin "not only set Dostoevsky apart from the tradition of Russian realism, but through a number of definitions actually took him outside the confines of realistic art."[21] Even worse, Dymshits com-plained, Bakhtin linked Dostoevsky only with modern West-ern literature and not with the socialist realist "heirs" of the Russian classical heritage. Not surprisingly, Dymshits blamed Bakhtin's past associations with the formalists for the "fail-ures" of the new edition. In their rebuke to Dymshits, I. Vasilevskaya and A. Myasnikov took the opposite view: they declared Bakhtin's book "antiformalistic."[22] Curiously, they argued their point on the basis of Konstantin Fedin's definition of formalism as "a negation of the ideological nature of art and a rejection of the principle of unity between content and form." Without directly taking up the issue of compatibility between socialist realism and polyphony they nevertheless ex-pressed their hope that polyphony would survive capitalism, and even urged Soviet writers to apply it in their work.[23]

It is against this background that Solzhenitsyn's interview with Ličko in 1967 should be viewed. The writer could hardly have declared his adherence to polyphony in so straightfor-ward a manner without being aware of Bakhtin's book and the controversy it had caused in the Soviet Union. In a sense, his statement may be viewed as a writer's contribution to the de-bate of literary scholars on the future of polyphony, a debate which continued long after Dymshits's original attack on Bakh-tin. Despite its brevity the statement makes it clear that Sol-zhenitsyn uses the notion of polyphony in much the same way as Bakhtin. His definition of the polyphonic novel as one with-out a single principal hero parallels, for instance, Bakhtin's assertion that Dostoevsky deliberately sought to assure in his novels a coexistence of different world views. The chief ques-

tion in regard to Solzhenitsyn's statement, therefore, is not
whether he had properly understood either Bakhtin or Dostoevsky, but rather, To what extent has he been able to imple-
ment polyphony in his work?

To answer this question I propose to investigate Solzhenitsyn's three major novels, *The First Circle*,[24] *Cancer Ward*,
and *August 1914*, which he referred to as polyphonic, with the
two-fold purpose of discerning their polyphonic and their Dostoevskian features, especially as these relate to each other. The
first two novels were completed in 1964 and 1967 respectively, and for a while Solzhenitsyn hoped they would be published in the USSR. This was not to be, however, and they
began circulating in *samizdat* (the underground distribution of
unpublished works). From there they found their way to the
West where they were published in 1968 both in the original
and in translations. Together with *One Day in the Life of Ivan
Denisovich* (hereafter referred to as *One Day*), the two novels
were chiefly responsible for the awarding of the Nobel Prize
to Solzhenitsyn in 1970. The following year the writer himself
authorized the Russian émigré publishing house YMCA-
Press in Paris to publish *August 1914*, the first "knot" of a
multivolume project on which he is still working. In my research I have relied on the Russian originals of the three novels; however, since most of the criticism is not to be found in
Russian, most of the references are to their English translations.

I have chosen to discuss *The First Circle* in greater detail
than the others because *August 1914* is part of a larger work,
and therefore must wait for any final judgment, and *Cancer
Ward* is the least novelistic of the three (that is why Solzhenitsyn subtitled it a *povest'*, a Russian word indicating an expanded short story rather than a full-fledged novel). I shall try
to demonstrate the polyphonic conception of *The First Circle*
in every aspect of its poetics—in its characterization, setting,
structure, and language. By comparing the novel's characters

with those from Dostoevsky's fiction—Stalin with the Grand Inquisitor, Rubin with Ivan Karamazov, Nerzhin with Alyosha, and Sologdin with Stavrogin—I do not mean to suggest that Solzhenitsyn was consciously trying to imitate the work of his great predecessor. However, once these characters were conceived of as bearers of enduring ideas, it seemed quite plausible to assume that they would have some important traits in common with the similarly conceived Dostoevskian figures. The discussion of *The First Circle* concludes with an attempt to define its genre. To *Cancer Ward* and *August 1914* there is devoted one chapter each, and their discussion focuses on certain aspects of style that I find crucial to their polyphonic conception.

CHAPTER I

Voices
from the Inferno

AT ONE POINT in *The First Circle* Muza, who is writing her
dissertation on Turgenev, asks her roommates:

> "Have you ever noticed what makes Russian literary heroes
> different from the heroes of Western novels? The heroes of
> Western literature are always after careers, money, fame. The
> Russians can get along without food and drink—it's justice
> and good they're after. Right?" (45:324)[1]

Though Muza receives no answer, the novel itself is so full of
heroes who are after "justice and good" that one need not
doubt that this particular tradition in Russian literature is very
close to the heart of the author. However, as far as the artistic
presentation of such heroes is concerned, there is reason to believe that it was not Turgenev who chiefly inspired him. At
another point in the novel the writer has Sologdin, an engineer, challenge Rubin, a philologist:

> "Would you care to debate some subject in the field of litera-
> ture? That's your field, not mine."
> "For example?"
> "Well, for example, how ought one to interpret Stavrogin?"
> "There are already a dozen critical essays—"
> "They are not worth a kopeck! I've read them. Stavrogin!
> Svidrigailov! Kirillov! Can one really understand them? They
> are as complex and incomprehensible as people in real life!
> How seldom do we understand another human being right from
> the start, and we never do completely! Something unexpected
> always turns up. That's why Dostoevsky is so great. And lit-
> erary scholars imagine they can illuminate a human being
> fully. It's amusing." (60:442)

Characteristically, the philologist dodges the challenge. Yet the engineer has made his point: the art of Dostoevsky is beyond the reach of all the "literary scholars" who say they can "illuminate a human being fully," and particularly all the socialist realist "engineers of human souls." Nevertheless, at least one Soviet literary scholar would have entirely agreed with the engineer: this was Bakhtin. And at least one Soviet writer would attempt to answer the challenge by making Dostoevsky's approach to characters his own—Solzhenitsyn.

Before we see to what extent the novelist was successful in this attempt, let us review briefly what Bakhtin has to say about Dostoevsky's approach to his characters.

Launching his thesis on polyphony as the distinctive feature of the Dostoevskian novel, Bakhtin first focuses on the novelist's "radically new attitude" toward his characters. He notes that critics often find themselves unable to distinguish the voice of the author from those of his characters, as if Dostoevsky had "coauthors" in Raskolnikov, Myshkin, Stavrogin, Ivan Karamazov, and the Grand Inquisitor. Bakhtin explains that this was not simply due to weaknesses in the methodology of criticism or to contradictions in the writer's personality, but rather to the writer's deliberate artistic strategy. Dostoevsky, according to Bakhtin, "like Goethe's Prometheus, creates not speechless slaves (as Zeus did), but *free* men capable of standing *side by side* with their creator, of disagreeing with him and even rebelling against him." Calling this strategy polyphonic, Bakhtin formulates it thus: "*The plurality of independent and nonconfluent voices, a true polyphony of equal voices, is the main distinctive feature of Dostoevsky's novels.*" [2]

This strategy of Dostoevsky the artist was motivated, according to Bakhtin, by the essentially personalist philosophy of Dostoevsky the thinker. Referring to the "underground man" Bakhtin observes that the hero of *Notes from the Underground* was the first hero-ideologist in Dostoevsky's work. One of his principal ideas, brought forth in his polemic with the socialists, was the idea that *man is not a finite and determined number* on which any reliable calculation can be based; man is free, and therefore capable of violating any advance definition of him.[3]

Dostoevsky's insistence on the unpredictability of man ("Something unexpected always turns up," as Sologdin says), did not, however, daunt his passionate desire to reveal "man in man," to uncover the true personality behind the mask of a person's socially determined role. It was just for that purpose that the novelist had to assume a radically new attitude toward his characters. He shifted the focus of characterization from a description of the social reality of his heroes, that is, from the approach taken by most of his contemporaries, to a presentation of their world views. As a result the very types of heroes changed, from "repenting noblemen" and "Gogolian clerks" to "underground men," "dreamers," and "men of ideas." Correspondingly, the *dominanta* (Bakhtin uses this formalist term) of portrayal shifted from an analysis of the biographical, social, and educational background of the characters to an illumination of their self-consciousness.

Since characters interested Dostoevsky less as products of social reality than as "ideologists,"[4] that is, as bearers of ideas to which they were utterly committed, his portrayal of "men of ideas" became at the same time a portrayal of their ideas. Whereas in a monological novel, argues Bakhtin, ideas usually constitute either its premises or its conclusions, or else serve as a means of characterization, in a polyphonic novel ideas themselves become objects for portrayal. In this sense only Dostoevsky's polyphonic novels could be called ideological novels, that is, novels about ideas *as they are embodied in people*. Dostoevsky was universally recognized as a great artist of ideas (*khudozhnik idei*) because, as Bakhtin says, he "knew how to portray somebody else's idea, presenting it fully developed, and yet retaining at the same time a distance from it, neither affirming it nor subordinating it to his own expressed ideology."[5]

Returning to Solzhenitsyn, even a quick glance at *The First Circle* shows that it is densely populated by ideologists of all kinds. Prominent among them are:

Rubin, who believes himself to be the only true spokesman for the "progressive" ideology at the sharashka (prison research institute);

Sologdin, Rubin's antagonist whose ideological preeminence at the sharashka is emphasized by his nickname, "Pythia of Mavrino," and by the influence he exerts on other prisoners;

Nerzhin, known at the sharashka as an inveterate skeptic, this "disciple of Socrates" is in quest of a more affirmative attitude toward life;

Rostislav Doronin, a twenty-three-year-old former student whose "character and . . . outlook on the world had been formed in a short but stormy life" (14:77) of police hunts and imprisonment; he views Stalinist society as a repetition of the cycle of Roman slavery, and generalizes all human history as "one continuous pestilence";

Kondrashev-Ivanov, a zek (sharashka inmate) painter and "ageless idealist," he rejects the fundamental Marxist belief that "the mode of existence determines the mode of consciousness" (42:297) in favor of a "fantastic" faith in the image of perfection innate in men;

Spiridon Egorov, a zek janitor of peasant stock, in whom Nerzhin sees "an alternative to the wisdom of his intellectual friends";

Innokenty Volodin, a Communist and "disciple of Epicurus" who later renounces his teacher's materialistic world view as the "philosophy of a savage" and "the babbling of a child";

Dushan Radovich, a Serbian Marxist and former member of

Comintern, whose thinking in the "free" Stalinist society is reduced to his motto, *Fumo ergo sum*, even though his "fumes" are still for Marx and the world revolution;

Yakonov, a boss at the sharashka, whose opportunistic attitude toward Stalinism is compared to that of Metropolitan Kirill toward the Tatar oppressors of old Russia;

Roitman, a deputy to Yakonov and a Jew, he now begins to feel "the whip of the persecutor of the Israelites" on his own back and asks himself the fundamental question of all ideologists: "Where should one begin to set the world aright? With others? Or with oneself?" (68:494);

Stalin himself, officially recognized as the only true living ideologue, he is convinced that "he alone on earth was a true philosopher" and therefore feels it his duty to "refute the counterrevolutionary theory of relativity" or, at least, to lay down the Marxist theory for linguistics.

Admittedly, not all the above ideologists can be put in the same category as the Dostoevskian heroes of ideas. Stalin, for one, although he was recognized at the time as the only true ideologue of Communism, has little in common with the Dostoevskian "Russian boys"; and Spiridon Egorov is definitely more committed to life than to any idea. Yet, taken as a group, they exhibit a number of features that Bakhtin considers indicative of the polyphonic mode of characterization.

First, the *dominanta* of their portrayal is placed not on an analysis of their social, ethnic,[6] or family background, but on a depiction of their self-awareness, their view of reality and of themselves. We learn nothing about Nerzhin's parents or about any outside influence in his youth, but we are informed that ever since he was a schoolboy he has been gripped by a single passion, "to learn and understand" what has been happening to his country. Yakonov's association with the Russian nobility did not prevent him from becoming an obedient servant of Stalin's "proletarian" rule, but Kondrashev-Ivanov, another nobleman, managed not to succumb either to socialist realism or to Marxist materialism. Rubin's adherence to the Revolution could be explained in part by his Jewish background; yet the novelist does not dwell on this, instead characterizing him through his betrayal of his cousin, through his painful awareness of that act, and through his attempt to justify himself in terms of "Party conscience." One could argue, perhaps, that Innokenty Volodin was influenced by his bourgeois mother, yet this influence is shown in the novel as a result, rather than a cause, of his changed attitude to life. It is about this change that Solzhenitsyn makes his most defiantly antisociological remark: "The ways of the Lord are unfathomable" (55:394). Like Dostoevsky, Solzhenitsyn leaves his heroes and their ideas free from any interference of sociological determinism.

Secondly, in agreement with Dostoevsky, the author of *The First Circle* treats the world views of his characters not as time- or place-bound ideologies but rather as basic human attitudes that have been observed throughout the history of mankind. Dostoevsky's approach was perhaps best expressed by Ivan Karamazov when he referred to the "absolute and everlasting" quality of the three questions that Satan put before Christ: "For in those three questions the whole future history of mankind is, as it were, anticipated and combined in one whole, and three images are presented in which all the insoluble contradictions of human nature all over the world will meet."[7] Solzhenitsyn, to use his own words, treats these world views *sub specie aeternitatis*,[8] associating the novel's characters with major figures of world culture. Innokenty, as already mentioned, is referred to as a "disciple of Epicurus" and later compared, tongue-in-cheek, to Rodin's *Thinker*. Nerzhin, a "disciple of Socrates," is associated with skeptics from Sextus Empiricus to Montaigne. In Rubin's eyes he is a follower of Tao and an admirer of the philosophy of Sankhya, but he himself suggests that his inspiration comes from such mathematical minds as Pascal, Newton, and Einstein. Stalin, on the other hand, seeing his only peers in Kant and Spinoza, aspires to refute Einstein's theory of relativity. Sologdin's ideological preeminence is underscored through his nickname, "Pythia of Mavrino." Finally, Rubin is a "Biblical fanatic," who ironically likes to quote the German iconoclast Martin Luther's "*Hier stehe Ich! Ich kann nicht anders*" (8:40). Though associations of this kind do not necessarily reveal the respective characters' true ideological profiles, they force the reader to think of them in the terms of universal history rather than in those of the social makeup of the USSR.

Thirdly, as in Dostoevsky's novels, the emphasis in *The First Circle* is not on single, isolated, and impersonal ideas, but on entire viewpoints embodied in hero-ideologists. Nerzhin, Rubin, Sologdin, and Volodin are just as committed to their viewpoints as are Kirillov or Shatov, Alyosha or Ivan. They truly are the "Russian boys" of the Stalinist period.[9]

In *One Day* the reality of Stalinist Russia is portrayed chiefly from the viewpoint of poorly educated Ivan Denisovich, who represents the Russian people rather than the Russian intelligentsia, but the very setting of *The First Circle* allows Solzhenitsyn to show reality from a number of intellectual vantage points. Just as Dostoevsky "was thinking not through thoughts but through viewpoints,"[10] so Solzhenitsyn stresses the importance of having one's own viewpoint. Nerzhin reproaches the "people" for lacking "that personal *point of view* which becomes more precious than life itself" (61:451). And when we read about Nerzhin—"Once a single great passion occupies the soul, it displaces everything else" (34:236) —we realize that this sentence holds a key to the conception of Solzhenitsyn's heroes of ideas. The reader would hardly doubt the readiness of Innokenty, who "had money, good clothes, esteem, women, wine, travel," to hurl "all those pleasures into the nether world for justice and truth . . . and nothing more" (84:630). Rubin may sound arrogant when he tells Sologdin that only he has "a real point of view," but the strength of his commitment to Communist ideas cannot be denied. No wonder that Sologdin calls him "the possessed one" (*oderzhimets*).

Yet another element of polyphonic characterization may be discerned in *The First Circle*, one having to do with the ways in which different ideologies are revealed. Just as Dostoevsky confronted his ideologists with each other, put them through a series of tests and trials, through all kinds of transgressions, temptations, violent passions, and let them live in the face of death, so Solzhenitsyn does not allow his heroes simply to indulge in idle philosophizing. Their professed ideas, like their own characters, are constantly tested in the crucible of the sharashka and on the thresholds leading either to physical death in the camps or to spiritual death in the "free" society. However, while Dostoevsky often had to contrive dramatic situations for the purpose of revealing "man in man," Solzhenitsyn has no such need. The conditions of everyday life in the sharashka, as in the rest of Russia, provided him with the most natural, most demanding and unavoidable series of tests that any psychologist could have devised. As far as confrontations with each other are concerned, the sharashka proved to be an especially suitable institution, for in no other place in the country was it possible for so many "wise men" to engage in ideological, Socratic dialogues. This is especially significant because such dialogues, in Bakhtin's view, are not only the main vehicle of polyphony but also its first prerequisite.

The above elements of polyphony, characteristic of Solzhenitsyn's cast of ideologists in *The First Circle*, are strictly formal. Important as they are for understanding his artistic strategy, they alone do not decide its ultimate success or failure. They leave unanswered the main question, which is whether the author of *The First Circle* was able to create "free men" with their "plurality of independent and nonconfluent voices"; whether he knew "how to portray somebody else's idea"; in other words, whether he succeeded in achieving the effect of polyphony once he possessed its means. To answer these questions I shall discuss in greater detail five major characters in the novel: Stalin, Rubin, Sologdin, Nerzhin, and Volodin. But first, before that, let us look briefly at Solzhenitsyn's view of Stalinist society that underlies the novel.

The vision of Stalinist society as hell on earth is essential for understanding *The First Circle*'s characterization. Its ironic sting is aimed at the Communist promise of paradise on earth. Although explicitly linked with such classics of world literature as Dante's *Divine Comedy* and Goethe's *Faust*, this vision is even more intimately connected with the Russian tradition of literary treatment of demonic and infernal themes, from Pushkin and Lermontov through Gogol and Dostoevsky, Vladimir Solovyov and Bely, to Bulgakov, Pasternak, and Tvardovsky.

The connection with Dostoevsky is particularly important, for the reality of totalitarianism depicted in *The First Circle* was, in its most essential features, foretold and prefigured by the author of *The Devils* and *The Brothers Karamazov*. According to Shigalyov, one of the "devilish" ideologists of socialism, the final solution for all social problems lies in the division of mankind into two distinct categories: "One-tenth will be granted individual freedom and full rights over the remaining nine-tenths, who will lose their individuality and become something like a herd of cattle. Gradually, through unlimited obedience and a series of mutations, they will attain a state of primeval innocence, something akin to the original paradise on earth, although, of course, they'll have to work." [11] Another Dostoevskian proponent of totalitarianism, this time not a socialist but a Catholic cardinal, the Grand Inquisitor, envisioned "the hundred-thousand voluntary sufferers" taking upon themselves the burden of power over "thousands of millions of happy infants."

Dostoevsky's foresight was based on his intimate acquaintance with the ideas of the revolutionary socialists of his time. During his lifetime, however, these ideas were not much more than a specter that haunted most European countries, in Russia making but few and feeble inroads. Yet the writer perceived the potential danger and, in *The Devils*, showed how a small gang of revolutionaries succeeded in turning a provincial capital into hellish havoc. In the writer's mind this boded no good for the future of Russia.

History proved him right: in less than fifty years the "sons" of the "devils" were firmly in control of the country. The slogans of the October Revolution—there was in them the promise of eternal peace and earthly bread for a united mankind—were strikingly similar to those of Shigalyov and the Grand Inquisitor. And the means to achieve this "paradise on earth" were similar too: the Marxist concept of the "dictatorship of the proletariat," when transplanted to Russia, would have meant a dictatorship of no more than one-tenth of the population over the rest, but since in practice the country was ruled by the Party rather than by the working class, it became more like the rule of the hundred thousand envisioned by the Grand Inquisitor.

The worst was yet to come. With Stalin's rise to power, the ideas of the two Dostoevskian visionaries bore their ultimate fruit: the absolute and unlimited power of the single "devil" and "mangod" became reality. Evidently hampered in their fantasies by the liberal environment of their age, both Shigalyov and the Grand Inquisitor did reserve individual freedom for "one-tenth" and "the hundred-thousand." Stalin had no such scruples and pushed their vision to its logical conclusion. Actually, Shigalyov anticipated it when he admitted that "having started out with the idea of unlimited freedom I have arrived at unlimited despotism." [12] Stalin simply took his spiritual father at his word, and unlimited despotism it was.

Unlike *One Day* which is concerned mainly with the physical aspect of the Stalinist hell, *The First Circle* focuses on its metaphysical, or ideological, content. In this sense Solzhenitsyn's *The First Circle* is not only as ideological as any novel written by Dostoevsky after *Notes from the House of the Dead* but also evinces a strong ideational continuity between the two authors. Nevertheless, the main conflict in *The First Circle* is not between socialists and atheists on the one hand and believers in Christ and Russia on the other, as was the case with Dostoevsky. It is not even a conflict of Marxists, Communists, and Stalinists versus those not believing in these isms. In fact, it is not a conflict between sets of ideas at all, but rather between a single totalitarian idea, the only one permissible in the country, and a variety of "impermissible" ideas banished from the "free" society to the nether world. In the light of Bakhtin's theory this conflict could be defined as existing between the official ideological monologue (for the whole Marxist-Leninist ideology was in fact reduced to the dictator's monologue) and a polyphony of ideological voices, including the Communist ones, monitored by the novelist from the nether world. More than was the case with Dostoevsky, polyphony serves for Solzhenitsyn not only as the chief medium but as the chief message as well. The novel itself vindicates Bakhtin's prediction of 1929 that "any attempt to render this world as completed, in the usual monological sense of this word, as subdued to one idea and one voice, is inevitably doomed to defeat."[13]

CHAPTER II

Stalin

or

the Epigone of the Grand Inquisitor

IN "THE FIRST CIRCLE" Stalin is shown at the peak of his power. The time is December 1949. The seventy-year-old dictator is brought into the novel's focus at the moment he tries to review his past in order to plan better for the years ahead. Viewing him from the standpoint of his own consciousness, the novelist remarks, "Like a legendary hero, Stalin had all his life been cutting off the hydra's eversprouting heads" (18:105). To be sure, the dictator does not recognize himself as a villain. He explains, for instance, his habit of working at night as a personal sacrifice: "A carefree country can sleep, but not its Father" (18:108). This "sacrifice" appears particularly magnanimous since the father is as old as a grandfather; just three days earlier the "whole Progressive Mankind" had celebrated his seventieth "glorious birthday." Yet the grandfather is neither thinking of an early retirement nor hoping for a personal reward for his unselfish service to mankind:

> Having set himself the goal of living to ninety, Stalin thought sadly of the fact that these years would bring him no personal joy, that he simply had to suffer another twenty years for the sake of humanity. (18:101)

Thus creating in his mind a heroic image of himself, Stalin is probably unaware of how close his "legendary" features bring him to another "legendary" figure, namely, Dostoevsky's Grand Inquisitor, a ninety-year-old "sufferer for humanity."

In addition to his desire to "suffer" till ninety, Stalin shares other important characteristics with the Grand Inquisitor. The latter combined, for instance, his mistrust of the "weak, vicious, worthless and rebellious" and "always ignoble race of men" with the wish to be its benefactor.[1] Stalin, too, was convinced that though "there were always dissatisfied people and there always would be," none of them could ever match his "iron will" because "their wrath was short-lived, their will not steadfast, their memory weak—they would always be glad to surrender themselves wholly to the victor" (21:130). Holding men in contempt, he mistrusted them to the extent that "mistrust was his world view" (20:122). Yet, he saw himself as a benefactor of mankind, called upon to fulfill the Communist promise of an earthly paradise:

> Only he, Stalin, knew the path by which to lead humanity to happiness, how to shove its face into happiness like a blind puppy's into a bowl of milk—"There drink up!" (21:130)

Dostoevsky's "benefactor," as we recall, also "knew the path by which to lead humanity to happiness." Having a low opinion of men he thought they would gladly surrender their freedom for the happiness to be found in the "loaves of bread." Although Solzhenitsyn mentions neither the Grand Inquisitor nor the loaves of bread, it is quite clear that Stalin's "milk" is but an updated version of the same offer with which Satan tempted Jesus in the wilderness. As according to Dostoevsky Satan spoke through the Grand Inquisitor, so he now appears to be speaking through Stalin.

Dostoevsky made the Catholic cardinal admit that he was lying in the name of Christ while actually serving Satan, "the terrible and wise spirit, the spirit of self-destruction and non-existence." Stalin's association with Satan appears to be just as close; indeed, one can hardly avoid the impression that he is portrayed as Satan himself. "The Ruler of Half the World," Stalin is provided with numerous satanic attributes, among them his nocturnal habits. Repeatedly emphasizing that "night was Stalin's most fruitful time" and that "all his best ideas were born between midnight and 4 A.M." (19:108), the novelist does not attribute this to chance: the dictator collects the books of his murdered opponents in his night office "so that he could be more spiteful in the nighttime when he made decisions" (21:134). Stalin's physical portrayal, too, is suggestive of the satanic. Now and then he is compared to the owl, to a nocturnal bird of prey, to the tiger, or to the raven. As vicious dogs are traditionally associated with the evil powers, so Stalin's henchmen and he himself are often depicted in terms of canine imagery. Stalin uses "the dog" as an invective for Abakumov (21:134). When he hears "four light knocks at the door, not even knocks, but four soft strokings, as if a dog were brushing against it" (18:104) he knows that his secretary Poskrebyshev wants to enter his office. He cannot even think about himself without resorting to canine imagery: "Growing old like a dog. An old age without friends. An old age without faith. An old age without desire" (21:134).

Anxious to stay as close to reality as possible, Solzhenitsyn never directly refers to Stalin as Satan or the Devil. He describes Stalin's old age as follows:

> That sensation of fading memory, of failing mind, of loneliness advancing on him like a paralysis, filled him with helpless terror. Death had already made its nest in him, and he refused to believe it. (21:134)

This passage may very well be read as a realistic account of Stalin's actual suffering in anticipation of his actual death in 1953; but it may also be seen as the crowning touch in the portrayal of Stalin as Satan, "the spirit of self-destruction and non-existence."

Apostasy is another feature that Stalin shares with his literary progenitor. Just as the Grand Inquisitor reminded Christ that he had been "preparing to stand among your chosen ones," and "thirsting 'to make myself of the number'" [2] so the Communist dictator recalls that until the age of nineteen he had grown up on the Old and New Testaments, on the lives of the saints and church history;

that

he helped celebrate the liturgies, he sang in the choir, and he used to love to sing Strokin's "Now You Are Forgiven";

and

how many times in the course of eleven years in school and in the seminary had he been drawn near the icons and looked into their mysterious eyes!

The photograph of the young Iosif remains imprinted on the mind of the dictator as well as the reader:

Dull, adolescent oval face exhausted from praying; the hair worn long, severely parted, in preparation for the priesthood, humbly smeared with lamp oil and combed down to his ears; only the eyes and strained brows giving any clue that this obedient pupil might become a metropolitan. (21:131)

However, instead of becoming one of many metropolitans of the Orthodox Church this "seminarist-careerist" chose a more ambitious path, the path of atheism and revolution, and eventually became the "sole and infallible" pontiff of world Communism.

There seems to be no limit of Stalin's ambition. In the twenty years after his seventieth birthday he plans to wage and win World War III and then proclaim himself Emperor of the Earth, following the example of his hero Bonaparte. "There was not the least contradiction here with the idea of world Communism," he thinks, perhaps still unaware that all this is in agreement with the Grand Inquisitor's "Caesarean" plan of uniting mankind into a single "anthill." His ambition soaring still higher, he hopes that in twenty years a medicine will be found which would make him immortal. He says that he personally would not mind dying after twenty years of suffering for the sake of humanity, but "how could he leave humanity?

In whose care? They'll make a mess of everything" (21:131). In his mistrust of doctors, and knowing all too well how the system he has created functions, he realistically concludes that "they wouldn't be able to do it in time," and resigns himself to the prospect of eventual death. But even then he would die as "the Greatest of the Great, without equal in the history of the earth." They would bury him in his native Caucasus, perhaps on the top of Mt. Elbrus, but in any case "above the clouds."

> Suddenly he stopped.
> And up there? Higher? He had no equals, of course, but if there, up there. . .
> Again he paced back and forth, but slowly.
> Now and again that one unresolved question crept into Stalin's mind. (21:131)

Having evoked the image of Stalin the Mangod aspiring to the "divine right" of immortality, the writer shows how his rivalry with God is accompanied by a struggle with Christ the Godman. For the "unresolved question" is the question of the existence of Christ. Despite Stalin's attempts to convince himself that "it had been proved that it was impossible to prove that Christ existed," this question remains for him unresolved because, as the writer puts it, "the fabric of our soul, what we love and what we have grown accustomed to, is created in our youth, not afterward," (21:131) and in his youth Stalin was a devout disciple of Christ. Deep in his heart he knows now, at the age of seventy, that Christ existed, just as well as he knew it in his youth; yet he does not want to admit it, for to do so would be to expose himself as a fallen angel and the Antichrist.

It could be argued, perhaps, that in the purely historical terms of Dostoevsky's "legend" Stalin must be identified not as a lineal descendant of the Grand Inquisitor, but with those builders of the new Tower of Babel who, according to the Grand Inquisitor, would raise the banner of earthly bread against Christ and eventually destroy his temple—that is, with the forces of atheistic socialism. The October Revolution in-, deed destroyed Christ's "temple" in Russia, and Stalin was to become the chief architect of the socialist Tower of Babel, advertised in the USSR as "the illuminated building of socialism." [3] Curiously enough, in the novel Stalin wants to live twenty more years because "the building was not completed." His concern was not without reason, for, according to the Grand Inquisitor, the tower never will be completed, at least not by its original builders. Only after they fail to fulfill the promise of "earthly bread," the cardinal says, will the hungry people turn to the leadership of church leaders who had at first been persecuted. Speaking on behalf of his supporters among the clergy, the Grand Inquisitor declares to Christ: "We shall finish building their tower, for he who feeds them will complete it, and we alone shall feed them in your name, and we shall lie to them that it is in your name." [4]

Having discovered an essential spiritual kinship between such religious leaders as the Grand Inquisitor who stood for a Christianity without Christ and such atheistic socialists as Shigalyov who sought a heaven on earth without God, Dostoevsky foresaw an eventual merger of those forces. The figure of Solzhenitsyn's Stalin seems to represent at least one step in that direction. In spite of the fact that Stalin's "inquisition" was historically different from the one fictionalized by Dostoevsky, he is nevertheless a spiritual descendant and an epigone of the Grand Inquisitor, or, in other words, a different historical manifestation of the same metaphysical phenomenon. Not only is he an apostate of Christ, like the Grand Inquisitor, but he actually flirts with the Moscow patriarchate that proclaimed him "the Leader Elected of God." Although his figure is in stature most obviously comparable with that of the leader of the Inquisition, he bears a strong resemblance to a number of Dostoevsky's socialist "devils" and atheistic "mangods." With Shigalyov he shares his somber dogmatism, the aplomb of a great philosopher, and a repulsive physical appearance. With Peter Verkhovensky he shares his mediocrity, banality, brutality, and a strong proclivity toward plotting and scheming. Just as Peter's last name is suggestive of his lust for power and a desire to lead (*verkhovodit'*)—and perhaps, at the same time, of superficiality—so the Leader of All Progressive Mankind wants most to restore to use, from among all the pre-Revolutionary words, the word *verkhovnyi*, the supreme. Moreover, Stalin's commitment to the idea of Communism is just as doubtful as that of Verkhovensky. His Napoleonic dream, though perfectly consistent with the cardinal's Caesarean plan, also links him to Raskolnikov. Finally, in his youth he was as much a "seminarist-careerist" as Rakitin, Alyosha Karamazov's tormentor and tempter. Thus it could be said that Solzhenitsyn's Stalin is not only an epigone of the Grand Inquisitor but also a historical product of his spiritual crossbreeding with other Dostoevskian "mangods" and "devils."

These similarities between Solzhenitsyn's Stalin and certain of Dostoevsky's characters point to the essential similarity of the ideas which they embody, which may be summed up as the definition of man's happiness as that of a full stomach, and —once it is proclaimed by the self-appointed "benefactors" as the highest goal of humanity—a readiness to use any means to achieve this goal. In the language of Dostoevsky's metaphysics these ideas, regardless of whether he saw them in the guise of a cardinal's cloak or veiled in the humanitarian phraseology of socialism, bear the mark of Satan and Antichrist. In our century they came to be called totalitarian, no matter whether they professed the goals of the Third International or the millenium of the Third Reich. By portraying Stalin, the chief standard-bearer of Communism, as a Satan in disguise, Solzhenitsyn continued Dostoevsky's work of stripping the wolf of sheep's clothing. This time the wolf was found draped in the red banner of Communism.

While the question remains open as to whether this similarity to Dostoevsky's "devils" was a product of the writer's deliberate effort or based on certain actual features of the historical Stalin, the similarity itself is as indisputable as the effect of the "satanic" that the reader perceives in the portrait. Such characterization is not only consistent with, but also complementary to, the more explicit association of the novel with Dante's *Divine Comedy* and Goethe's *Faust*. One realizes, for instance, that Stalin's night office in the outskirts of Moscow is his Judecca. Just as Dante's Satan presides over his domain while being frozen in Lake Cocytus, so Stalin the Omnipotent rules over his domain while seized by helpless terror in the confinement of his "spaceless" office. As to the boundaries of his province, they seem to be firmer around the "paradise" where "free" citizens live than around the "nine circles" of hell that Stalin created for his opponents. And just as in *Faust* evil creates good in spite of itself, so Stalin's malevolent intention in creating the sharashka produced at least one good result: it was the only place in the country where his monologue was answered. The author of the novel is anxious to preserve the "polyphony" of the answers.

Solzhenitsyn's portrayal of Stalin is perhaps not the best example of his polyphonic approach to characters. One could argue, for instance, that it lacks the ambiguity of the Grand Inquisitor that has led some critics to ascribe the Inquisitor's views to the author. Moreover, its bitter irony and sarcasm seem to preclude that fairness which distinguishes Dostoevsky's approach to his heroes of ideas. We should not forget, however, that Solzhenitsyn's task in the portrayal of Stalin was essentially different from Dostoevsky's because he had to bear witness to (to describe) a historical realization of Dostoevsky's fictional idea. One should also bear in mind that Solzhenitsyn did not even intend to portray Stalin as a hero of ideas. On the contrary, he aimed at exposing Stalin as a traitor to the Communist idea he supposedly embodied. More than once the novelist suggests that the "only true classic" of Marxism-Leninism deviates markedly from the path followed by all the founding fathers of that ideology. At one point he has Nerzhin say that Stalin's program of collectivization is contrary to Marx (5:26). Apropos of Stalin's policy that "only legal marriage should be recognized, as had been the case under the czars," the novelist comments: "It did not matter what Engels thought about it in the depth of the sea" (21:133). Most significant is Stalin's disagreement with Lenin, the man whose direct heir and successor he was supposed to be. Just as the Grand Inquisitor wanted to *correct* Christ, so, characteristically, in *The First Circle* Stalin's "own memory told him how often he had warned and *corrected* the rash and too easily trusting Lenin" (18:101, emphasis added). The novelist traces Stalin's disagreement with Lenin to the pre-October days of 1917. With bitterness Stalin recalls how Lenin's "arrogant" April theses overturned "what had already been done, and how they had laughed when Stalin proposed forming a legal party and living at peace with the Provisional Government" (18:104). Now, in 1949, he finds other faults with Lenin. He ridicules, for instance, Lenin's slogan that "every cook, every housewife, should be able to run the state!" Not only had Lenin "been confused on this point," but his policy "had produced a mess" (19:109). According to Stalin, the state should be run by the "chosen cadres" with him, the Leader, at the helm (compare with the Grand Inquisitor's "hundred-thousand"). Only the fear that "it was still too early" prevents Stalin from openly declaring that Lenin had been wrong and probably anti-Party.

Solzhenitsyn portrayed his Stalin not as a man possessed by the idea of Communism, but as the man who took the idea into *his* exclusive possession and prostituted it for his idea-less lust for power. In this respect the portrait of Stalin vindicates the opinion of Alyosha, and Dostoevsky, about the Grand Inquisitor and his ilk. Alyosha saw through all the "mystery and lofty sadness" with which Ivan shrouded them and declared: "It's the most ordinary lust for power, for filthy earthly gains, enslavement—something like a future regime of serfdom with them as the landowners—that is all they are after." [5]

Though polyphony provides for the autonomy of various ideological voices, it should not be confused with a sort of moral or philosophical relativism. Nor does it require that an author maintain equanimity toward his characters. Just as Dostoevsky showed a greal deal of sympathy for Ivan but not for Smerdyakov, for Kirillov and Stavrogin but not for Shigalyov and Verkhovensky, so Solzhenitsyn shows great sympathy for many characters, including Communists, but not for the "leader."

As to the question of the historical authenticity of Stalin's portrait, many critics find it superior to Tolstoy's Napoleon. Edward Brown, for instance, comes to the conclusion that whereas Tolstoy "warped historical truth in order to reduce the stature of Napoleon," Solzhenitsyn "has revealed a human being remarkably like the real Stalin." Without directly attributing the achievement to polyphony, Brown makes a number of observations that seem to confirm that attribution. When he says, for instance, that the Napoleon of *War and Peace* is an abstraction, "an episode in Tolstoy's historical argument," and "an object lesson in his polemic with the historians" he pinpoints exactly the same weakness that Bakhtin found so characteristic of the homophonic or monological novel. "Solzhenitsyn, on the contrary," Brown goes on to say, "expounds no theory of history and is not trying to prove anything" beyond wishing "to capture, in the character and ambience of a single human being, the sense and spirit of a particular age." Furthermore, the technique of "inner monolog" and "intellectual mimicry" which, according to Brown, distinguishes Solzhenitsyn's Stalin, is highly consistent with the novel's overall polyphonic strategy. [6] In a similar way, Alexander Schmemann points out that whereas Tolstoy's Napoleon is shown mainly from outside, Solzhenitsyn's Stalin is more convincing because the novelist was able to penetrate deeper and show him from inside. Comparing Solzhenitsyn's portrait with that of Tolstoy, he says that this Stalin may have been invented, but the invention is not from thin air nor is it superimposed on him.[7]

But whether superior to Tolstoy's Napoleon or not, Solzhenitsyn's Stalin is a considerable achievement in the art of portraying historical figures, and this achievement is due largely to the novelist's polyphonic strategy. Dorothy Atkinson perhaps best summed it up. Noting that in Solzhenitsyn's polyphonic novels "we are auditors of the inner voices of numerous characters" she praised him for his "recognition of the fact that no man considers himself a villain" and that everyone "is the hero of his own epic." In an apparent reference to such characters as Stalin she concluded: "As a compassionate humanist Solzhenitsyn is capable of understanding what he cannot as a moralist condone."[8]

A better test of polyphony, however, is to be found in the portrayal of other characters, namely, of the true idealists who are committed to their ideas. Not surprisingly in a society where "everything is permitted" to but one man, all true "heroes of ideas" are reduced to an underground existence. One of them is the "Biblical prophet" Rubin who, in contrast to Stalin, is portrayed as a true embodiment of the Communist idea.

CHAPTER III

Rubin

or

Ivan in the Hands of the Grand Inquisitor

LEV GRIGORYEVICH RUBIN is a Communist, even a Stalinist, and believes that among all the prisoners of the first circle he is the best spokesman for the "progressive ideology" of Marxism-Leninism. Though he shares Stalin's ideology, a quite different man is hidden behind this ideological facade. Although Stalin was officially believed to be the truest embodiment of the Communist idea, the real idea he embodies is the "satanic" idea of the Grand Inquisitor, that is, the "lust for power and filthy earthly gains," in Alyosha's words. He is a false "hero of ideas." Rubin, on the other hand, though the name of Communist has been denied him from the moment of his arrest, is a true hero of the Communist idea. He is so strongly committed to it that he is called a "Biblical fanatic" and "the possessed one." Whereas Stalin claims exclusive possession of the Communist idea, Rubin is virtually possessed *by* the idea. Continuing the interpretation of Stalin's reign as "satanic," one could view Rubin's fate as similar to that of Ivan, had the latter fallen into the hands of his "legendary hero."

To begin with, Rubin's "leader" is as much an emanation of his fantasy as was Ivan's cardinal. Just as Ivan created his "legend" about the historical Inquisition in order to justify his socialist and atheist path to "universal happiness," so Rubin attempts to justify his own, and the country's, predicament under Stalin in an allegorical ballad which tells

how Moses had led the Jews through the wilderness for forty
years, in deprivation, thirst, and famine, and how the people
became delirious and rebelled; but they were wrong and Moses
was right, knowing that in the end they would reach the promised land. (29:199)

Rubin's "Moses" is, of course, Stalin, "the Jews" are the
Russians, "forty years" represent the period of time elapsed
since the Bolshevik Revolution of 1917, and "the promised
land" is the envisioned triumph of world Communism. Obviously, Rubin expects the "people," including his prison
mates, to be more patient and to place their future in Stalin's
hands. At another point, when Rubin declares Stalin to be both
"the Robespierre and Napoleon of our Revolution wrapped up
in one" (8:41), he actually anticipates the dictator's own
"Napoleonic dream" later in the novel, a dream that is quite
in line with Ivan's "Caesarean" image of his hero. Just as
Ivan is forced to admit that the essence of his "legend" could
be summed up as "Everything is permitted,"[1] so Rubin is
goaded into the admission that the real motto of Communism
is "The end justifies the means," the same guideline that has
been commonly ascribed to the medieval Inquisition, and that
Dostoevsky echoed in the legend. Finally, though he is a zeal-
ot of Communism and Stalinism, Rubin not only ridicules the
Stalinist system of justice (in his travesty of the Prince Igor
epic) but, in fact, even compares it with hell. Solzhenitsyn
merely borrows Rubin's analogy with the Dantean inferno and
elevates it to the novel's title theme. In this respect, too, Rubin
is not unlike Ivan, the "coauthor" of "The Legend of the
Grand Inquisitor," one of the most important chapters of *The
Brothers Karamazov*. Just as Ivan, while admitting that his
cardinal was on the side of Satan, still insists that he was a
true "Benefactor," so Rubin, while elaborating on his "hellish" analogy, implies Stalin's ultimate benevolence in the
creation of the first and all other circles of hell.

However, unlike Ivan, who bore the hell of his "legend"

only in his mind and his heart, Rubin actually has to live in the country of *his* legend and personally bear the consequences of the hell unleashed on that country. One of the consequences is his imprisonment. But why has this Stalinist been put in prison? Because in the country where he lives everything is indeed permitted to Stalin, and because "That was Stalin's signature —that magnificent equating of friends and enemies which made him unique in all human history" (27:184). The writer not only emphasizes the uniqueness of Stalin's rule "in all human history," but also suggests that the rule of evil is the rule of arbitrariness. As to Rubin's particular "crime," we learn that he somehow began to feel pity for the retreating Germans, evidently because he took too seriously the Marxist teaching about internationalism and class solidarity.

> For this, Rubin had been arrested. Enemies in his own administration accused him of agitating, after the January 1945 offensive, against "blood for blood and death for death." (3:12)

His very capacity for feeling pity disqualified him from being one of Stalin's cadres and doomed him to imprisonment. Another "crime" was his refusal to become an informer. When advised by Major Myshin, the boss of the informers at the sharashka, to write denunciations in ink rather than pencil, he proudly replies: "I have already proven my devotion to Soviet authority in blood, and I don't need to demonstrate it in ink" (25:167). At first sight these two "crimes" seem to vindicate his assertion that in his personal behavior he has not followed the motto "The end justifies the means" which he believes to be the ethical foundation of Communism. The question arises, however, of whether it is at all possible to separate one's personal integrity from one's belief in the social benevolence of the motto. To answer this question Solzhenitsyn lets the reader see Rubin's past as revisited in his own memory.

Accused by Sologdin of having personally followed the motto, Rubin spends a sleepless night, haunted by memories "which he had no wish to awaken" (66:480). He recalls, for instance, his first arrest in 1929, when he was sixteen years old, after helping his married cousin hide some type fonts. He discovered then that the prison was filled neither with anti-Soviet nor counterrevolutionary people, but with veterans of the Revolution who considered Stalin "another czar on our backs" and the traitor who forfeited the goals of Lenin and the Revolution. In spite of his sympathy with these anti-Stalinists, however, Rubin did not become one of them. On the contrary, upon his release, "anxious to expiate his guilt" and with "a Mauser on his hip," he took an active part in Stalin's collectivization of peasants in the Ukraine. That he had to use the Mauser against the peasants had hardly troubled his conscience; but if it had, he could have excused himself by reasoning that the Mauser was just a means, "in a social sense," since it was used against a "class enemy." At that time he was proud that "he did not turn in his cousin; he made up a story about finding the fonts under a staircase" (66:477). The time came, however, when Rubin's ethical principle was put to the test in an unmistakably personal sense, and he failed miserably. Four years after his first arrest he was made to confess to the Party "when and where his cousin had belonged to the opposition organization, and what he had done" (66:480). He informed on his cousin even though he knew that the Party meant the GPU, and that this was "vengeance against those who had once disagreed" (66:479).

Since in the past, then, Rubin could not avoid personal complicity with the motto "The end justifies the means," he has no wish to awaken his memory. But, as the novel has it, "What will one sleepless night not drain from the miserable soul of the man who has erred?" It drains from Rubin the confidence that his actions had been justified, and evokes instead "the feeling that his wounds were retribution" (66:481) for what he had done to the Ukrainian peasants and to his own cousin. In this respect, Rubin's unwanted encounter with his memory during a sleepless night of headache and delirium after his "duel" with Sologdin is reminiscent of Ivan's suffering from the qualms of his conscience in the wake of the murder of his father. But it would be premature to conclude, as Rubin does, that "since he now understood that what he had done was dreadful" and "had atoned for it" through his imprisonment, he would not do it again. The very next day he participates in the phonoscopic hunt of those who, he feels, are innocent, and lends his services to those who, in his opinion, "were worthy of being blown up by an antipersonnel grenade." He does so because "one has to serve them, and one's country, its progressive idea, its banner" (33:227). Though he tries to justify himself, saying that he saved three men out of five, the fact of his complicity in an injustice is indisputable. Thus Rubin's own fate suggests that personal integrity and honesty are incompatible with what he believes to be the ethical motto of Communism: "Our ends are the first in all human history which are so lofty that we can say they justify the means by which they've been attained" (64:469).

To Rubin's credit it must be said, however, that just as Ivan could not foresee that the principle "Everything is permitted" would be exploited by the most ruthless and unprincipled of men, so Rubin does not see that his belief in "The end justifies the means" has inextricably bound him to the people who use the motto for their own, selfish ends. A basically decent and honest person, Rubin, like Ivan, refuses to follow the dictates of his own conscience and allows himself to be corrupted by his reason. His situation as a rationalist is further aggravated by the fact that his reason, unlike Ivan's, has already been put in the straightjacket of the official ideology. Characteristically, he is least dogmatic when he speaks not as an ideologist of Communism but as a philologist and literary critic.[2] He disagrees, for instance, with the official Soviet critics when they interpret Goethe's *Faust* "in a socially optimistic sense." According to them, Faust exclaimed "Oh, moment stay! You are

so fair!" because he was so happy to have started draining the
swamps in order to make humanity happy. In actual fact,
Rubin says,

> "there wasn't any service to humanity at all. Faust pronounced
> the long-awaited sacramental phrase one step from the grave,
> utterly deceived, and perhaps truly crazy. And the lemurs im-
> mediately shove him into the pit." (7:37)

Rubin's own interpretation of *Faust*, however, is loaded with
an irony which he does not perceive, for what he says about
Faust turns back on himself. In Rubin's mind, too, "a great
idea" for making humanity happy had been kindled, and for
that end he has been willing to use such means as the Mauser
pistol and the betrayal of his own cousin. At the moment he
accepted the Party as "our conscience" and equated the Party,
the world revolution, and the happiness of mankind with Stalin, he in effect bartered away his individual conscience; he
has pawned his soul to the Mephistopheles Stalin. When he
later tries to regain his soul, by disagreeing with Stalin's policy
toward the Germans, Stalin does not keep his part of the contract and throws him in jail, just as Mephistopheles did with
Faust, "only to bury him and be rid of him, no longer hoping
for his soul" (7:37). To the end, like his Faust, "utterly de-
ceived and perhaps truly crazy," Rubin continues to sing
"You are so fair!" to Satan and the society he has created. As
to Rubin's subsequent fate, it is quite likely that because he is
a "cosmopolite," if for no other reason, he will be shoved
deeper into the pit by the "lemurs" of the sharashka, in spite
of his cooperation with them in the field of phonoscopy, which
he considers his great service to humanity. Though he has
played the role of a Damascene sword in the hands of his master he has not been sharp enough, owing to the qualms of his
conscience. What is especially ironic about Rubin is the fact
that, despite his "melancholy notion that there is no such thing
as happiness, that it is either unattainable or illusory," it is

happiness that he seeks as a Communist. Nerzhin appears to be speaking for the author when, upon hearing Rubin's interpretation of Faust, he exclaims:

> "Oh, Lev, my friend, I love you the way you are right now, when you argue *from your heart* and talk intelligently and don't try to pin abusive labels on things." (7:37, emphasis added)

That is virtually the only time Nerzhin approves of Rubin's reasoning. Yet they part as friends. Here is their final conversation, at the time Nerzhin is about to leave the sharashka:

> "Listen, friend," he said, "for three years we haven't agreed once, we've argued all the time, ridiculed each other, but now that I'm losing you, maybe forever, I feel so strongly that you are one of my most—most—"
> His voice broke.
> Rubin's big black eyes, so often sparkling with anger, were warm with tenderness and shyness.
> "So that's all in the past," he nodded. "Let's kiss, beast."
> And he took Nerzhin's face into his black pirate's beard. (86:657)

In this scene is the key to the author's attitude toward Rubin and toward his characters in general. It is the attitude of Nerzhin: not to judge a man according to the ideology he professes (for ideologically, they "haven't agreed once"), nor even solely on the merit of his actions, past and present (for Nerzhin would have found most of Rubin's actions at least morally questionable, if not wholly evil), but rather in terms of his innermost motivation. Like Dostoevsky, Solzhenitsyn tries to reveal for the reader the "man in man" and, if the inner man is still not fully revealed, he gives him the benefit of doubt that the sociologically and ideologically determined outer man may not deserve. Sologdin may have been right in comparing Rubin to "a puppy on a chain" obediently serving his master (64:471).[3] But if Rubin is such a puppy, he is so not for the sake of milk but for the sake of an idea. Thus the fate of Rubin refutes rather than confirms Stalin's view of mankind. And just as Dostoevsky allowed Alyosha to give Ivan a kiss, a symbolic gesture of forgiveness and trust, so Solzhenitsyn allows Nerzhin to exchange a kiss with Rubin, a gesture of friendship cutting across political and ideological lines. Such an attitude is part and parcel of the overall polyphonic strategy that secures for Rubin, whose ideology the author unequivocally rejects, a treatment so sympathetic and fair that some critics have mistaken him for one of the author's spokesmen.[4]

Finally, it must be pointed out that the character's last name, Rubin, seems to be a carefully chosen charactonym, suggestive of a number of attributes. Besides the red color of his Communist convictions it suggests the butchering function (from *rubit'*) of the Damascene sword he wanted to be; the brilliance, if not the depth, of his jewellike intellect; and perhaps the "cosmopolitanism" of a Jew, since it is a typically Jewish name encountered in many countries.

CHAPTER IV

Sologdin

or

the Way of a Superman

ONE WAY to characterize Sologdin is to describe him in terms
of his ideological antagonism to Rubin. The latter considers
him to be the main proponent of "metaphysics" and "idealism" at the sharashka. Lest one should be confused about the
meaning of these labels, Rubin also brands him reactionary,
priest-lover, and obscurantist. The author emphasizes Sologdin's importance as an anti-Stalinist ideologist by having him
challenge Rubin to a duel-debate. The ideological antagonism
of the two debaters is further emphasized by its graphic description as a confrontation between Sologdin's "precise
blond goatee" and Rubin's "big black beard." Before the debate degenerates into a personal squabble, Sologdin emerges
victorious. First he vanquishes his Stalinist opponent in the
field of Marxist dialectics "with a weapon torn from his
hand." Then he skillfully goads Rubin into the admission that
the ethical motto of Communism is "The end justifies the
means," a motto that clearly echoes Ivan Karamazov's "Everything is permitted." What is more, Sologdin's counter-
motto—"The higher the ends, the higher must be the means!
Dishonest means destroy the ends themselves"—seems to reflect Solzhenitsyn's own view. Sologdin's role as the author's
spokesman against Stalinism becomes even more evident
when he debunks Rubin for trying to justify the Stalinist
means:

> "Morality shouldn't lose its force as it increases its scope!
> That would mean that it's villainy if you personally kill and be-

tray someone; but if the One-and-Only and Infallible knocks
off five or ten million, then that's according to natural law and
must be appraised in a progressive sense." (64:469)

It is doubtful, however, that the novelist was mainly concerned with a characterization according to political ideology.
For one thing, Rubin himself is not primarily so characterized.
Solzhenitsyn's portrayal of Stalin and Rubin shows that he can
penetrate the facade of ideology and show the man behind it.
Thus, to say of Sologdin that he is an idealist and anti-Stalinist
would mean neither more nor less than to say that Rubin is a
materialist and Stalinist. But, then, what kind of idea is shin-
ing through Sologdin's precise blond goatee? What sort of
man is hidden inside the zek engineer's coveralls pasted with
the labels of reaction and anti-Communism? What word, in
Bakhtin's sense, is uttered by the "Pythia of Mavrino?"

Though Rubin intended the above nickname to be ironic,
actually considering him not an oracle but a liar and pretender,
there are indeed a few Pythic, enigmatic, and ambiguous
things about Sologdin. He appears different to different people
at different moments. Whereas Rubin accuses him of being a
liar and pretender wearing the mask of Aleksandr Nevsky, in
Nerzhin's eyes he appears now as an icon image of Nevsky,
the Russian saint and warrior prince, then as a wise Socrates
laying down his scriptural rules for overcoming difficulties. In
the eyes of the jailed engraver he is "not stupid but an entirely
mediocre person" (52:367). Finally, his boss Yakonov sees
him first as a "diabolical engineer," then discovers his own
image reflected in Sologdin's "imperturbable, incorruptible,
immaculate" eyes. Meanwhile, Sologdin himself may have
dropped a hint as to where the key to his enigma may be found
when, challenging Rubin to a debate in the field of literature,
he first asks, "How ought one to interpret Stavrogin?" (See
above, chapter I.) There are reasons to believe that he admires
Stavrogin from more than a literary standpoint. If it is at all
possible to elucidate one enigma with the help of another,

Sologdin may be explained with the help of Dostoevsky's Stavrogin.[1]

To begin with details, Sologdin, like his literary hero, is a man of exceptional beauty, strength, vitality, and talents. Like Stavrogin, he is not just handsome but "unnaturally, almost indecently handsome" (52:367), and his face reminds Rubin of a mask. His beauty is matched, as in the case of Stavrogin, by an extraordinary physical strength and vitality. In fact, his survival in the northern camps is described as bordering on a miracle. Like Stavrogin, he also seems to be endowed with an "unwavering will power subject only to his reason" (30:210). Because of this willpower and his outstanding engineering talent, he alone is able to find a solution which has for years eluded the sharashka. Yet, in spite of his nearly miraculous achievements and abilities, "Sologdin never tired of telling everyone that he had a weak memory, limited abilities, and a total lack of will" (52:367). This, of course, also reminds one of Stavrogin's indulgence in false humility. As Stavrogin often acts just to test his strength, so Sologdin says about his invention that "so far I have done this only to try out my strength. For myself" (29:204).

As a man of great handsomeness, he also has Stavrogin's irresistible attraction for women. First imprisoned "because of an enemy's jealousy," he was later "promoted" to the camps on account of his rivalry with a prison guard over a woman. At the sharashka he again finds himself committing adultery, with Larisa Emina, a draftswoman assigned to inform on him. He further resembles Stavrogin in that he is not a mere skirt-chaser but rather allows Larisa to seduce him. In any case, he "puts the horns" on Larisa's husband, a high-ranking officer of the secret police, just as Stavrogin does with many a husband. (Among other things, the name of Stavrogin alludes to the Russian idiomatic expression *stavit' roga*, meaning to seduce somebody's wife.)

Sologdin further resembles Stavrogin in his role of a "cor-

rupter" of minds. At least Rubin thinks so, suspecting him of
influencing Nerzhin in the direction of "metaphysics" and
"idealism." Having involved both Nerzhin and Rubin in a
woodcutting morning exercise, he turns it into a sort of seesaw
Socratic dialogue about esoteric questions like the mystery of
good and evil and the "blessing of prison." Not for nothing
does Nerzhin admit that he has "acquired some of Sologdin's
unhurried comprehension of life," and that Sologdin had "first
nudged him into thinking that a person shouldn't regard prison
solely as a curse, but also as a blessing" (24:158). The scene
at the sawhorse seems to confirm Sologdin in the role of Nerzhin's spiritual mentor. First he grants his approval to Nerzhin's decision to abandon the road of skepticism, then gives
his blessing to his writing of the "Notes on History," and
finally entrusts him with his "scriptural rules" on overcoming
difficulties. Rubin himself is not entirely immune to Sologdin's
influence. Though he has been avoiding the sawhorse dialogues, he finds himself drawn, against his will, into the duel-
debate with Sologdin, and afterwards he cannot help admitting
to himself that no matter how violently he has refuted Sologdin's accusations against him, "there was some justice in
them."

Sologdin resembles Stavrogin in a number of other details.
Like his literary hero, Sologdin proves himself a formidable
"duel-fighter," even though his duels are of necessity verbal.
Solzhenitsyn continuously compares him to a duel-fighter during his confrontations with both Rubin and Yakonov. Sologdin
even argues for the restoration of real duels. Again, like
Stavrogin, he is portrayed as an eccentric, and, in fact, is
known at the sharashka as a character (*chudak*). Though his
eccentricities never go as far as, say, biting Yakonov's ear,
they are just as puzzling as Stavrogin's pranks. Finally, just as
Stavrogin appears under the name of Prince Harry and Ivan
Tsarevich, so Sologdin is repeatedly associated with the an-

cient knights, foreign and Russian, and especially with Prince Aleksandr Nevsky.

These similarities between Sologdin and Stavrogin in the details of portrayal are hardly accidental. They point toward a crucial likeness of the idea that each personifies, the idea of a strong individual who stands, or purports to stand, above the mediocrity of human multitudes and "beyond Good and Evil," in the phrase of Nietzsche, who popularized the idea through the notion of a superman. Having rejected Rubin's philosophy of collectivism and class struggle, Sologdin has gone to another extreme, that of self-centered individualism and spiritual elitism which would allow "strong individuals" to put themselves above the human masses and to exempt themselves from any moral law. Perhaps the name of Sologdin suggests the self-centered hero's emphasis on solo action. Solzhenitsyn mocks Sologdin's exaggerated view of himself immediately after he parodies Rubin's Communist notion of "the people":

> And Sologdin knew equally well that "the people" is an over-all term for a totality of persons of slight interest, gray, crude, preoccupied in their unenlightened way with daily existence. The Colossus of Spirit does not rest on their multitudes. Only unique personalities, shining and separate, like singing stars strewn through the dark heaven of existence, carry within them supreme understanding. (61:449)

Expressed in his own language, Sologdin's idea confirms him as a modern superman and a spiritual kin to Stavrogin, whom he apparently admires from more than a literary standpoint. It is this idea that shines through the "precise blond goatee" of this recent Soviet specimen of "the blond beast." It is this idea that ultimately determines his ethical conduct. Without it the portrait of Sologdin as an anti-Stalinist can hardly be understood.

In accordance with this idea, Sologdin sets out to accomplish the impossible, truly superhuman task of obtaining his

release from prison. To do that he has to overcome two major
difficulties: he must produce something extraordinary, and he
must ensure that this achievement will not be plagiarized by
his overseers but will be credited to him personally. Harness-
ing his engineering talents, he manages to overcome the first
difficulty by solving the problem of absolute encoding that has
eluded all the collective efforts of the sharashka. The second
difficulty he manages to overcome by burning the outline of
his invention and then promising to restore it only if given the
credit. The reader's sympathy is wholly on his side when
Sologdin skillfully outmaneuvers his captors and makes
Yakonov promise him a full share of credit. However, his
personal triumph over his captors is at the same time a moral
defeat for him, because to achieve it he has to make a moral
compromise. Indeed, from the very beginning he has been
aware of a "certain moral question" involved in his invention.
As he explains it to Professor Chelnov:

> There is very little industrial significance in it, but a great deal
> that relates to the palace. When I think of the *customer* who
> will pick up our transmitter, . . ." (29:204)

The customer, of course, is Stalin; the palace is the Kremlin;
and the moral question implies that the transmitter will be used
against Sologdin's fellow countrymen. However, Sologdin's
Übermensch-like attitude allows him to disregard the fate of
"human multitudes." In order to overcome the external resistance of prison walls, he decides to eliminate in himself all
the internal resistance of a moral nature. (Ironically, he does
so in accordance with his "rules," by which Nerzhin was so
impressed.) It could therefore be said that when Sologdin
makes his deal with Yakonov, he indirectly concludes a contract with Stalin/Satan. Even though, in contrast to Rubin, he
concludes it himself in the hope of outplaying his captors at
their own game, the fact remains that by doing so Sologdin
forfeits his ethical alternative to Stalinism, "The higher the

ends, the higher must be the means." He may have proved himself a superman, but he also shows himself to be something less than a man. Although Rubin's verdict on Sologdin,

"You're the one who is lying! Everything with you is just a big act! Your idiotic 'Language of Maximum Clarity!' And your playing at chivalry and knighthood! And getting yourself up to look like Aleksandr Nevsky! Your sawing firewood— that's an act, too!" (64:469)

strikingly resembles Marya Timofeevna's indictment of Stavrogin as a liar, a pretender, and the False Dmitry, Solzhenitsyn makes it function differently in the novel. For one thing, he has much more sympathy for Sologdin than Dostoevsky has for Stavrogin, largely because the two "supermen" find themselves in entirely different situations. Whereas Stavrogin was a free man who could always have told his "devils" to go to hell, his spiritual kin of the Soviet period is put in hell by the "devils." Stavrogin was free to choose between good and evil, but Sologdin knows that if he should choose good, it may cost him his life. Stavrogin was largely a sinner; Sologdin is above all a victim. The former is shown in the eclipse of his "superhuman powers" and characterized by a deadness of spirit; the latter has to demonstrate a superhuman vitality in order to survive. In fact, both as a superman and as a "diabolical engineer" Sologdin may be said to have been born in jail, for prior to his arrest "he had been a kid concerned more with how he looked than with anything else" (29:202). It is only through the struggle for survival in the jails and camps that he learns of good and evil, and, eventually, how to transcend them. If Stavrogin is his spiritual father, Sologdin's mother is the country of camps. Unlike Stavrogin he does not have to look hard for obstacles on which to try out his strength. The umbilical cord of his endless term, which seems forever to tie him to Mother Russia's womb of camps, serves for him as a natural obstacle calling forth a superhuman effort. Sologdin's situation, therefore, hardly warrants the same harsh verdict that Stavrogin receives from Marya Timofeevna and Dostoevsky.

Furthermore, there is great irony in Rubin's accusations, for they boomerang against him. By calling Sologdin a failure, he apparently means to allude to his lack of engineering talent and, by contrast, places himself at the "fountainhead of science." Ironically, at this very moment Sologdin has already accomplished his engineering feat but prefers not to talk about it. As to Rubin's own "science of phonoscopy," it can hardly be called more than a half-success. He is also wrong in his prediction that Sologdin will "crawl on his belly" to beg for freedom. In fact, Sologdin demonstrates just the opposite: in his confrontation with Yakonov he puts himself in a position of strength vis-à-vis his boss, who desperately needs his discovery, and he demands rather than begs for his freedom. Also, Sologdin's Language of Maximum Clarity, extravagant as it may be, is certainly superior to Rubin's party-line jargon which Sologdin justly calls the Language of Apparent Clarity. Lastly, Rubin is wrong about Sologdin's indulgence in sawing firewood. What appears to Rubin a theatrical act serves Sologdin as a means of maintaining his physical prowess and as a ploy to secure an exchange of opinion in the absence of informers.

Contrasting with Rubin's indictment of Sologdin is the attitude of Nerzhin. In spite of his awareness of Sologdin's moral compromise, Nerzhin does not condemn him. On the contrary, when the time comes for Nerzhin to leave the sharashka, he parts as friends with Sologdin, just as he does with Rubin. In an effort to save Nerzhin from the camps, Sologdin offers to put in a word for him with Yakonov. Nerzhin replies:

> "Thank you, Dmitri. I had that chance. But for some reason I'm in a mood to try an experiment for myself. The proverb says: *'It's not the sea that drowns you, it's the puddle.'* I want to try launching myself into the sea." (86:658)

The chance Nerzhin refers to is the opportunity to work on cryptography which Yakonov had offered him. To that offer Nerzhin had characteristically replied, "Get thee behind me, Satan!" thus rejecting any sort of contract or moral compromise with Stalin and his henchmen (9:49). But having made his choice, Nerzhin does not want to impose it on others, does not want to condemn Sologdin for his acceptance of a similar offer. This does not mean, however, that he endorses either Sologdin's or Rubin's way of using the sharashka as a springboard to freedom, and, in fact, he seems to warn Sologdin that the "puddle" of the sharashka may spiritually drown him. But while making it clear that he personally prefers a different way, he refuses to judge Sologdin. It is clear that Nerzhin rather than Rubin reflects Solzhenitsyn's own attitude toward Sologdin.

Characteristic of the author's attitude toward Sologdin is also the fact that he is the only prisoner of Mavrino who at the end of the novel can look forward to an early release. This fact is both symbolic and ambivalent in its symbolism. On the one hand, it seems to vindicate Sologdin's way, the way of a superman, as the only effective way of getting out of prison— that is, with the help of extraordinary talents, willpower, and the ability to suppress internal resistance to moral qualms. On the other hand, given the fact that the "free" society is basically hostile to Sologdin's individualistic ideas, his exit will mean not the end but the beginning of his trials. The author seems to be unwilling to prejudge the outcome. Like the reader, he seems to be wondering, Does Sologdin see his future release as an end in itself, or as a means? If he considers it the end, it would mean an end for him as a superman. If it is a means, will he use it to "make a million" as Rubin insinuates? Will he continue to express his eccentric opinions? Will he continue to speak his Language of Maximum Clarity? Will he dissipate his "superhuman" powers and talents in skirt-chasing or harness them in the struggle for human rights? Will his moral compromise turn into a permanent neutrality, as with Stavrogin, between good and evil? Or will the crusader continue to challenge the Stalinists to ideological duel-debates? (In his "duel" with Rubin, he extols the Crusades as "a magnificent triumph of spirit over flesh. An incessant striving, sword in hand, toward sacred goals!") If so, his face will remind one of the icon image of Aleksandr Nevsky or Dmitry Donskoy, both of whom knew how to face difficulties and win victories for Russia. If not, then one could indeed agree with Rubin that he is merely a liar, a pretender wearing the mask of a Russian prince, as his literary hero Stavrogin turned out to be.[2]

At the end the reader realizes that although he knows a great deal about Sologdin, he does not know everything. Together with Yakonov he can only surmise that behind the pupils of Sologdin's "imperturbable, incorruptible, immaculate" blue eyes, the "whole astounding world of an individual human being" remains largely undisclosed. What Bakhtin says about Dostoevsky's approach to his characters—"There is always something in a man that only he himself can reveal in a free act of self-consciousness and confession"[3]—seems to be just as applicable to Solzhenitsyn's Sologdin. As if in agreement with this aspect of polyphonic strategy, Solzhenitsyn frees Sologdin from his authorial authority, thus giving him a chance to prove himself different from his model.

CHAPTER V

Nerzhin

or

the Way of a Saintly Hero

GLEB VIKENTYEVICH NERZHIN offers yet another response to Stalin, and another way out from the impasse of Stalinism. His conflict with Stalin is of long standing. "Through some strange inward sense, he had since adolescence been hearing a mute bell—all the groans, cries, shouts" of Stalin's victims, and an "inviolable decision took root in him: to learn and understand" what was going on. He wondered, for instance, why the old Bolsheviks, who made the Revolution, had not only begun to "drift into nonexistence," but "let themselves be arrested and appeared in court and unaccountably confessed, loudly condemned themselves with the worst vilifications, and admitted serving in all the foreign intelligence agencies in the world" (34:235).

When we meet him in the novel, Nerzhin is on the eve of his thirty-first birthday. About his past we learn that he graduated from a university, married, then fought as an artillery captain before he was arrested for his "turn of mind" at the end of the war. Now he is serving his fifth year "in harness," the last three of which he has spent at the sharashka where he is employed as a mathematician in the Acoustics Lab.[1] As to his youthful passion "to learn and understand,"

> Everything was realized and fulfilled, but Nerzhin was left with neither his work, nor time, nor life—nor his wife. Once a single great passion occupies the soul, it displaces everything else. There is no room in us for two passions. (34:236)

Whatever Nerzhin has learned has been "not from the philosophy I've read but from stories about real people that I've
heard in prison" (8:39). His prison experience has led him to
reject not only the Communist goals of the Stalinist society but
any materialist philosophy of life. Contrary to Rubin's allegation that he has been influenced either by Sologdin's "metaphysics" or by certain idealist philosophies of the ancient
world, Nerzhin asserts himself as his own philosopher:

> "It isn't the philosophers of the Vedanta or the Sankhya, but I
> personally, Gleb Nerzhin, a prisoner in harness for the fifth
> year, who has risen to that stage of development where the bad
> begins to appear the good. And I personally hold the view that
> people don't know what they are striving for. They waste
> themselves in senseless thrashing around for the sake of a
> handful of goods and die without realizing their spiritual
> wealth." (8:40)

To Nerzhin's passion for learning has now been joined a
determination to bear witness to the suffering of Russia under
Stalin. In his spare time and under the constant threat of being
caught, he keeps writing his "Notes on History," which he
considers his "first coming of age." Through them the reader
discovers that Nerzhin views Stalin as Russia's "butcher"
rather than a "therapist" (5:26).

The routine of Nerzhin's "peaceful existence" is suddenly
interrupted by his summons to Yakonov, the boss of scientific
research at the sharashka. As a talented mathematician, he is
offered a position on a cryptography project. The offer is very
tempting. Not only would it give Nerzhin a chance to "achieve
maturity in his own field," but, he is told,

> "As a cryptographer, if the work is successful, you'll be freed
> ahead of your term, the conviction will be removed from your
> record, and you will be given an apartment in Moscow." (9:50)

Should he reject the offer, however, he would most certainly
be deported to the camps. Yet Nerzhin decides to reject the
offer, and tells his superiors why:

"You're beginning at the wrong end. Let them admit first that
it's not right to put people in prison for their way of thinking,
and then *we* will decide whether we will forgive *them*." (9:50)

This explanation notwithstanding, one may still think of
Nerzhin's decision as irrational, foolish, and quixotic. As
Sologdin sees it, "You behave not as a mathematician but as
a poet." Unlike Rubin and Sologdin, the "poet" Nerzhin rejects the offer of cooperation with his captors and thus refuses
a moral compromise with Stalin, that "inflated, gloomy giant"
whom he has resolved to combat.[2] In this he is indeed poetic,
somewhat Dantean, somewhat Quixotic, somewhat Faustian.
Like Dante he is resolved to descend from the first circle to
the hell of the camps, is determined to bear witness to what he
sees; and as Dante was sustained in his journey across the Inferno by his love for Beatrice, so Nerzhin feels better prepared
for the camps after his faith has been reaffirmed by his beloved
wife, Nadezhda (Hope). Like Don Quixote, a knight and a
poet who was always ready to charge against the windmills of
evil, Nerzhin feels compelled "to grapple with the riddle of
the inflated gloomy giant who had only to flutter his eyelashes
for Nerzhin's head to fly off" (9:49). Finally, he is consumed
by the same passion to "learn and understand" that consumed
Faust in his striving for the secrets of the "evergreen tree of
life."[3]

However, the figure of Nerzhin cannot be understood solely
in terms of his association with the poetic myths of world
literature. There are grounds for believing that these associations are secondary to Solzhenitsyn's conception of Nerzhin as
an essentially Christlike figure. Built up gradually and unob-
strusively, this image is inconspicuously sustained throughout
the novel.[4]

The reader is first made aware of it in the scene in which Nerzhin tries to sum up his "pros" and "contras" in regard to the
cryptography offer. The choice presents itself to him as a
question of the meaning of life:

But why live a whole life? Just to be living? Just to keep the
body going? Precious comfort! What do we need it for if
there's nothing else?
   And good sense said, "Yes," but the heart said, "Get thee
behind me, Satan!" (9:49)

While the passage may be read as a paraphrase of "Not by
bread alone," it also contains a verbatim quotation from the
Gospels, namely, the rejection formula "Get thee behind me,
Satan!" that Christ used in his reply to the threefold temptation in the wilderness. Since Nerzhin has just expressed his
readiness to grapple with the "inflated, gloomy giant," that
is, with Stalin, his reply amounts, on a metaphysical level, to
a rejection of Stalin/Satan's offer of milk or bread.
   A further similarity with Christ may be seen in Nerzhin's feelings about the ultimate implications of his decision:

Now, when he could reflect on the conversation in Yakonov's office, Nerzhin understood everything more clearly.
His refusal to participate in the cryptographic group was not
a mere incident but *a turning point in his life*. It was certain
to result, perhaps very soon, in a long and arduous journey to
Siberia or the Arctic, *to death or to a hard victory over death*.
   He wanted to think about this sudden break in his life. What
had he managed to do during this *three-year respite* in the
sharashka? Had he sufficiently tempered his character before
this new *leap into the abyss of camp*?
   It so happened that the next day would be Gleb's *thirty-first
birthday*. (He had, of course, no heart to remind his friends
of the date.) *Was this the middle of his life, almost the end of
it, or only the beginning*? (14:75, emphasis added)

Not unlike Christ before the Crucifixion, Nerzhin thinks of his
uncompromising decision as a turning point of his whole life.
The "long and arduous journey" that he is facing reminds one
of Christ's Via Dolorosa. While common sense would tell
Nerzhin that at the end of his journey he can expect nothing
but death or, at best, bare survival, he dares to believe, as
Christ did, in the possibility of a "victory over death" and the

beginning of a new life. Even in age he is rather close to Christ at the time of Golgotha, and his three years of relative freedom and respite at the sharashka seem to correspond to the three-year period allotted to Christ for accomplishing his mission and preparing for his "leap into the abyss." Finally, Nerzhin's birthday coincides with Christmas Day, 25 December according to the Gregorian calendar.

There is a further resemblance in that Nerzhin, after making the fateful decision, finds himself momentarily overpowered by a feeling of weakness and even thinks that "after all, it was not too late to correct matters, to agree to join the cryptography" (14:75). Characteristically, when he later regains his moral strength he does so through compassion toward a fellow prisoner. Having noticed that Rostislav Doronin, a younger friend whom he has taken under his wing, has come close to a total lack of faith (*neverie*), he tells him:

> "You're losing sight of everything solid, of every goal. One can certainly doubt, one is obliged to doubt. But isn't it also necessary *to love something?*" (14:79, emphasis added)

As if in reward for this, Nerzhin is suddenly, against all prison regulations, allowed a visit by his wife, Nadezhda, on Sunday morning, 25 December; the visit comes as both a birthday and a Christmas present. Although she informs him of her intention to divorce him *pro forma*, as he himself had earlier advised her, he now feels reaffirmed in his faith and love and is more than ever determined to go to the camps rather than to join cryptography, and he tells her not to be surprised "if they send me away from here, far away, and if my letters stop entirely." After that, the dialogue quickly reaches its culmination before it is broken off by the guards:

> "Can they do that? Where?" Nadya cried out.
> What news! And he was telling her only now!
> "Only God knows," he said, shrugging his shoulders meaningfully.

"Don't tell me you've started believing in God?!"
(They haven't talked about anything!)
Gleb smiled. "Pascal, Newton, Einstein."
"You were told not to name any names!" the guard barked.
"Let's break it up!" (37:258)

The culmination, of course, is Gleb Nerzhin's declaration,
transparently veiled by the names of great scholars, of his faith
in God. It reinforces the impression that behind the secular
exterior of the mathematician a religious drama is taking place.

The scene of Nerzhin's birthday party is most meaningful
when it is understood in the light of this drama, which in its
reminiscence of the Last Supper adds to his portrayal as a
Christlike figure. At this party Nerzhin twice violates the tradition by refusing to drink to his own health, even though he
knows that he is well on the road to "death or a victory over
death." Instead, he proposes two toasts, one "to the friendship which thrives in prison vaults," another to the wives and
sweethearts of the prisoners who have bound themselves to
their men with the bond of love. Although the scene lacks the
motif of betrayal, an essential element of the Last Supper, it is
full of the spirit of the New Testament. Nerzhin's toasts, for instance, seem to parallel Christ's message of love, friendship,
and brotherhood. (In them, significantly, Nerzhin addresses
his guests as "brethren.") It must be also pointed out that the
scene takes place in a former Christian chapel, turned prison,
and in a cell located just below the altar vault. While it is true
that at the improvised "Lyceum table" Nerzhin has not twelve
disciples but only half a dozen friends,[5] it may be noteworthy
that they are seated on two bunks at the sides of the table, three
on each side, while he as the birthday celebrant is seated at the
head of the table on the windowsill. He is seen then against
the background of the cross-barred window, and thus singled
out visually as a Christ figure.

They drink to friendship, and to love, and the reader realizes that these seven friends of different ideological and political orientation are not just indulging in a pathetic Russian drinking ritual.[6] Rather they are making a symbolic gesture of defiance against a social order which suspects as ideologically subversive any manifestation of genuine human love and friendship across ideological barriers. The abnormality of the situation is symbolized in the image of the black snow introduced at this moment; it falls outside as the seven friends drink to friendship and love.

> The snow itself couldn't be seen, but the lamps and the searchlights of the zone cast the black shadows of falling snowflakes on the windowpanes.
> Somewhere beyond that curtain of heavy snow was Nadya Nerzhin.
> "Even the snow we see is black," Kondrashev-Ivanov said. (53:372)

At the other end of Moscow, Nadya watches the same snowfall from the window of a student dormitory. There she stands as if *"crucified on the black cross of the window frame"* (47:337, emphasis added), for the suffering she has to bear is no less than her husband's. She has just told her friend, Shchagov, a former front-line soldier, that her husband is a political prisoner. As if in a gesture of repudiation, Shchagov immediately leaves the room. Nadya's ears are filled with the music of despair. However, a few minutes later, Shchagov returns:

> He had a bottle and two glasses with him.
> "Well, soldier's wife," he said heartily, "don't lose heart! Here, take a glass! If you've got a good head on your shoulders, there'll be happiness yet. Let's drink—*to the resurrection of the dead!*" (47:337)

Captain Shchagov's toast not only reciprocates Captain Nerzhin's toasts as a counterpoint in the polyphonic development of the theme of "victory over death," but also alludes to the

Calvary of all political prisoners in Stalin's Russia and more specifically to that of Nerzhin.

The final touch in Solzhenitsyn's portrayal of Nerzhin as a Christ figure comes at the end of the novel in the description of his departure as one of twenty condemned zeks, to the "abyss" of the camps:

> Yes, the taiga and tundra awaited them, the record cold of Oymyakon and the copper excavations of Dzhezkazgan; pick and barrow; starvation rations of soggy bread; the hospital; death. The very worst.
> *But there was peace in their souls.* (87:673, emphasis added)

Nerzhin is certainly more at peace with his conscience, his inner self, than either Rubin or Sologdin. This is partly because he has acquired "the fearlessness of those who have lost everything" but chiefly, as the novel has it, because

> even Christ in the garden of Gethsemane, knowing his bitter fate full well, nonetheless prayed and hoped. (87:666)

To designate Nerzhin as Christlike is not necessarily to say that he is a Christian in the commonly accepted sense of the word; at least there is no direct evidence to that effect in the novel. In this respect he is distinctly different not only from Alyosha Karamazov but also from Solzhenitsyn's own Alyoshka the Baptist in *One Day*, two Christians in a more or less traditional sense. Nerzhin may be aware of the Gospels and even inspired by Christ—the story "Buddha's Smile," which he wrote in collaboration with Potapov, relates the episode of a prisoner swallowing the pages of the Sermon on the Mount from the Gospels—yet his faith in God is founded neither on the memories of his childhood, nor on an elder's spiritual guidance, nor on communal religious experiences. His is newfound faith, acquired through his suffering in the hell of an atheistic society, tempered in the fire of that hell, verified by the data collected in his mathematical mind, and affirmed through his dialogues with the "select" wizards of the nether world. Paraphrasing the author, one could say that his is the faith "which is not easy to come by but which endures."

Solzhenitsyn seems anxious to demonstrate that the believer Nerzhin is much more in tune with the scientific discoveries of the twentieth century than the atheist Rubin whose allegedly scientific ideology is no more than an anachronism. When Nerzhin denounces Stalinism, Rubin accuses him of meddling "in matters you know nothing about." The mathematician Nerzhin is quick with a rebuttal:

> "Listen here, enough of these legends about people who discovered the neutrino and weighed Beta Sirius without ever having seen them being so infantile they can't orient themselves in the simple problems of human existence. We have no choice. If you historians no longer concern yourselves with history, what is left for us mathematicians and technicians to do? I see who wins the prizes and who gets the academic salaries. They don't write history; they just lick a certain well-known spot. So we, the scientific intelligentsia, have to study history ourselves." (8:42)

Nerzhin clearly asserts himself as a spokesman for modern progress and for the technocratic segment of the Soviet intelligentsia (which, by the way, in recent years has been increasingly active in the forefront of the Soviet human rights movement). Characteristically, when in the novel Nerzhin actually declares his belief in God, he refers not to the fathers of the Church but to the fathers of modern science—Pascal, Newton, and Einstein. The reference to Einstein, the founder of the theory of relativity and a Jew, seems especially significant, suggesting that the source of Nerzhin's religious inspiration is not limited to Russia's Orthodox Christian heritage. Ironically, the Russian Nerzhin is spiritually much closer to Einstein than is the Jew Rubin, a dogmatist possessed by the "absolute truth" of Marxism.

Nerzhin's admiration for Einstein and the theory of relativ-

ity does not mean, however, that he is either a philosophical or
a moral relativist. In fact, in his conversation with the young
Rostislav Doronin, he rejects all philosophical schools which
are based on the notion of the relativity of moral values, and
tells him why:

> "No matter how clever and absolute the systems of skepticism
> or agnosticism or pessimism, you must understand that by their
> very nature they doom us to a loss of will. They can't really
> influence human behavior because people cannot stand still.
> And that means *they can't renounce systems which affirm
> something, which summon them to advance in some direc-
> tion.*" (14:78, emphasis added)

Among those "systems which affirm something" one can certainly name several world religions including Christianity and,
perhaps, secular beliefs in progress, democracy, and the free
world. It is obviously not these that Nerzhin wants to renounce,
for none of them has caused his current troubles. What is
really on his mind is the philosophic system of Marxism-
Leninism which summons, even forces, people to advance in
no uncertain direction.

Realizing that neither skepticism nor agnosticism nor pessimism nor any other secular system of thought is capable of
stopping the onslaught of the atheistic religion of Communism, Nerzhin appears to be groping for a new faith which will
not "doom us to a loss of will" and which will "influence
human behavior." Though he has been known at the sharashka
as an inveterate skeptic, he realizes that "skepticism can never
provide firm ground under a man's feet" and decides to abandon that road in favor of a more affirmative ideology. In his
quest for the "firm ground" he has absorbed into himself
modern and ancient philosophies from the West and East, the
ideas of Tao and Sankhya, Pyrrho and Sextus Empiricus,
Montaigne and Lev Tolstoy.

Among all the philosophers, however, Nerzhin seems closest to Socrates, and at one point the writer refers to him as a "disciple of Socrates." In using his skeptical attitude to split "the rockheads" of the official dogmatism and to choke the "fanatical voices" of men's blind convictions, he is indeed following the ancient teacher. He is like Socrates, too, in playing the role of a midwife, helping to bring about the birth of truth through dialogues, as well as through his commitment to a clear conscience and his faith in the immortality of truth and justice, and, finally, in making a decision, which, to the uninitiated, is an expression of foolishness and the death-wish, and then knowing how to face the prospect of death with peace in his heart. However, keeping in mind that Socrates himself has often been called the Christ of ancient Greece, Nerzhin's closeness to this philosopher does not detract from, but rather adds to, his portrayal as essentially Christlike.

Having conceived of Nerzhin as a Christ figure, Solzhenitsyn provides him with certain features that make him a Russian Christ, or rather a Russian saintly follower of Christ. Physically, he appears humble, ordinary, somehow lacking in color, especially when compared with the imposing figures of Rubin and Sologdin. He looks older than his age. His hair is neither black like Rubin's nor blond like Sologdin's, but an intermediate color (*rusye*).

> There were already many deep wrinkles in his face—whole wreaths of them around his eyes, at the corners of his lips, long furrows on his forehead. His skin looked faded because of the lack of fresh air. But it was most of all his economy of movement that made him seem old—that wise economy with which nature husbands a prisoner's strength against the drain of a concentration-camp regime. (5:21)

Realistic as it may be, the portrait is yet suggestive of the humble image of a Russian saint of the so-called kenotic type. Nerzhin's deportment also conforms to the spirit of self-abnegation, humility, and voluntary martyrdom that distin-

guished the kenotic saints. His first name, Gleb, may be read
as an allusion to Prince Gleb who, together with his brother
Boris, heads the list of Russian saints. The writer seems to be
saying that people like Gleb Nerzhin continue the line of Russian sainthood into the Soviet period. In fact, at one point his
wife sees a sort of halo (*oreol*) around Nerzhin's head, and
then thinks that it rather "suits him" to be in prison.

Returning to our main thesis, that the artistic strategy of
The First Circle is similar to that employed by Dostoevsky in
his polyphonic novels, it must be pointed out that the presence
of a Christ figure is neither required by nor does it prove the
presence of polyphony. However, one can only agree with
Bakhtin that the person of Christ has played an extremely important role in Dostoevsky's "form-determining ideology." According to Bakhtin, "The image of the ideal man or the image
of Christ is seen by him [Dostoevsky] as the solution of ideological quests. This image, this supreme voice must crown
the world of voices, organize and subordinate it."[7] Although
Bakhtin concedes that Dostoevsky never quite succeeded in
giving an adequate artistic representation to that image, one
can hardly avoid the temptation to compare Nerzhin with Dostoevsky's last attempt to create a Russian Christlike hero,
namely, with Alyosha Karamazov.

At first glance the two appear rather dissimilar. One is formally Christian, indeed a novice, while the other is only groping for some kind of faith. They are quite different in age,
education, occupation, and experience; one is a bachelor, the
other is not; one has hardly heard a shot fired, the other has
gone through the cruelest of wars. Also, they are faced with
entirely different situations, one being a free citizen, the other
a prisoner; and they live in two entirely different Russias. So
if there is indeed some similarity between the two, it is not in
the details of their portrayal, but rather in their deportment,
ethics, insistence on learning from life and on going to the

people. And, of course, both are inspired by the same ideal of self-abnegation and personal sacrifice.

What is even more important in respect to our thesis, however, is the fact that Nerzhin resembles Alyosha through his structural role in the novel as a friend and confidant of other characters. He is the bridge between the Communists and the reactionaries, the technical and humanist intelligentsia, between the intellectual elite of the country and its grass roots, between male and female, old and young. He lends his sympathetic ear to twenty-three-year-old Rostislav Doronin and to the old Bolshevik Adamson, "winding up the twentieth" in Stalin's jails; to the heroic optician Gerasimovich and the "ageless idealist" Kondrashev-Ivanov, a painter. He makes Sologdin confide to him his "scriptural rules," but he also appreciates Rubin when "you argue from your heart and talk intelligently and don't try to pin abusive labels on things." He helps the peasant zek Spiridon deliver his "homespun truths," and with the apolitical "robot" Potapov he writes the story "Buddha's Smile." To his birthday party he purposely invites a select company of widely divergent ideological persuasions, makes them exchange views, and even brings about agreement in some areas. In short, he functions in the novel as a living practitioner and catalyst of polyphony and dialogic communication. (For more on this subject see chapter 7.)

When the time comes for Nerzhin to leave the sharashka he exchanges kisses with both Rubin and Spiridon, though the two are poles apart and do not communicate with each other at all. Then he tries to make peace between Rubin and Sologdin, two ideological antagonists:

> Troubled by the ill will between his companions, Gleb said quietly in the total silence of the library, "Friends. You must make it up."
> Neither Rubin nor Sologdin moved.
> "Dmitri," Gleb insisted.

Sologdin raised the cold blue flame of his gaze. "Why do
you direct your remarks to *me*?" he said, acting surprised.
"Lev!" Gleb repeated.
Rubin looked at him vacantly. "Do you know," he asked,
"why horses live a long time?" After a pause he explained:
"Because they never go around clarifying their relationships."
(86:658)

Even though Nerzhin does not succeed in bringing peace between the two, his peacemaking effort is in itself very significant. Not only does it confirm Nerzhin as Christlike, but it also
shows how close Solzhenitsyn's conception of such a figure is
to Dostoevsky's Alyosha, with his insistence on the necessity
of showing an "active love."

In a sense, Nerzhin goes even further than Alyosha in his
practice of active love. While on the one hand he is a meek,
kind, reflective, compassionate, idealistic, and even quixotic
person,[8] he is at the same time shown to be very strong-willed,
dynamic, mature and practical. In this respect he is different
not only from the prevailing male heroes of nineteenth-century
Russian literature but also from Solzhenitsyn's own kenotic
characters such as Matryona and Alyoshka the Baptist. He
may be as meek or as saintly as they, yet he lacks their fatalis-
tic passivity, a trait that is so often considered a part of the
Russian national character. Not only is he a man of action, but
the course of action he chooses seems quite effective. This is
evident from the description of how Nerzhin is remembered at
the sharashka:

> Just as at funerals people remember everything good the de-
> ceased ever did, so now they remembered, in praise of Ner-
> zhin, *how he would stand up for their rights, and how often he
> had defended the prisoners' interests*. There was the famous
> story of the sifted flour, when he had inundated the prison
> administration and the Ministry of Internal Affairs with com-
> plaints that each day he *personally* was given five grams of
> sifted flour less than he should have received. According to
> prison regulations, collective complaints and complaints on

behalf of others were both prohibited. *Even though the idea was that the prisoner was to be retrained in the direction of socialism, he was forbidden to be concerned with the common cause.* In those days the zeks of the sharashka had not yet eaten their fill, and the struggle for the five grams of flour aroused far keener interest than international affairs. The fascinating epic ended with Nerzhin's victory: the "captain in charge of under-drawers," as they then called him, the assistant to the prison supply officer, was fired from his job. From the sifted flour each man in the sharashka got each day they cooked extra noodles twice a week. The zeks also remembered Nerzhin's struggle to extend the Sunday exercise periods. (86:656, emphasis added)

In this passage Nerzhin is exemplified as a practitioner of active love and a champion of the common cause, and in it is shown, too, how much more difficult is his situation than that of Alyosha Karamazov. The passage may also be read as an endorsement of Nerzhin's way, that of a saintly hero, as a rather effective way of combating the Stalinist system of jails and camps without yielding to moral compromise. Unlike Rubin and Sologdin, Nerzhin wins his victories with a clear conscience. No matter how small they are, his victories demonstrate that not all means, not even all legal means, of fighting against the system are precluded. Right up to his last moment at the sharashka Nerzhin continues to fight, to stand up for his and everybody's rights:

Nerzhin himself hardly listened to all these eulogies. For him the moment of action had come and energy was erupting in him. Now that the worst had happened, any improvement depended on him alone. (86:656)

First, he presses the demand that he and his twenty friends departing for the camps should be given the last meal due them at the sharashka. When the demand is finally met and the meal is brought in, there is a "stir of victory" among the inmates, because "this last chance to eat meat meant not only the last full stomach before months and years of thin gruel; it also

meant their human dignity" (87:667). Second, he demands
that Major Shikin return to him a book of Esenin's poetry that
had been taken away in violation of prison regulations, "and
the major of State Security yielded to this doomed, helpless
zek, being sent to a slow death" (86:653). This victory is
especially important to Nerzhin, for he sees in it "a symbol of
success at the moment when everything was in ruins." It is a
symbolic fulfillment of the inscription his wife Nadezhda had
written on the book, "And so everything lost will return to
you!" Finally, it represents a symbolic pledge of allegiance to
Esenin's dictum, "The white rose of truth will never be recon-
ciled with the black toad of evil." Nerzhin may or may not
attain his victory over death, but he will not cling to the sharashka at the cost of a moral compromise with the black toad
of evil.

Although the symbolic implications of the charactonym,
again, are unobtrusive and in no way imposed on the reader,
Solzhenitsyn has perhaps crystallized his conception of the
character in Nerzhin's full name. Thus, Gleb may be read as
alluding to his saintly qualities of self-abnegation and readiness for self-sacrifice in the spirit of his patron saint; Nerzhin
may be read as suggesting that the tradition of Russian sainthood is not subject to corrosion and decay (a negative from
rzha: rzhavchina, meaning "rust"); and his patronymic Vikentyevich (related to Latin "victor") seems to suggest that
the way of Nerzhin, the way of a saintly hero, may prove
victorious in coping with Soviet totalitarianism.

CHAPTER VI

Innokenty Volodin's Crime and Punishment

IF THE STORIES of Rubin, Sologdin, and Nerzhin show the predicament of being a prisoner in Stalin's Russia, the story of Innokenty Volodin illustrates the predicament of a free citizen in that country. As his last name seems to suggest, he belongs to the elite who possess (*vladeiut*) Russia, to those who have ruled it since their godfather Lenin put them in power in 1917. Born two years after the Revolution, Innokenty belongs to that group chiefly on the merit of being a son of "the celebrated hero of the Civil War," the Red sailors' leader Artyom who, under his first name, symbolizes in the USSR the "revolutionary spirit of the Russian proletariat." To be sure, Innokenty has been taught to feel proud of his father's "struggle for the ordinary people against the few who lived steeped in luxury" (55:396). Yet, ironically, his own life is also steeped in luxury, in sharp contrast to the lot of the ordinary Soviet citizen. At the age of thirty he is already a lieutenant colonel and state counselor in the Ministry of Foreign Affairs, and thus belongs to "that circle of society in which people do not know what it means to walk or take the subway" (55:394). Besides, he is happily married to a pretty blond named Dotnara, that is "Daughter of the Working People" (*doch' trudovogo naroda*), so that "their happiness together became a legend among their friends." In short, "everything seemed to be at his fingertips."

Under the circumstances one would hardly expect to find Innokenty among those "dissatisfied people" who, as Stalin admitted, have always existed and always will exist. But the writer reminds us, in the words of the Old Testament, that "the ways of the Lord are unfathomable." After years of total contentment, Innokenty has suddenly begun to feel an acute dissatisfaction with his whole way of life. He notices in himself "the lack of something, he didn't know what." The library of his deceased mother, her books, letters, diaries, and "Notes on Ethics," eventually help him to find that something. From her letters and diaries he learns, for instance, that her marriage to his father "had not been a marriage, but more like the passage of a hurricane, like everything else in those years," that she inhabited "a whole separate world of her own," and "had always loved another man," whom she was unable to join. As a result of reading her "Notes on Ethics" he comes to the conclusion that pity is not a shameful and humiliating emotion as all Soviet children are taught in school[1] but "the first action of a good soul," and that "the most precious thing in the world" is "not to participate in injustices." He cannot help noticing that his mother and her friends used "old-fashioned" language and wrote with capital letters "Truth," "Beauty," "Good," "Evil," and "Ethical Imperative." In her library he also becomes acquainted with pre-Revolutionary books, art magazines, publishers, writers, and poets "as forgotten as if they had dropped into Hell."

> For several days he would come and sit on that bench in front of the open bookcases, breathing it all in, poisoning himself with the air of his mother's world, that world into which, long ago, his father, in a black raincoat, his belt hung with grenades, had entered with a search warrant. (55:398)

Clearly, Innokenty's discovery of his mother's separate world is tantamount to his discovery of his spiritual Mother Russia.

The "poisonous air" of the spiritual world of pre-Revolutionary Russia has a profound effect on Innokenty's world view and his subsequent fate. He realizes that "just as the essence of food cannot be conveyed in calories, the essence of

life will never be captured by even the greatest formulas"
(55:399); this leads him to estrangement from one of the main
premises of the official ideology, namely, that the essence of
life had been captured once and for all by the formulas of
Marxism-Leninism-Stalinism. His ideological estrangement is
accompanied by his rejection of Soviet ethics; he arrives at his
own "Ethical Imperative":

> Up to then the truth for Innokenty had been: you have only
> one life.
> Now he came to sense a new law, in himself and in the
> world: you also have only one conscience.
> And just as you cannot recover a lost life, you cannot re-
> cover a wrecked conscience. (55:399)

Innokenty's "Ethical Imperative" clearly implies a challenge
to the materialistic code of ethics underlying the behavior of
the indoctrinated Soviet citizen. Although Solzhenitsyn does
not mention the socialist realist "classic" author Nikolai
Ostrovsky by name, a Soviet reader would certainly realize
that Innokenty's "You also have only one conscience" serves
as a counterpoint to Ostrovsky's "You have only one life,"
part of a lengthy quotation that everyone learns by heart as if
it were a catechism.[2] Innokenty's departure from the official
ideology and ethics is followed, in his personal life, by estrangement from his wife. The Daughter of the Working People (actually, her father is Makarygin, a high-ranking state
prosecutor and member of the ruling elite) has ironically by
this time degenerated into Dotty, a name which in the Soviet
context suggests an affinity with the "bourgeois and capitalist" Western culture. While "a breeze of renewal" seems to
breathe on Innokenty from the world of pre-Revolutionary
Russia, Dotnara is more interested in the newest fashions in
Paris and in high society parties where "they would leap to
their feet for the initial toast to Comrade Stalin, and then eat
and drink a great deal, oblivious of Comrade Stalin, and then

play cards stupidly" (55:398). Innokenty now recalls that his
mother never gave her consent to their marriage. When it approaches the brink of divorce he knows that "his mother had
finally done what she wanted: rising from her grave, she had
taken her son away from her daughter-in-law" (55:399).[3]
The statement has symbolic overtones as well: in the struggle
for his soul, Innokenty's dead Mother Russia, now spiritually
revived through his memory, has won out over her unwanted
daughter-in-law, the so-called Daughter of the Working People, that is, the new, Stalinist Russia. Incidentally, in contrast
with Stalin, who has restored such elements of the old Russia
as orderlies, the officer corps, shoulder boards, and the title
"supreme," not to mention Russian chauvinism and anti-
Semitism, Innokenty wants only to restore the notions of
Truth, Good, and Beauty; as to the "old-fashioned" notion of
conscience he wants to elevate it into a "new law" for himself
and the world.

Innokenty's newly acquired "ideology" is soon tested in
the crucible of action. As a high ranking diplomat about to be
sent to France, he has been informed of the Dobroumov "es-
pionage case": Dobroumov has promised to give his French
colleagues a sample of a new medicine he discovered. Instead
of simply warning the well-meaning doctor against keeping
his promise, the MGB has decided to catch him in the act,
and then use this as a pretext to crack down on all unautho-
rized contacts with the West. In other words, the Dobroumov
case is to be a signal for Stalin's wider campaign against
"cosmopolitanism" and "toadyism" to Western powers. Convinced of Dobroumov's innocence, Innokenty decides to call
him on the phone anonymously and warn him that he is being
framed. Reason tells him that this will hardly save Dobroumov,
while the risks to himself are enormous. Nevertheless, he
stands firm in his decision and phones the Dobroumovs' apartment, because "if one is forever cautious, can one remain a
human being?" Hamlet's "to be or not to be" has been re-

placed in Innokenty's case by the no less crucial dilemma: whether to be a *homo soveticus* as he was raised to be or to remain a human being as his mother's notes have taught him? The first course would mean to act with the utmost caution, as people do who are intimidated throughout their lives, to be mindful of the interests of the state and of the world revolution, and to remember that one has only one life. The second would mean to act according to his own conscience. He chooses the second because he senses in himself the "new law" of a clear conscience, and also because he prefers his mother's "pity is the first action of a good soul" to Gorky's "pity degrades men," and because she advised him "not to participate in injustices."

The trials of Innokenty the ideologist do not end with his arrest. Thrown into the Lubyanka prison he feels himself in the jaws of death. But even in this "legendary pit of horror" he wants "to think his way through to some important, yet unperceived thought" (84:630). As in Stalin's case, the idea of immortality crosses his mind:

> Suddenly it was as though a film had been removed from his brain, and what he had read and thought about during the office day emerged with full clarity:
> "Faith in immortality was born of the greed of unsatisfied people. . . . The wise man finds life's span sufficient to complete the full circle of attainable pleasures. . ."
> But was it really a matter of pleasure? He had had money, good clothes, esteem, women, wine, travel, but at this moment he would have hurled all those pleasures into the nether world for justice and truth . . . and nothing more. (84:630)

The quotation is from Epicurus (ca. 341–270 B.C.), a Greek philosopher highly regarded by the Marxists for his materialism and atheism; in fact, Marx himself had written a dissertation on him. Innokenty used to consider himself a "disciple of Epicurus" as long as he was enjoying all the privileges of the Soviet "new class." However, his first confrontation with the reality of Stalinism has made him doubt the wisdom of his teacher, and in the Dobroumov case he has acted contrary to Epicurus' advice not to participate in public life. Now, feeling that faith in immortality is essential if justice and truth are to prevail, he dismisses Epicurus' philosophy as contrived and irrelevant to our time. A few more hours of suffering in the hell of Lubyanka, and he undergoes the experience of "that second wind thanks to which an athlete's straining body feels refreshed and tireless" (84:642). It climaxes in what the writer calls the "supreme perception," that is, a suddenly increased ability to think and perceive ideas, which makes him decisively reject his teacher.

> Another of Epicurus' thoughts—unrefuted and difficult to grasp yesterday in freedom—floated in his mind:
> "Inner feelings of satisfaction and dissatisfaction are the highest criteria of good and evil."
> That meant, according to Epicurus, that what one liked was good and that what one didn't like was evil.
> The philosophy of a savage.
> Stalin enjoyed killing—did that mean that for him killing was a virtue? And since being imprisoned for trying to save somebody did not, after all, produce satisfaction, did that mean it was evil? (84:643)

Innokenty answers no because by now "Good and Evil have . . . been substantively defined." Though we never learn how they have been defined, the notions of "Good" and "Evil" themselves clearly echo the "old-fashioned" language of his spiritual Mother Russia. The writer concludes the story of Innokenty's spiritual regeneration thus:

> From those heights of struggle and suffering to which he had been lifted, the wisdom of the ancient philosopher seemed like the babbling of a child. (84:643)

We learn nothing more about Innokenty's newly acquired outlook; yet it would hardly be preposterous to conclude that his is an essentially idealist world view based on the notions of an individual conscience, faith in the immortality of justice and truth, and the necessity of discriminating between good and evil. This may or may not be a Christian world view, but it is clearly inspired by the Christian spirituality of the "old Russia," his Mother Russia. The image of a prisoner who from the "heights of struggle and suffering" looks down on the "wisdom" of the philosopher of materialism and atheism and affirms his faith in the immortality of truth and justice is bound to evoke the image of another prisoner who, from the Cross of Calvary, rejected the wisdom of this world.

In the figure of Innokenty the writer shows the transformation of a member of the Soviet ruling elite into a conscientious rebel against the Stalinist system, a transformation closely paralleled by his development as an ideologist. At first he is characterized by the nickname "Epicurean" his high-society friends used to call him. At this stage he is not actually an ideologist at all, though he wholly embraces the Communist doctrine. Then comes his dissatisfaction with himself and his way of life, because "the ways of the Lord are unfathomable." In his mother's library he discovers the real Epicurus and becomes aware of the existence of values other than those he had grown up with. The next stage comes after "he had reached a point where he felt less tossed about from one writer's ideas to another's"; at this stage he begins to sense the "new law" of a clear conscience. After he has acted in accordance with this law he discovers that his action was contrary to Epicurus' advice not to participate in public life; yet he still likes to think of himself as a "disciple of Epicurus." Only after his arrest and induction into the hell of Lubyanka does he finally dissociate himself from the ancient progenitor of materialism and atheism.

Stripped of his clothes, the last vestiges of his identification with the Soviet "epicurean" elite, he is first compared, tongue-in-cheek, to a "neutral" philosopher, Rodin's *Thinker*. Later, after a sleepless night in which he faces the prospect of torture and possibly death, he gains his "second wind" and the power of "supreme perception." Finally, from the heights of struggle and suffering he renounces the philosophy of Epicurus as the "philosophy of a savage" and the "babbling of a child." At this last stage he truly lives up to the implications of his name: an innocent human being who treads the road of suffering and self-sacrifice for his fellow men.

Neither Innokenty nor any other ideologist in the novel has the chance to engage in an actual duel-debate with Stalin. None of them is allowed to break through the isolation of Stalin's Judecca, to open the shell of his self-imposed solipsism, to interrupt his ideological monologue. However, given the fact that Stalin was considered the infallible pontiff of Communism, the responses of the novel's "heroes of ideas" to the Communist reality inevitably turn into dialogues with the dictator and the ideology he was believed to embody. Thus, Solzhenitsyn's portrayal of Innokenty appears to be formed of a series of counterpoints to Stalin's ideological voice, especially to his definition of man and man's happiness. As a member of the Soviet elite he had all the "milk" Stalin could offer, but refused to drink it. He was treated all his life as a favorite "blind puppy," but he wanted to have his eyes opened and made a conscious choice to "remain a human being." A product of Soviet education and—unlike Stalin—raised as an atheist, his soul has nevertheless been won over by his spiritual Mother Russia. He had no personal grudge against Stalin, yet he was not "glad to surrender wholly to the victor." Instead he revolted. And though his revolt may seem totally unreasonable and futile, it nevertheless shows that no Grand Inquisitor can define man once and for all, force him into a certain program, and then make permanent use of him as a dependable brick in a new Tower of Babel.

The Biblical quotation, "The ways of the Lord are unfathomable," that Solzhenitsyn uses in lieu of providing either psychological or sociological motivation for Innokenty's spiritual regeneration may be seen as the leitmotif in his portrayal, a leitmotif that accords with Dostoevsky's method of character development in which mystery and miraculous transformation are essential. Both writers evidently start from the premise that man's character and aspirations cannot possibly be regarded as set in a mold for all time, that he is unpredictable and incalculable, and that the irrational element in him is just as important as the rational. Although it is hard to pinpoint any particular predecessor for Innokenty among Dostoevsky's characters, he belongs to the same category of heroes of ideas as Shatov, Kirillov, Ivan Karamazov, and Raskolnikov.

Once he comes to feel in himself the "new law" that says that a clear conscience is no less precious than life itself, he surrenders himself totally to that law. Both estrangement from his wife and his political crime against the state are shown as concrete manifestations of his general ideological conflict with Stalin's Russia. The fact that Solzhenitsyn makes him go through the tribulations of crime and punishment has, however, strong ironic overtones. The writer seems to be saying that even though his heroes are just as strongly committed to their ideas as their predecessors, their spiritual adventures are different and take place in an entirely different environment.

Unlike the crime of Raskolnikov, his fellow trespasser of the nineteenth century, Innokenty's crime is not to murder a human being but to attempt to save one. His inner motivation for the crime is not to assert himself as a mangod but to "remain a human being." The crime itself signifies for him not a Napoleonic exemption from a law designed for ordinary human weaklings but a return to a universal ethical law. If before committing his crime Raskolnikov needs to lull his conscience by all kinds of rationalizations, Innokenty commits his "crime" as a result of the awakening of his conscience. Only after he suppresses his rational voice that tells him of the futility of his effort and of great personal risks, only after he yields to his heartfelt pity for Dobroumov, does Innokenty act.

Whereas Raskolnikov receives consolation and sympathy from a harlot, Innokenty can expect nothing of the kind even from his wife. Furthermore, there is no need in the novel for a Porfiry, because the MGB's main purpose is not to identify the culprit positively, but to be able to report to Stalin that people have been caught and punished.[4] Finally, even if the novelist tells us nothing of Innokenty's subsequent fate, we know that his punishment is not a *nakazanie*, that is, an instructive punishment, but a *kara*, a punishment of malice and revenge, the word Stalin preferred to use.

This perhaps best explains the charactonym Innokenty: he is not innocent of his crime, for he has indeed committed it and has no regrets about it, but the nature of his crime is innocent —that is, when judged by other than Stalinist standards. It is noteworthy that the name was given to him by his mother: her memory made his crime inevitable. By committing it, he simply lived up to his name and, ultimately, to the spiritual legacy of his Mother Russia.

CHAPTER VII

"No Main Hero"

or

a Galaxy of Stars

IN EXPLAINING his concept of polyphony, Solzhenitsyn focuses on his special approach to characterization, defining the polyphonic novel as a "novel without a main hero":

> If a novel has a main hero the author inevitably pays more attention and devotes more space to him. How do I understand polyphony? Each person becomes the main hero as soon as the action reverts to him. Then the author feels responsible for as many as thirty-five heroes. He does not accord preferential treatment to any one. He must understand every character and motivate his actions. (See Introduction, n. 6)

As I stated earlier, Solzhenitsyn's approach seems to parallel what Bakhtin calls Dostoevsky's "radically new attitude" to characterization whereby a "plurality of independent and non-confluent voices, a true polyphony of equal voices" is achieved. Consideration having been given to five major individual portraits in *The First Circle*, two interrelated questions remain to be answered. The first is whether this truly is a novel in which no single character can be called the main hero. Secondly, if the novel's characters are indeed organized into a polyphonic rather than a homophonic unity, how is this done? These questions are the subject of this chapter.

Most critics agree in attributing the novel's success chiefly to Solzhenitsyn's ability to create a large set of convincing, diversified, individuated, and vital characters. As if to dispel the allegation that the success of *The First Circle* outside Russia is due mainly to its anti-Stalinist topicality rather than to

its artistic merits, V. S. Pritchett says: "Twenty years ago
Koestler gave us his theatrically conceptualized account of
Stalinism and the purges in *Darkness at Noon*: Solzhenitsyn
makes the subject more spacious, and, as a real novelist must,
places it in the lives of men and women. He shows the lives
out of which opinion has grown." His view is seconded by
Harrison Salisbury, for whom the novel's characters are "flesh
and blood"; while according to Jeri Laber the novelist not
only "reveals the life styles and the spiritual state of the 50-
odd characters," but does so "with economy and control, yet
with such great attention to detail that one never finds it necessary to refer to the guide at the beginning of the book."
Donald Fanger calls the novel's characters "a series of inter-
locking portraits, of separate arrested fates." They "may be
ultimately exemplary," Fanger says, but "none of the characters exists simply to show or prove something. The emphasis
throughout is on what the author calls at one point 'the whole
astounding world of an individual human being.'" [1]

What is more, a number of critical reviews seem to confirm
the overall polyphonic effect of the novel, even when not
using the term. More specifically, it has been pointed out that
Solzhenitsyn shows an unusually high degree of sympathy for
many characters, including the sharashka jailers. Maurice
Friedberg notes that "Solzhenitsyn displays little rancor for
the jailers in the sharashka; in fact, his attitude toward some of
them approaches sympathy"; and according to C. J. McNaspy,
the writer is "compassionate, not abusive. Most of the characters, even the jail guards, are shown with some sympathy."
Finally, Mary Ellmann is deeply impressed by Solzhenitsyn's
ability to feel compassion: "And sympathy then, through his
talent, is roused as though we were by nature sympathetic!
The illusion is one of no novelist at all, of an effortless bond
between character and reader." [2] The effect thus described
amounts to that of a self-effacing author, one of the main objectives of polyphonic strategy: in order to create "free men"

and to ensure the polyphony of their independent ideological voices, the writer must avoid interposing his "voice," his world view, between his characters and his readers. This is the effect which is conspicuously lacking in the novels of Lev Tolstoy, but for which Dostoevsky's novels have been highly praised. While Tolstoy seems to do everything to make certain that the reader can positively identify his, the author's, voice, Dostoevsky's voice is not so easy to discern. As Bakhtin puts it, "For some critics the voice of Dostoevsky is consonant with that of one character or another; for others, his voice represents a peculiar synthesis of all the ideological voices; still others believe that he simply allows his voice to be muffled by the voices of his characters."[3]

Similarly, the task of discerning the author's voice in *The First Circle* poses a challenge as soon as one goes beyond the purely political aspects of Stalinism. Some critics speak about Solzhenitsyn's advocacy of quietism, stoicism, or Tolstoyanism; others view him as the latest offspring of the Russian populism; still others identify him with either "ethical socialism" or Orthodox Christianity.

Particularly revealing is the dispute among critics about the novel's heroes. Although most identify Nerzhin as the main hero, he frequently must contend for that position with other characters, especially with the Communist Rubin. The *Times Literary Supplement* reviewer went so far as to equate the two as joint spokesmen for the author. As to the literary model for their mutual relationship, the *TLS* reviewer finds it in Lev Tolstoy: "Like *War and Peace*, *The First Circle* rests heavily on the dialogue of two main characters . . . both of them in a sense embodiments of two different facets of the author's personality. Gleb Vikentich Nerzhin is Solzhenitsyn's Pierre, Lev Grigoryevich Rubin his André." That the question of the main hero's identity is not just a technical one, but has to do with determining the direction of the novel's main ideological thrust, is evident from the *TLS* reviewer's summary of their

dialogue: "Whereas Rubin believes passionately that history
will eventually sort out the anomalies of the Stalinist system
and put communism back on to its proper, gloriously constructive path, Nerzhin prefers to take refuge in quietist philosophy." In this reviewer's judgment, "Solzhenitsyn opts neither
for Nerzhin's withdrawn solipsism nor for Rubin's collective
optimism. The problem remains honestly unresolved." [4]
    At the opposite pole stands Helen Muchnic. There is no
doubt in her mind that Nerzhin is the hero of the novel. As to
Rubin, far from being one facet of the author's personality, he
"is a scholar who perverts his knowledge, an honest man who
becomes an informer, a humane man who, because of his
ideas, acts brutally." For her there is no "honestly unresolved" problem, no chance of Solzhenitsyn's opting for
Rubin's "collective optimism." Quite to the contrary, she
says, in Rubin "more eloquently than if he had been by nature
false, petty, and cruel, the basic principles of communism, the
logic of dialectical materialism, and the official ethics of the
Soviet State, stand condemned." In terms of the nineteenth-
century Russian literary tradition Muchnic finds Rubin similar
to Raskolnikov and Turgenev's Bazarov, for, like them, "he
is inflexible in his philosophical and political beliefs" and is
"a man corrupted by his intellect." In contrast to those critics
who, like that of the *Times Literary Supplement*, see Rubin
and Nerzhin as a variation of Tolstoy's famous duo, she emphasizes their sharp ideological antagonism. "As men the two
are friends," say Muchnic, but "as thinkers, enemies. . . .
Nerzhin is a humanist, Rubin is a doctrinaire." She then attempts to explain this in terms of the modern, post-Revolu-
tionary tradition: "They are in this respect something like
Pasternak's Zhivago and Strelnikov, on the one hand, an independent, enlightened man opposed to Russian Communism
on the ground of humanity, on the other, its exponent and advocate, a hidebound, rigid follower of the official doctrine." [5]
    The discrepancy of opinion about Rubin and Nerzhin is

widespread: Are the two modeled after Pasternak's Strelnikov and Zhivago or after Tolstoy's Bolkonsky and Bezukhov? Do both speak for the author or does Solzhenitsyn glorify one and condemn the other? Do they represent two facets of the author's personality?

Faced with these questions one is immediately reminded of the never-ending debate concerning Dostoevsky's fictional ideologists. In regard to *The Brothers Karamazov* the debate still continues, despite the author's explicit statement in his preface that Alyosha was to be the main hero of the novel. In the light of Bakhtin's thesis, however, the question of the main hero appears rather irrelevant, for in a polyphonic novel the author's central idea is expressed not so much through one character or another as through the work's structure. Thus, though the religious ideas of Alyosha (and Father Zossima) may very well be closest to the "voice" of Dostoevsky—and in this respect his prefatory statement is not a case of intentional fallacy—the writer conveys his main idea, which goes beyond his personal, changeable and "sinful" convictions and biases, by allowing other ideologists, including the ones with whom he totally disagrees, to speak up for their ideas as persuasively as if they were his own—for example, the ideas of the Grand Inquisitor as voiced by Ivan. Thus he avoids the pitfalls of solipsism as a thinker, and the pitfalls of the homophonic, or "monological," art as a novelist, instead implementing in his novels a true polyphony of autonomous voices and granting his "men of ideas" freedom to expound their views indefinitely. In accordance with the supreme message of his metaphysics, namely, that freedom of choice is fundamental for the religion of Christ, Dostoevsky the novelist, though he makes no secret of his own choice, leaves it to the reader to choose a personal hero.

In a similar way, when Solzhenitsyn contends that there is no single main hero in his polyphonic novels, he seems to be suggesting that one will search in vain for the principal message of these novels in one character or another without taking into account the polyphonic arrangement of characters in the whole. Perhaps, by refusing to endorse any single character, Solzhenitsyn goes even further than Dostoevsky, for though Bakhtin nowhere says that a polyphonic novel must not have a single main hero, it can be safely assumed that polyphony would tend to minimize such a role as understood in a homophonic novel.[6]

Why cannot Nerzhin, for instance, be considered the main hero? To answer this question, this rather loose notion must be more precisely defined; specific criteria must be set up by which a character may be qualified for the role. Solzhenitsyn himself suggested as one standard the amount of attention and space devoted to a character. A second criterion obviously is the degree to which a character may be said to be the author's principal spokesman, the chief protagonist of his ideas.

Judged by the first standard, Nerzhin hardly measures up to such established principal heroes of Russian literature as Bazarov in *Fathers and Sons*, Nekhlyudov in Tolstoy's *Resurrection*, Melekhov in Sholokhov's *Quiet Flows the Don*, not to mention such title characters as Goncharov's Oblomov, Pushkin's Onegin, Lermontov's Pechorin, Pasternak's Zhivago, and Solzhenitsyn's own Ivan Denisovich. Although Nerzhin perhaps receives slightly more attention and space than Rubin or Sologdin or Volodin, Solzhenitsyn was surprisingly even-handed in his treatment of them.

But would not Nerzhin qualify as the author's principal spokesman? Isn't he in this sense the main hero of *The First Circle* as Bezukhov is of *War and Peace*, Levin of *Anna Karenina*, Shtolts of *Oblomov*, and Insarov of *On the Eve*? The answer must be both yes and no. Yes, because he is most closely identified with the author: biographically, ideologically, and as a potential "author" of the novel. No, because the emphasis in the novel is not on his, or anybody else's, world view, but on a coexistence of different world views.

While thematically this emphasis is most strongly expressed through Nerzhin's toast to friendship across ideological lines, through his "midwifery" and peacemaking efforts, structurally it is carried out through a polyphonic arrangement of the "wise men" in the "first circle."

So, if Nerzhin is the main hero of the novel, then he is a rather unusual one. Perhaps he can be called a self-effacing main hero in much the same sense as Solzhenitsyn is a self-effacing author. Or, since the notion of a *main hero* stems from a monological, or homophonic, conception of art and is hardly compatible with polyphony, Nerzhin may be distinguished among other characters as *the author's personal hero*, that is, a character who stands closest to his creator and yet is independent from him and in no way imposed on the reader as *the* hero. (Alyosha Karamazov would also appear to be such a character, for he is so imposed only in the preface, not in the novel itself.)

Once this distinction is made, the discrepancy of opinion about *The First Circle*'s major characters appears in a different light. While I am convinced that the *Times Literary Supplement* reviewer is wrong in equating Rubin and Nerzhin as dual spokesmen for the author, the error itself seems to indicate Solzhenitsyn's success in producing the effect of independent characters, one of the chief objectives of polyphonic strategy. On the other hand, while basically agreeing with Helen Muchnic's assessment of the two characters, I think that her analogy with Pasternak's Zhivago and Strelnikov is just as misleading as the *TLS* reviewer's analogy with Lev Tolstoy's Bezukhov and Bolkonsky.

The latter is misleading because Nerzhin and Rubin are not two facets of Solzhenitsyn's personality as Bezukhov and Bolkonsky may be said to be of Tolstoy's. As to the analogy with Zhivago and Strelnikov, it seems to me misleading in spite of the fact that as individuals they are quite close to Nerzhin and Rubin respectively. For one thing, only the sec-

ond part of Muchnic's definition of the Nerzhin/Rubin relationship, "As men the two are friends, as thinkers, enemies,"
applies to Pasternak's pair, whom the reader remembers not as
two friends but rather as two distant rivals in a love drama.
Even more important, however, is the fact that while Solzhenitsyn has indeed managed to distribute his attention and space
so evenly and treated the Communist Rubin so fairly that he
can be—and has been—taken for his spokesman, in Pasternak's novel there can be no doubt as to who gets the most attention, space, and all other authorial favors. Compared with
the title hero, the figure of Antipov-Strelnikov appears rather
bleak, schematic, and auxiliary. The whole novel is, in fact,
dominated by Yurii Zhivago. No other character can match
him as an ideologist, since the philosophy of his uncle and
Sima Tuntseva is virtually identical to his own, and since the
revolutionary ideology is expressed by the subsidiary and
episodic figures of Samdevyatov, Liberii, and Klintsov-
Pogorevshikh.

This difference between Pasternak's and Solzhenitsyn's approaches to characterization is all the more striking in that both
authors appear to be inspired by Dostoevsky: both view the
events of their time in the light of Dostoevsky's prophecies,
both conceive certain characters as descendants of his fiction,
both seem to favor the art of Dostoevsky over that of Tolstoy.
Viewing the revolutionary Klintsov-Pogorevshikh through the
eyes of his hero, Pasternak says, for instance, that he reminded
Zhivago of "something long familiar to him. Similar radical
views were advanced by the nihilists of the last century, and a
little later by some of Dostoevsky's heroes, and still more re-
cently by their direct descendants, the provincial educated
classes" (chapter 5, section 16).

Also, in the dialogue between the Tolstoyan Vyvolochnov
and Zhivago's mentor, Vedenyapin, the latter apparently
speaks for Pasternak in arguing for Dostoevsky's aesthetics,
"The World will be saved by Beauty," and expresses his pref-

erence for symbolism in art. It is no accident that Solzhenitsyn, in turn, used this prophetic dictum of Dostoevsky as the main theme of his Nobel lecture (see the epigraph to this book).

If the same inspiration produced rather different results, then, it must be because the two writers assimilated different elements from Dostoevsky. While Solzhenitsyn proved more susceptible to what Bakhtin calls the most distinctive feature of Dostoevsky's art, that is polyphony, Pasternak's novel, in spite of its apocalyptic allusions and Dostoevskian symbolism, remains essentially in the category of monological, or homophonic, art. Although Pasternak asserts that Moscow was to be the heroine of his novel, one can hardly avoid the impression that the events of half a century of Russian history are shown almost exclusively from Yurii Zhivago's idiosyncratic viewpoint, which is equivalent, or nearly so, to that of the author. By contrast, Nerzhin, though he may be just as close to his creator—he is certainly closer to Solzhenitsyn biographically —is shown as one of many victims, one of many ideologists, one of many "wise men" in Limbo. His view of Stalinism, his way of combating it, and ultimately his way of life, are offered to the reader among a number of convincing options from which to choose.[7] While the *Times Literary Supplement* reviewer may be wrong, as I think he is, in his assessment of the main ideological thrust of *The First Circle*, in *Doctor Zhivago* the reader is left no freedom to make such an error.

In my analysis of the individual characters in *The First Circle* I have tried to show that they may best be understood through comparison with the "men of ideas" of Dostoevsky's polyphonic novels, particularly *The Brothers Karamazov*. The same holds true in trying to define the relationships between the characters, to identify the underlying system in which they are arranged. Thus, the relationship between Nerzhin and Rubin is best explained in terms of that between Alyosha and Ivan Karamazov. Although the latter are brothers by blood,

Dostoevsky's emphasis is clearly on the brotherhood of men. On the other hand, Solzhenitsyn lets Nerzhin—at his birthday party—address his friends as "brothers." Therefore, what Muchnic has said about Rubin and Nerzhin—"As men the two are friends, as thinkers, enemies"—may be applied just as well to the relationship between Ivan and Alyosha. The parallel could reasonably be extended to include the elder of the Karamazov brothers, Dmitry: in *The First Circle* he is Dimitri Sologdin. These two share such important traits as vitality, physical prowess, and attraction to women. (Solzhenitsyn interestingly uses the same diminutives, Mitya and Miten'ka, in reference to Sologdin that Dostoevsky used for his Dmitry, although the alternative Dima is actually more popular in the USSR.) However, Solzhenitsyn's Sologdin is also proof that the parallel cannot, and should not, be pursued dogmatically or too far. He may share certain features with Dmitry Karamazov, but his ideological profile—his *Übermensch*-like voluntarism, spiritual elitism, and moral stance beyond good and evil—brings him much closer to Stavrogin.

Whether Solzhenitsyn intended it or not, Sologdin, Rubin, and Nerzhin seem to form a triad, a troika, and, like Dmitry, Ivan, and Alyosha, may be interpreted as the three sons of Russia. Obviously *The Brothers Karamazov* is far more than the account of a criminal case in a family of the Russian gentry, no matter how intriguing for the reader it may be on that level. Essentially it is a novel about Russia's spiritual crisis in the face of what Dostoevsky felt was a crime perpetrated against humanity by the atheist proponents of social revolution. Having denounced God in the name of a false humanitarianism, as the Grand Inquisitor did, they committed deicide; by substituting "Everything is permitted" for God, they paved the way for regicide, parricide, fratricide, and the internecine wars of the Revolution. In the three brothers Dostoevsky portrayed then three basic responses to the situation of crisis.

In a similar way, Solzhenitsyn's *The First Circle* is not simply a novel about a certain penal institution under Stalin, no matter how harrowing and truthful the depiction is. It is also a novel of Russia's spiritual death and resurrection, an artistic résumé of the period transformed into a "myth of human affairs," to use the expression that George Steiner applied to Dostoevsky's novels. As has already been mentioned, Rubin and Sologdin were modeled on two of Solzhenitsyn's close prison friends, the literary critic Lev Kopelev and the engineer Dmitry Panin, and Nerzhin is a strongly autobiographical figure. Significantly, after serving their sentences, all three became involved in one way or another in the human rights movement. The relative prominence of the "troika" in the novel may be corroborated with a piece of extrinsic evidence: when several years a photograph of the three friends was taken, they inscribed it "The Three Musketeers of Sharashka—Twenty Years On." [8] It could as well have been inscribed "Three Sons of Russia" or even "*Tri bogatyria*," that is, the three Russian fairy-tale knights. For one can see in these three characters' fate the common fate of the true Soviet Russian intelligentsia. Products of the same educational system, they encompass the main branches of intellectual pursuit —the humanities, science, and engineering. (Even the fact that one of the three is a Jew seems emblematic of the important role that Jews have played in the Soviet intellectual community.) The three may be said to represent, embryonically, the chief components of the human rights movement: Rubin anticipates those who have been trying to humanize the system from within the party; Sologdin may stand for those technocrats who have insisted on ideological immunity; and Nerzhin is a predecessor of those who have emphasized the need for a spiritual renascence.

Just as in Dostoevsky's characterization the brothers transcend their social class and are shown as concrete Russian embodiments of abstract universal ideas, so all the particularities of Solzhenitsyn's three heroes' biographical, social, and ethnic backgrounds are transcended and they become personifications of three basic responses to the situation in which they find themselves—in the hands of Stalin, the "Grand Inquisitor."

Rubin's attitude is that of a philosophic materialist, rationalist, positivist, collectivist, internationalist, and atheist, all combined, however, with an idealist's faith in Stalin the Mangod. His antagonist Sologdin's credo is "metaphysics," voluntarism, individualism, nationalism, and spiritual elitism; though he may be favorably disposed toward religion, because, like all the other elements of his credo, it is suppressed, he has nothing to oppose to Rubin's belief in the Mangod but a belief in himself as a superman. Skeptical of all established philosophies, Nerzhin seems to occupy a middle ground between the two. He is neither a philosophic materialist nor an idealist but a sort of "materialist metaphysician" whose faith is founded on the natural sciences and on his personal experience. To the extremes of Rubin's collectivism and Sologdin's individualism he opposes his own brand of personalism: whereas his friends are ready to sacrifice other people in order to assert either the "collective" or the "supreme individual," Nerzhin would sacrifice only himself for his belief. As to the extremes of internationalism and nationalism to which Rubin and Sologdin respectively tend, Nerzhin avoids them through his conviction that a man becomes a part of his nation only after he forges in himself the soul of a human being. Nerzhin is the only one of the three who declares his faith in God, and yet he is much more broad-minded and openhearted than either of his friends. In this respect he is a true "polyphonist"—to use Bakhtin's notion in a nonliterary sense—distinguished from both Rubin's "monologism" and from Sologdin's duel-dialogues.

Ultimately the three heroes of the sharashka parallel Dostoevsky's three brothers in representing three basic human types:

(1) Ivan/Lev Rubin, a man of intellect, a rationalist, a positivist, who believes himself to possess the apple of knowledge; (2) Dmitry/Dmitri Sologdin, a man of will, an epitome of irrational, instinctual vitality and a strong animalistic drive for self-preservation; (3) Alyosha/Gleb Nerzhin, a man of heart, soul, and spiritual wisdom. As such they can also be reduced to the archetypes of "scholar," "warrior," and "saint." The division, of course, is not meant to be absolute: each type may have features of the others. Nor is one fated to belong forever to a certain type, for one has the freedom and responsibility to choose his own way. And one's type is certainly not determined by his social place, occupation, or achievement. Thus, Rubin is a "scholar" though his scholastic record may not be better than the mathematician Nerzhin's; Sologdin is a "warrior" though, unlike the other two, he has never taken part in a war;[9] and Nerzhin is a "saint" though he may not formally belong to any religion; in fact, he becomes a "saint" only after he chooses to act as one.

Although Solzhenitsyn the man seems to favor the choice of Nerzhin, Solzhenitsyn the novelist neither imposes him on the reader nor condemns the other choices. Quite to the contrary, all three heroes of the sharashka, like the three brothers Karamazov, appear to the reader credible choices. Together with Nerzhin, Solzhenitsyn seems to be pleading not only for a permanent coexistence of the three but also for friendship between them. In this sense, all three may be considered to be protagonists of the novel with a common enemy and antagonist in Stalin. Their mutual antagonisms, no matter how serious, are decidedly overshadowed by their common fate as inmates of the sharashka and prisoners of Stalin's Russia. The dictator's intolerance of and hostility toward independent voices, including those of other Communists, constitutes the main ideological conflict in the novel. Just as Stalinist society leaves no room for the Dostoevskian notion of crime and punishment, it also leaves no room for "heroes of ideas": the three

Karamazov brothers, or Kirillov, Shatov, and Stavrogin, would all have found themselves no higher than the "first circle" of Stalin's Russia, all victims of a single idea—that of the Grand Inquisitor.[10]

The other ideologists in the novel tend to fall into one of the three types personified by Rubin, Sologdin, and Nerzhin, according to the choices they make during crucial moments when their futures are at stake. Each of the three has his doubles both within and without the sharashka's walls.

The tragedy of Rubin, a "cosmopolitan" devotee of the chauvinist Stalin, is echoed in the portrait of his "free" boss Adam Roitman, a Stalin Prize laureate, major of the MVD, and a Jew. In the face of an impending campaign against "cosmopolitanism," he begins to doubt his lifelong beliefs in the redeeming power of Communism and to think that one should start setting the world aright not with a revolution but with oneself. Like Rubin he remains "free" and "undefined" to the end: though the reader feels that Roitman is moving away from Stalinism, there is no telling when or whether he will ever take a firm anti-Stalinist stance. Among the prisoners Rubin has his double in the old Bolshevik Adamson, who may be wavering in his Communist convictions but still encourages Rubin to stick to his.

Sologdin's most obvious double is Yakonov. The two engineers are pitted against each other in the "duel" which the prisoner wins. Yakonov cannot help admiring the audacity and talents of the "insignificant slave." At one moment he sees in Sologdin a "diabolical engineer," at another, he sees his own image reflected in the pupils of his "immaculate" blue eyes. Just as the name Sologdin betrays the solo nature of the jailed individualist, so Yakonov alludes to the ethical egotism (*yakan'e*) of his boss.

Innokenty Volodin is Nerzhin's closest double on the outside. Each follows the dictates of his conscience, each listens to his heart rather than his mind, each refuses to compromise with Stalin, each chooses the way of self-sacrifice. They are downward bound, a species doomed for extinction—that is, from a materialist, or realist viewpoint. However, from an idealistic, or spiritual viewpoint, they present the most viable alternative to Stalinism, the surest way out of the impasse. They may not survive physically, but they achieve that liberation of the soul without which all resistance to Stalinism is meaningless. Characteristically, both achieve spiritual heights during their descent into the inferno. Besides Innokenty, the path of Nerzhin is chosen on the outside by Agniya, Yakonov's former sweetheart (notice her name's symbolism: in Greek it means "chaste and innocent," in Latin a "lamb"); in the sharashka it is chosen by Bobynin, Khorobrov, and Gerasimovich (whose closeness to Nerzhin is particularly enhanced in the complete, ninety-six-chapter version of the book).

Of course not all characters in the novel can be identified with the heroes of ideas discussed above. Some of them are clearly conceived, and vividly portrayed, as primarily social types: the peasant zek Spiridon Egorov who values family life above religion, patriotism, and socialism; the vacuum specialist Zemelya, the "Sunny Soul," a representative of the working class; the Party secretary Stepanov, Solzhenitsyn's antithesis to the socialist realist conception of a party leader; the prosecutor Makarygin, a member of the new class of Communist *nouveaux riches*; the state security men Shikin and Myshin, paired by the prisoners as a sinister and comical tandem Shishin-Myshkin. A number of other characters provide the reader with a glimpse into Soviet student life, acquaint him with the plight of the prisoners' wives or with the problems of a soldier returning from the fire of war to the flames of peacetime competition. Apparently, Solzhenitsyn has purposely selected his characters so as to create not only a representative set of ideologists but also a broad panorama of the whole society. As he himself has pointed out in the interview with Ličko, the novel is built vertically, that is, from Stalin, through the party and secret police apparatus, to the zek janitor Spiridon.

Many critics have observed an extraordinarily large, heterogeneous, yet unified set of characters as one of the chief distinguishing features of *The First Circle*. Attempts have been made to link this feature with the novelist's artistic method. Deming Brown explains it in terms of Solzhenitsyn's deliberate "strategic choice," enabling him to achieve the effect of a "microcosm" through "the close interaction of characters with very diverse social, occupational, political, cultural, and ethnic backgrounds." György Lukács more specifically identifies Solzhenitsyn's strategy with the "new method of epic composition" initiated by Thomas Mann in *The Magic Mountain* and introduced in the USSR through Makarenko's *Pedagogicheskaia poèma* (Pedagogical poem). Lukács argues that Solzhenitsyn, whether or not he was aware of the two works, availed himself of this method first in *One Day* and *Cancer Ward* and then developed it further in *The First Circle*, in which he managed to portray a truly representative cross-section of society and thus brought into focus a total picture of Stalin's Russia. Earl Rovit defines Solzhenitsyn's strategy as "a temporalization of space," and points out that this strategy allows the novelist to project a wide gallery of characters as "mirrors of all the levels of social life as well as the breadth of different psychological types." Finally, Miroslav Drozda sees *The First Circle* as a novel of "destroyed biographies" in which each character exists for the sake of his "ethical monography" rather than his biography; he calls the novel an "ethical monography of the epoch." [11]

Although all these explanations of Solzhenitsyn's method of characterization have some validity, they seem incomplete so long as they ignore the fact that *The First Circle*'s characters are combined into a polyphonic rather than homophonic unity. Even Drozda, while correctly pointing out that the novel's chief concerns are "axiologic"—that is, ideological in the

Dostoevskian sense—fails to notice that the "ethical monographies" have different ideological accents and coexist in a pluralistic world. What Bakhtin said about Dostoevsky's polyphonic novels, in contradistinction to the homophonic novels of his contemporaries, applies to *The First Circle* as well:

> In his novels there is not the unfolding of a multitude of characters and fates, contained within a single objective world and illuminated by the author's single consciousness, but rather *a plurality of equal consciousnesses with their worlds* is combined [in Dostoevsky's novels] into a unity of coexistence, within which each [consciousness, each world] retains its autonomy.[12]

Perhaps the following analogy may help to distinguish a polyphonic conception of art from a monological one. If the monological novel can be pictured as a solar system in which the sun represents either the main hero or the author himself, dispensing his favors on other characters according to their relative proximity to him, the polyphonic novel is a galaxy of stars. Each character is a star, each is the sun of his own system. Some of the stars are brighter than others, or so it would appear from afar. But the brightest stars are not necessarily the biggest nor the best. In fact, some of them might be "anti-stars." A few of them, perhaps just one, may be considered favorites of the author; but then one realizes that all stars are independent worlds. *The First Circle* displays for the reader such a galaxy.

In addition to its overriding presence in characterization, polyphony permeates all other elements of the novel, including the setting, structure, and the verbal texture. Before any conclusions can be drawn as to *The First Circle*'s genre and its place in Russian literature, it is necessary to review briefly how polyphony enters each of these elements of the novel.

CHAPTER VIII

Duality of Setting:
Authenticity and Symbolism

Не исключена такая возможность, что
на земле — ад. Тогда всё понятно.
А если — нет? Господи, тогда как?

One cannot help thinking that what
we already have on earth is a hell.
Then everything is clear. But if
not? Oh, Lord, then what?

Andrey Sinyavsky

A BELIEF that there must be more than one way of understanding the world is essential to the polyphonic conception of art, and it governs the setting of a polyphonic novel. As Bakhtin says,

> Polyphony by itself as coexistence and interaction of autonomous and internally incomplete consciousnesses, required a different artistic conception of time and space, a "non-Euclidian" conception, to use Dostoevsky's own expression.[1]

Bakhtin defines the "non-Euclidian" conception of time and space more precisely as Einsteinian. Noting that Dostoevsky's novels are full of elements belonging to different "worlds" (*raznomirnost' materiala*), that the world of doggerel is combined with the world of Schiller's dithyrambs, and the intellectual horizon of Smerdyakov is shown side by side with that of Ivan, Bakhtin compares a polyphonic novel with the "Einsteinian universe," into a complex unity of which, he argues, different systems of measurement (*sistemy otscheta*) are combined, as it were, in a polyphonic novel.[2] In another place, arguing against Engelgardt's assertion that Dostoevsky's novels are an arena for the dialectic development of a single spirit in the manner of Hegel. Bakhtin insists:

> The world of Dostoevsky is profoundly *pluralistic*. If one wants to find a central image for his world, an image in line with his own ideology, then it is to be found in a *church as a communion of nonconfluent souls* where the sinners and the righteous meet; or, perhaps, in *the image of the Dantean world*, where diversity is projected to eternity, where there are the nonrepentant and the repentant, the condemned and the saved. Such images are in line with Dostoevsky's style, or more precisely, with his ideology, whereas the image of a single spirit is profoundly alien to him.[3] (emphasis added)

In *The First Circle* Solzhenitsyn not only indicates his admiration for Einstein as a thinker, but also boldly exploits the Dantean world as an underlying image for the whole novel. Furthermore, the pluralistic quality of the Dostoevskian world is expressed in his conception of the novel's setting, an aspect playing a special role in his polyphonic novels, as he made clear when he qualified them as novels "strictly defined in time and space." Accordingly, *The First Circle* is set within highly specific chronological and geographical coordinates. The entire action transpires in no more than three days: from mid-afternoon on Saturday, 24 December, until noon on Tuesday, 27 December 1949. Although most scenes take place in the Mavrino Special Prison on the outskirts of Moscow, some important episodes occur at authentic locales like the MVD-MGB apartment house on Kaluzhskaya street, at the Lubyanka and Lefortovo prisons, the Stromynka student dormitory, and Stalin's residential dacha outside Moscow. Emphasizing the chronological authenticity in the novel is the fact that the days of the week described are given in accordance with the perpetual calendar for that year.

Although such authenticity of setting has greatly contributed to the success of *The First Circle* as a documentary and realistic novel, it would be wrong to view the work merely in these terms. As Konstantin Mochulsky wrote of Dostoevsky's *Notes from the House of the Dead*, which also was acclaimed for its realistic portrayal of prison life:

> Both the author's devices and his goal are different. "Objectivity" is only a means for augmenting the given impression; factual authenticity is considered as a foundation of artistic authenticity. The matter-of-fact and annalistic quality of the style heightens the illusion of documentation.[4]

The same is true of *The First Circle*: its factual authenticity is not a goal in itself, but a foundation of artistic authenticity. While the novel is indeed "strictly defined in time and space," this should not be understood in terms of chronology and geography alone, but also in terms of its artistic definition.

To begin with, the restriction of the action in the novel to a very short time span should not be attributed to chance but rather to a deliberate artistic strategy which is thoroughly consistent with the Dostoevskian—and, by implication, polyphonic—conception of time. *War and Peace* covers a period of more than ten years, *Anna Karenina* goes through the seasons for half a decade, and Turgenev's "fathers and sons" display their differences in the course of several months, but the main events of *The Idiot*, *The Devils*, and *The Brothers Karamazov* take place in twenty-four hours, forty-eight hours and five days respectively. This difference in the temporal organization of the material is directly attributable to a difference between artistic world views of the respective authors. In contrast to Lev Tolstoy and most of his contemporaries, Dostoevsky saw the world primarily in space and not in time. Therefore, Bakhtin says, the main category of Dostoevsky's artistic strategy was "not development, but coexistence and interaction."[5] Though agreeing with other critics that Dostoevsky tended toward a dramatic rather than an epic form, Bakhtin nevertheless warns against confusing a polyphonic conception of time with the dramatic principle of temporal unity. Whereas the dramatic form presupposes a single "monologic" world, Dostoevsky uses short bursts of time to dramatize different worlds or, at least, different ways of measuring the same world.

In *The First Circle* the selection of three particular days in a particular year also has a significance going beyond a mere desire to establish factual authenticity. For the purpose of characterizing the three days, Solzhenitsyn resorts to different scales of time, or in Bakhtin's words, to different "systems of measurement": a Soviet scale, a Christian scale, and a scale based on universal history.

According to the Soviet time scale 1949 is the year of Stalin's seventieth birthday, the thirty-second year after the Revolution, the year of the Communist takeover in China (the fact that sustains Rubin in his convictions), the year in which the power of Stalin—and by implication, of Communism—reaches its peak at home and abroad. Continuing this line, the month and the days are defined by their proximity to Stalin's birthday, which is also the deadline for the annual production plan. Ironically, the anniversary of Lenin's death, 21 January, figures in the novel as the ultimate deadline for the secret telephony project.

On the Christian time scale the novel is set not just in the year 1949 but in 1949 A.D., and more precisely in a three-day span centering on the birth of Christ. The prisoners argue heatedly as to the exact date of His birth: "On the twenty-fifth of what year was Christ born, or supposed to have been born?" (52:366). In this way Solzhenitsyn draws the reader's attention to the fact that the action taking place seventy years after Stalin's birth is at the same time happening in about Anno Domini two thousand. Characteristically, the novel is not set around the Russian Orthodox Christmas but according to the more universal Gregorian calendar. Although Russians nor-

mally do not celebrate Christmas on 25 December, the sharashka prisoners do, at least by implication: first, by celebrating
the birthday of Nerzhin, portrayed as a Soviet Russian Christ;
and second, because this particular Christmas Day falls on a
Sunday—synonymous in Russian with resurrection—and
therefore the prisoners work only half a day.

The spiritual aspect of time is further augmented by reference to an apocalyptic time scale. The tone is set early in the
novel through a seemingly casual exchange of remarks between two prisoners:

> "But how can I possibly eat if human beings are going
> around somewhere with numbers on their caps? It's the Apoca-
> lypse!" (2:6)

Although there are no more direct references to the Apoca-
lypse, the ominous shadow of the prophecies of St. John the
Divine is cast over the rest of the novel.[6]

On the secular scale of world history the period of Stalinism
is defined as a cyclical repetition of the Roman slavery. Referring to the recent facts of Soviet history Rostislav Doronin
offers Nerzhin his version of the theory of cycles:

> It has all happened before. They put Gnaeus Naevius in prison
> to make him stop writing free and courageous plays. And the
> Aetolians declared a false amnesty to lure émigrés back and
> murder them. Even in Roman days they discovered the truth,
> afterward forgotten, that it is uneconomical to let a slave go
> hungry, that one has to feed him. All history is one continuous
> pestilence. There is no truth and there is no illusion. There is
> nowhere to appeal and nowhere to go. (14:78)

Nerzhin disagrees only with Doronin's conclusion that "there
is no truth." Besides, he could have pointed out to his younger
friend that this was not a simple cyclical repetition, but a repetition on a more sophisticated level. Even though there were
historical precedents to the "personality cult," Stalin the
Mangod was worshipped as no one else had been "during the

three billion years of the earth's crust" (18:99). The "never before" motif is especially reinforced when the writer places the inhumanity of the Stalinist penal system within the context of Russian and world history.

The temporal setting of the novel is also defined by the opposition of one's "own" time to that belonging to the state (*vremia svoe i kazennoe*). The former is actually confined to a few hours after 6 P.M. on Sunday, and even then, "This period of repose was such that a person not initiated into that life might think *it was a torture devised by the devil*" (48: 338, emphasis added). Stalin, the devil, naturally laid claim to all time as belonging to the state, in other words to him, in regard to "free" citizens as well as prisoners. He particularly claimed the night as his own:

> There was only one person, behind a dozen walls, who could not sleep at night, and he had taught all official Moscow to keep vigil with him until three or four in the morning. Knowing the nocturnal habits of the Sovereign, the three score ministers sat up like schoolboys in expectation of a summons. So as not to get sleepy, they called out their deputies, and the deputies harassed their section heads; reference librarians on stepladders pored over their card catalogues, filing clerks dashed down corridors, secretaries broke pencil points. (1:1)

That is why a number of important scenes take place at night: Nerzhin is summoned to Yakonov late in the evening, Yakonov in turn is summoned to Abakumov at midnight, and a couple of hours later Abakumov is received by Stalin. It is possible, however, to resist Stalin's claim: during this same night Nerzhin tells Stalin "Get thee behind me, Satan!"; Yakonov, feeling the effects of Abakumov's punch in the nose, devotes the rest of the night to the memory of Agniya, his conscience; Rubin achieves the deepest insights into his own nature during the torments of a sleepless night; Roitman finds himself prey to "that nighttime lucidity which renders useless all efforts to get to sleep" (68:488).

Like the artistic definition of the temporal setting of the novel, that of the spatial setting points to a coexistence of different worlds, or of different ways of looking at the world. The main locus of the novel is defined geographically and historically with a degree of precision suggesting authenticity:

> The sharashka took its name from the nearby village of Mavrino, which had long been absorbed into the Moscow city limits. The sharashka had been established on a July evening a little more than three years ago. Some fifteen zeks had been brought in from concentration camps and delivered to an old manor house in the Moscow suburb, encircled for the occasion by barbed wire. (5:22)

In other places we learn that it takes a half-hour bus ride to reach the center of Moscow; that the Moscovites used to come to the nearby grove on Sundays; that there are exactly 281 prisoners in the sharashka, a few dozen free employees, and about fifty guards; that it has passed from the jurisdiction of Beria's MVD to that of Abakumov's MGB. Such details also give the impression of authenticity even though the name Mavrino itself is fictional.[7]

However, as with Dostoevsky's *Notes from the House of the Dead*, factual authenticity in the spatial setting of *The First Circle* only serves as a basis for artistic authenticity. Solzhenitsyn's depiction of the locale takes the reader into a realm of significance outside the limits of conventional realist fiction. Without losing its identity as a Stalinist institution, the Mavrino Special Prison emerges in the novel as

—an enchanted castle, in which the Evil Enchanter, "the man of steel," has fettered the spiritual "knights" of Russia with a steel chain (the sharashka happens to be located in what was formerly a "noblemen's nest");

—a laboratory of modern scientific progress paid for with the slavery of its creators;

—a lyceum, a prison academy in which the ultimate ques-

tions of existence are discussed more freely than in the so-
called "free" society outside;

—a chapel, in which the imprisoned "monks" give the
blessing to their fettered life and where the mysteries of Christianity are reenacted in the blue light under the altar vault (as
one of the prisoners says in chapter 13, which is symbolically
entitled "The Blue Light," the blue light bulb "gives a soft
light, and it reminds me personally of the blue icon lamp my
mother used to light at night when I was a child");

—a new ark, in which a few righteous men escape the flood
of Stalinism, preserve their sanity in the midst of universal
confusion, and look for their Mount Ararat on which to plant
the seed of a new mankind.

Each of them characteristic of a different reality—fairy-
tale, social, philosophical, religious, prophetic—these images
are organized around the central, title image of the novel, the
first circle, about which a few words should be said. Explicitly
derived from Dante, it is not an extraneous mythic embellish-
ment on the portals of an ostensibly realist novel but an essential fixture of its central meaning. Above all, it helps to locate
precisely the place of the sharashka, of Stalinist Russia, on the
metaphysical map of modern history. And more remarkably,
it is introduced into the novel neither by the narrator nor by his
alter ego, Nerzhin. When one of the zek newcomers expresses
his disbelief in the reality of the sharashka, saying that it is
either a dream or "Perhaps I'm in heaven," Rubin corrects
him:

> "No, dear sir," said Rubin, "you are, just as you were
> previously, in hell. But you have risen to its best and highest
> circle—the first circle. You ask what a sharashka is? Let's say
> the concept of a sharashka was thought up by Dante. Remem-
> ber that Dante tore his hair trying to decide where to put the
> wise men of ancient times. It was a Christian's duty to toss
> those pagans into hell. But the Renaissance conscience
> couldn't reconcile itself to the idea of enlightened men being

packed in with all sorts of sinners and condemned to physical torture. So Dante thought up a special place for them in hell." (2:10)

This analogy contains an admission of the hellish nature of the Stalinist penal system, all the more significant in being made by a Communist who still believes in Stalin. Yet Rubin invents the analogy not in order to condemn Stalin or Communism but to justify and even glorify both. For him Stalin is a new Dante, and Communism equals a modern Renaissance. As a Communist it was Stalin's duty to toss "those pagans," that is, nonbelievers in Communism, into hell side by side with "all sorts of sinners." (Rubin believes himself to be imprisoned because of a judicial error.) However, true to the dictates of his Communist Renaissance conscience, Stalin showed himself so benevolent toward the "wise men of ancient times," that is, the Russian intelligentsia, that he saved them from the physical torture of slave labor camps and assigned them instead to such "special places" as the Mavrino sharashka.

According to the polyphonic principle of "independent voices," the omniscient narrator does not comment directly on Rubin's analogy but lets another prisoner counter it:

"Ah, Lev Grigorich, you're too much of a poet," said Valentine Pryanchikov. "I shall explain to the comrade what a sharashka is much more clearly. You need only remember the newspaper piece that said: 'It has been proved that a high yield of wool from sheep depends on the animals' care and feeding.'" (2:10)

There the chapter, rightly entitled "Dante's Idea," ends. The rest of the novel is suspended between the two opposing explanations, and it is left for the reader to arrive at his preference.

The difference between the two is not just one of form, that is, poetic versus journalistic, but also one of essential meaning. Characteristically, Pryanchikov does not dispute Rubin's association of the Stalinist penal system with hell. He merely rebukes Rubin's attempt, transparently veiled in poetry, to find a noble motivation for the sharashka's existence. Instead, he sees the sharashkas as a logical outcome of Stalin's utterly cynical, "economic" approach to intellectual dissent. Pryanchikov's view is corroborated throughout the novel, most notably through an authenticated account of the sharashka concept's historical origin (13:72) and through Doronin's reference to the "economical truth" that one has to feed the slaves in order to increase their productivity.

Thus, while the writer ostensibly borrows the title image of the novel from Rubin, he does so with a great deal of irony. He endorses Rubin's analogy between hell and the Stalinist penal system, but fuses with it a meaning essentially different from the one Rubin intended. When at the end of the novel the notion of the first circle reappears, it is Nerzhin who voices it. Reaffirming Rubin's distinction between sharashkas and camps he goes so far as to say that the Mavrino sharashka is "almost paradise." The expression is obviously ironic, for it alludes to Rubin's belief in the "promised land" of Communism, and because from a materialistic viewpoint the conditions of life at the sharashka are almost the same as those on the outside. The ultimate irony of the situation, and of the title image, however, consists in the fact that Nerzhin, though familiar with the logic of the materialist world, chooses to defy it and to act according to a different logic. For him the "almost paradise" of the sharashka is no more than a "puddle" in which one is more apt to drown spiritually than in the hellish "sea" of the camps, where, conversely, one is not likely to survive physically. That is why there is peace in his soul when he descends from the first circle deeper into hell. And that is why, if one applies not a materialist but a spiritual "system of measurement," the real hell of the novel must be identified with the "free" society over which Stalin/Satan presides from the Judecca of his isolated dacha. In that case, the sharashka might be thought of as the first circle of a Dantean *purgatorio* in which the intellectually arrogant are cleansed of their pride. But whatever logic one applies, the fact remains that the novel's title casts a dark shadow over the whole Soviet experiment.

It must also be pointed out that Solzhenitsyn's concept of the first circle is significantly different from Dante's. This is not only because the "first circle" of the sharashka was created out of malevolence rather than benevolence, or because it is a transit point rather than a place of eternal confinement. Essentially it is different because the "wise men" of the sharashka do not merely coexist, as they do in Dante, but interact as well. (Although Dante's "wise men of antiquity" are said to be engaged in discussion, the poet does not use the opportunity to introduce their ideological dialogues.) Sologdin observes that prison is virtually the only place in the country where people can argue. Nerzhin proposes his toast to the "friendship which thrives in the prison vaults." Even Rubin benefits from the sharashka, for here he can give a freer rein to his literary imagination. Thus the title image may also be seen as symbolic of polyphony itself. It is noteworthy that Bakhtin differentiated between Dostoevsky's polyphonic method and Dante's "formal polyphony." Arguing that the Dostoevskian novel represents "artistically organized coexistence and interaction of spiritual diversity" rather than development of a single spirit, he pointed out that

> the worlds of his heroes, different planes of his novels, in spite of their different hierarchic accent, are expressed in the very structure of the novel where they are placed side by side on the level of coexistence (like Dante's worlds) and interaction (*that is absent in Dante's formal polyphony*), and not one after another as stages of development.[8] (emphasis added)

Finally, Solzhenitsyn's concept of the first circle accords with his general polyphonic strategy in one other respect. By focusing on the first circle he chose not only the best one, leaving the reader to imagine the rest, but also the one at the locus of transition between different worlds. As a halfway house, the sharashka offers an ideal place and situation for the trial of men and ideas.

Just as the temporal setting of the novel transports the reader to Christmas Eve, to the threshold of a new year, and, perhaps, to one of the turning points of our century, so the spatial setting invites the reader to set foot on the first step to hell, or to purgatory, allows him to look out through the "illuminator," or porthole, of the Noah's Ark, albeit with no Ararat in sight, and leaves him poised between good and evil, between Stalin's power pyramid and the penal pit.

Solzhenitsyn's artistic definition of the setting not only is consonant with the notion of the plurality of the world, a feature of Dostoevsky's polyphony, but also is distinguished by symbolism that reminds one of Dostoevsky, rather than of Lev Tolstoy, Goncharov, and Turgenev. But the novel's abundance of authentic detail has prevented many critics from paying sufficient attention to its symbolism. Once Pasternak declared that at the time described in *Doctor Zhivago* "everything metaphorical became literal" (*vse perenosnoe stalo bukval' nym*).[9] The same holds true for Solzhenitsyn and *The First Circle*, where according to Heinrich Böll "the unity of reality and symbol is not invented or imagined; it emerges from the existing material like the solution of a mathematical equation."[10] In fact, the symbolism of the novel's setting is so deeply embedded in a matrix of authentic details that many a reader ignores it altogether. Overwhelmed by the wealth of detail in the description of the sharashka, he assumes that it is all documentary realism. But once he notices that he has been taken into an enchanted castle, a laboratory of modern progress, a chapel fenced in barbed wire, and a new Noah's Ark, he can hardly help feeling the chill emanating from this modern, manmade hell.

CHAPTER IX

Structure:

A Cathedral, an Ark, a Vicious Circle

Там,
Где соборно
Строят незримый
Храм,
Там и корни
Руси родимой.

Where
An invisible temple
Is being built
In the spirit of unity,
There are the roots
Of our native Russia.

Vyacheslav Ivanov

Нам четырех стихий приязненно господство;
Но создал пятую свободный человек.
Не отрицает ли пространства превосходства
Сей целомудренно построенный ковчег?

We are used to the dominion of the four elements;
But a free man has created the fifth.
Hasn't he defied the primacy of space
By this immaculately constructed ark?

Osip Mandelshtam

IN HIS ATTEMPT to define *The First Circle*'s structure, Heinrich Böll, himself a Nobel Prize winner, resorted to the metaphor of a cathedral. Like a cathedral, he said, it has "an enormous span, numerous girders, and several dimensions: fictional, spiritual, political, and social." Compared to this "cathedral" even the best novels of recent Western literature appear to be only "decorative side chapels," "niches" and "elegant single-family homes." The huge cathedrallike structure of this novel, says Böll, allows the novelist to "sum up and illuminate an enormous amount of suffering and history." What is more, the structure itself as a form of artistic expression shows that "here not only a great writer is at work, but also a mathematician, one who is familiar with scientific formulae." Integrated not so much by novelistic means but rather in the sense of mathematics and physics, the novel seems to be founded on "materialist metaphysics." [1]

The analogy has a number of implications that are relevant to our previous discussion. Employing basically the same image that Bakhtin used to describe the structural pattern of Dostoevsky's polyphonic novels (see chapter VIII), it suggests that Solzhenitsyn's "cathedral" has as much room for the coexistence of several dimensions as does Dostoevsky's "church," a place "where the sinners and the righteous meet." Böll's definition of the novel's underlying philosophy as "materialist metaphysics," odd as it sounds, also suggests the coexistence of two realities usually thought to be mutually exclusive; and his assertion that Solzhenitsyn uses extraliterary, nonnovelistic devices is again reminiscent of the great structural complexity of Dostoevsky's polyphonic novels.

Of course, the cathedral analogy is not the only metaphor which can explain the novel's structure. Böll himself suggests two others, the sea and the rosette. While he apparently uses the "sea" in contradistinction to Tolstoy's "epic river," the more graphic metaphor of a "rosette" is suggestive of the independence and interdependence of the numerous "petals" of the novel, that is, of its different dimensions, or of its several main heroes. [2] As Böll says, the novel invites so many different comparisons because it has so many dimensions. To his metaphors could be added others, such as the ark and the vicious circle. In fact, every image Solzhenitsyn uses in his artistic definition of the setting can also be used as a metaphor for the novel's structure, because the structure is largely governed by setting. Yet no single metaphor or combination of metaphors would suffice without an analysis of the novel's interior structure.

Thus, *The First Circle*'s internal or plot structure is much more complex and important as a unifying element of the novel than it may at first appear. Most critics seem to believe that the only plot is to be found in Innokenty's phone call, which they find rather loosely connected to and of little relevance for the rest of the novel. In fact, however, there are a number of interrelated plots more or less tightly knitted together. Besides the detective plot of Innokenty's phone call, the narrative includes a sort of production novel, a political novel, and a romance. Each of these will be briefly described in order to explain their function in the context of the novel as a whole.

1. "Innokenty's Crime and Punishment," a detective novel, surfaces throughout *The First Circle* at more or less regular intervals, in about a dozen chapters. The detective plot includes such incidents as Innokenty's phone call to Doctor Dobroumov's apartment (chapter 1); Ryumin's suggestion to charge the sharashka with the task of identifying the culprit (15); Yakonov's decision to pass the buck to Roitman, and Rubin's cheating on the test that qualifies him as the voice-print reader (31); Rubin's request for additional tapes (33); the taping of Innokenty's phone call to his wife (55); Rubin's identification of Shevronok as a more likely culprit than Volodin, and the decision by General Oskolupov to arrest "both the sons-of-bitches" (80); and, finally, Innokenty's arrest and induction into the hell of the Lubyanka (82).

While Innokenty's phone call sets in motion the whole Stalinist apparatus, it also functions in the novel as a sort of sonic depth finder in the "sea" of Stalin's Russia. Together with the temporal and spatial delimitations it has a unifying function, although not in the sense of a conventional detective story that intrigues the reader with an unsolved but soluble problem. Innokenty's problem is "solved" even before he commits his crime; his fate is sealed in advance because the state security does not need to identify the culprit positively. As Edward Brown justifiably asks, "How can there be suspense if you know that someone, whether innocent or guilty—possibly even an incidental character who couldn't have had anything to do with the crime—will surely be caught and punished. How can interest be maintained if the police don't really have to find out who done it?"[3] In spite of this Solzhenitsyn takes full advantage of the artistic possibilities inherent in the genre, and uses the detective plot much as Dostoevsky does in his polyphonic novels: to show the spiritual adventures of a "criminal," to reveal "man in man" in a state of crisis, and—to a lesser extent—to make others respond to his "crime."

2. "The Secret Telephony," a production novel, revolves around a Stalin-sponsored project in which the task of voice-print identification, central to the detective plot, is merely a side incident. In January 1948, the narrator says,

> someone suggested to the Father of Western and Eastern Peoples the idea of creating a special secret telephone intended for his use only—an instrument so constructed that no one could understand his telephone conversations even if they were monitored. With his august finger, the nail of which was yellowed by nicotine, the Father of Peoples pointed on the map to the Mavrino unit, which until then had been used to create portable transceivers for the police. His historic words on this occasion were: "What do I need those transceivers for? To catch burglars? Who cares?"
> He announced a time limit: the first of January, 1949. Then he reflected a moment and said, "All right, you can have till May first." (10:51)

Six months later, when the novel begins, there is still no breakthrough in sight. Since the sharashka has fallen under

the jurisdiction of the MGB, its minister Abakumov fears
that the matter will surface any moment when he next meets
Stalin. He decides therefore on a course of action including a
summons for the sharashka's bosses (chapter 15: "The Troika
of Liars") and prisoners (16: "No Boiling Water For Tea";
17: "'Oh, Wonder-Working Steed'") and a punch in Yakonov's nose. Although Stalin's senility makes him forget to
ask Abakumov about his pet project, the matter does not lose
its urgency. The sharashka's bosses continue to live under the
Damoclean sword of the ultimate deadline set by Abakumov:
21 January 1950, the anniversary of Lenin's death. The matter
becomes even more complicated because of the rivalry between Yakonov and his deputy Roitman: the two do not get
along "for some illogical, deep-rooted reason." As a result,
the project has been approached independently in two competing laboratories:

> Roitman gathered up everyone he could to work in the Acous-
> tics Laboratory on the vocoder, which in Russian was called
> the "artificial speech device." In retaliation, Yakonov picked
> through all the other groups and gathered all the most skill-
> ful engineers and the best imported equipment into Number
> Seven, that is, into Laboratory Seven. Tentative starts on other
> solutions to the problem were wiped out in unequal battle.
> (10:57)

This rivalry, anything but an example of ideal "socialist
competition," constitutes the main vehicle of the "production" plot. In the hope of knocking Roitman down, Yakonov
passes on to the Acoustics Lab the extracurricular assignment
of voice identification. Ironically, in spite of the fact that it
is Rubin of the Acoustics Lab who fulfills the assignment,
Yakonov and his supporters emerge victorious at the end. Also
ironically, Yakonov's "scientific" victory over Roitman has
nothing to do with the sharashka's collective effort as a socialist realist writer would have it, but is chiefly due to his deal
with Sologdin. Belonging to neither of the competing teams,

Sologdin solves the problem of encoding on a strictly individual basis. However, this "scientific" victory would mean little for Yakonov if it were not at the same time a political victory, but this takes us into another "novel."

3. "Stalin's Glorious Anniversary," a political novel, has to do with the dictator's last fit of political rage at the time of his seventieth birthday. We are given to understand that at the time the aging dictator felt an acute urge to do something extraordinary to ensure his immortality. For that purpose he wants to live twenty years past his seventieth birthday. His twenty-year plan includes waging and winning "the last world war," and providing the "blind puppy" of humanity with a bowl of milk. Afterward he is sure to become a Bonaparte of world Communism and Emperor of the Planet. All events in the novel happen in the shadow of a particular promise that Stalin has made to his minister of state security: "You will have a great deal of work soon, Abakumov. We are going to carry out the same measures as in 1937. Before a big war a big purge is necessary" (20:129).

When the novel begins, the preparatory steps of the coming purge are already in progress. The reader realizes that the Dobroumov affair which stands at the center of the "detective novel" is not an isolated incident but a beginning of the MGB's "campaign against cosmopolitanism and toadyism toward Western powers." Jewish intellectuals and party members, "all those famous, protesting, goateed Talmudists, kinless, rootless, with nothing positive about them" (21:133), as Stalin thinks, are to be a prime target of this campaign. The Jewish employees of the sharashka prove to be no exception. As early as Saturday, 24 December, the sharashka's party secretary, Stepanov, is asked on the phone by "a certain official very highly placed" what he is planning to do about "the Judeans" or "kikes" at the sharashka. Stepanov, who up to this point has supported Roitman against Yakonov because the

latter is not a party member, quickly realizes that he has failed
to detect an important new drive. By the following Monday
Stepanov is already prepared to denounce "the Roitman fac-
tion." After being "dressed down" he apologizes to Yakonov
for allowing "a group of, shall we say, rootless cosmopolites
to build their nest in our party organization." As a result,
"Yakonov's affairs, which had been so hopeless just the day
before, had made an about-face" (73:536). Roitman, on the
other hand, can now expect only the worst in spite of the fact
that it was "his" zek, Rubin, and his Acoustics Lab that had
just accomplished the important task of voice-print identification. Thus the "political novel" affects the outcome of the
"production novel."

As far as the prisoners of Mavrino are concerned, their fates
are more affected by another aspect of the senile Stalin's madness. Though he forgets to inquire about the sharashka's progress in secret telephony, he does not fail to instruct Abakumov
to "put a stop to the vacation-resort conditions in political prisons." At this point, the narrator says in parenthesis, "Abakumov wrote assiduously. The first in a long series of gears had
begun to turn" (20:127). Next Monday at dawn new prison
regulations are handed down to the Mavrino zeks that mean,
among other things, that "the thin thread of communication"
with their relatives "could be maintained only at the cost of
police denunciation of them" (69:502). Nerzhin realizes that
he must cease all correspondence with his wife.

> The sensation of being caught in a vise—not a poetical,
> figurative vise but an enormous locksmith's vise with teeth
> milled into it, with jaws for squeezing a man's neck—the sen-
> sation of having that vise close around him took Nerzhin's
> breath away.
>   It was impossible to find a way out. Every course was fatal.
> (69:504)

With bitter irony the zeks call the new regulations a New
Year's present. This irony is contrapuntal to the fact that a few

days earlier, on his birthday, Stalin had received a unique tele-
vision set made by the zeks of Mavrino as a gift "from the
Chekists."

4. "Gleb's Passion," a romance, is centered around Nerzhin's relationship with Simochka, a free employee at the
sharashka and lieutenant of the MGB. Since she is duty-
bound to spy on him, the relationship has strong ironic un-
dertones. However, such a relationship is not unusual at the
sharashka. On the contrary:

> The security officers did not know about the twenty-two wild,
> irrational women, free employees, who had been allowed into
> that somber building. . . . no one knew that all twenty-two,
> despite the swords hanging over their heads, had found a secret
> attachment here, were in love with someone and embraced him
> in secret, or had taken pity on someone and put him in touch
> with his family. (34:231)

Solzhenitsyn deliberately emphasizes the irrationality of love
and pity, for he considers these feelings the only vents that
help to refresh the stuffy air of "that somber building"
founded on the rational and utterly cynical idea of intellectual
exploitation. Apparently sharing this emphasis with such visionaries of totalitarian rule as Dostoevsky, Zamyatin, and
Orwell, he seems to suggest that "irrational love" may eventually help to undo the spell cast over the enchanted castle of
Russia. The exchange of a kiss between Gleb and Simochka
provokes his comment:

> Thus it could be said that a cunningly wrought steel chain
> broke at the link which had been forged from the heart of a
> woman. (6:32)

Short of securing his release from prison, this break in the link
could benefit Nerzhin in several ways, by enabling him: to
work more freely on his notes and, possibly, smuggle them
out; to satisfy his need for physical love; to satisfy his desire

for procreation. When the novel ends, however, none of these benefits have materialized. In fact, Nerzhin takes no advantage at all of the "broken link."

The plot lines of the romance are suspended between late Saturday evening when Gleb succeeds in extracting from Simochka the promise of an assignation behind closed doors (chapter 12: "He Should Have Lied") and late Monday night when he appears only to tell her that he loves his wife (81: "No, Not You"). Between these two points there is only one important event: on Sunday, Gleb is unexpectedly allowed a visit from his wife during which he regains his faith in their love. He is caused to reflect on the meaning of life in general and, in particular, on the implications of his incipient love affair with Simochka. His thinking occurs not only inwardly but also outwardly, that is, through dialogues with his friends, with Rostislav Doronin, Sologdin (before the visit), Kondrashev-Ivanov, and Spiridon (afterward). Nerzhin's soul-searching produces two important results. First, his decision to go to the camps rather than to surrender to the temptation of cryptography becomes irrevocable. Secondly, he decides to renounce Simochka's love, a decision that seems, perhaps, especially quixotic.

> Nine out of ten men would have ridiculed Nerzhin for his renunciation after so many years of deprivation. Who would have compelled him to marry her afterward? What was to stop him from seducing her right now? But he was happy he had acted as he had. He was moved . . . as if it were someone else who had made the great decision. (81:601)

The adjective "great" is not accidental here, nor is the allusion to "someone else": they suggest that Nerzhin is guided by a higher power, perhaps by God whom he invokes while informing his wife about the first decision, that is, not to join Cryptography. The writer also suggests that the two decisions are equally important for Nerzhin, perceiving them as two sides of the same coin; for, unlike Rubin, Nerzhin does not apply a double standard to his personal and his social behavior. For him both fall under the same jurisdiction, that of a man's conscience. He explains to Simochka:

> "Simochka, I don't consider myself a good person. When I think of the things I—like everyone else—did at the front in Germany, I realize I am not a good man. And now with you . . . But this is how I learned to behave in the so-called normal life. I had no idea what good and bad were, and whatever was allowed seemed fined to me. But the lower I sink into this inhumanly cruel world, the more I respond to those who, even in such a world, speak to my conscience. She won't wait for me? So be it! So be it! Let me die uselessly in the Krasnoyarsk taiga. But if you know when you die that you haven't been a complete bastard, that's at least some satisfaction." (81:600)

Thus, Nerzhin's romance functions within *The First Circle* as a vehicle for revealing the man and his idea. It is consistent with Solzhenitsyn's conception of Nerzhin as a man of a single passion, an idealistic Christlike figure whose actions appear quixotic because they break with the logic of the materialistic world. It provides the book with a framework for the treatment of such themes as spiritual versus physical love, the sublimation of human energy under the forcibly imposed monastic conditions of prison life, and the irrationality of love. It also allows the novelist to take the reader out of the sharashka to a Soviet college classroom where Simochka passes her exam with the help of "cribs," to a student dormitory where Nadya lives, to the Makarygin's apartment where Nadya's friend Shchagov goes after he drinks with Nadya "to the resurrection of the dead."

These four "novels," or rather four concurrent plots, since none of them, of course, is a full-fledged novel, play an important structural role within *The First Circle*'s polyphonic unity.[4] Each spans the whole book. Each consists of a number of incidents, episodes, and scenes leading to a climax and resolution. Each belongs to a different novelistic genre adopted by the author for his own use. Most importantly, each "novel" offers a field of action for a hero, or heroes, who would otherwise remain in the background. In the detective novel Innokenty and Rubin share the attention, if not the scene. In the production novel the individualistic Sologdin steals the limelight from both Yakonov and Roitman, in fact, from the "collective" of the prison institute. Only a side figure in either of these two "novels," Nerzhin has center stage in the love story. The chief instigator of the political novel, Stalin, casts his spell over all the characters and all the "novels." The four overlapping "novels" roughly correspond to the four dimensions of *The First Circle* mentioned by Böll: "Innokenty's Crime and Punishment" to the fictional dimension, "The Secret Telephony" to the social, "The Glorious Anniversary" to the political, and "Gleb's Passion" to the spiritual. In this respect, the four plot lines might be likened to four arches converging under the main dome of the novel's "cathedral." Linked by numerous girders and beams, all four are built on the foundation of a common setting; all four balance and reinforce one another; and all four support with grace and assurance the lofty dome of the cathedral. Thus, they all contribute to the impression of the unity of diversity that a polyphonic novel must produce.

Important as they are, however, the concurrent plot lines alone do not account for the polyphonic effect of *The First Circle*'s cathedrallike unity. The two scenes that frame the whole book—the arrival of the newcomers to the sharashka and departure of the recalcitrant ones to the camps—are seemingly unrelated to any of the four plots, yet they serve the same unifying purpose; what is more, they contribute to the effect of a vicious circle which also is one of the novel's major themes. Among other unifying devices, besides those embodied in setting and plot structure, the most prominent are the juxtaposition of characters, episodes, and scenes; the contrapuntal development of themes; symbolism of name and of chapter titles; and the recurrent usage of images and expressions. (Still other examples are provided in the preceding chapters as well as in those that follow. Although Solzhenitsyn's use of them reminds me of Dostoevsky rather than Tolstoy, I have no quarrel with what Robert Belknap said about *The Brothers Karamazov*: "In no case can an author escape using one of the arsenal of devices which has been developed over the centuries by the predecessors of the novelists, the historians and the epic poets.")[5]

The novel includes, for instance, several scenes of celebration—a "Protestant Christmas," Makarygin's Order of Lenin party, Nerzhin's birthday party, and Stalin's seventieth anniversary. All of them are skillfully juxtaposed. The "Protestant Christmas" party has its irony in the fact that Rubin, a Communist, Jew, "victor," and prisoner, tries to brainwash the defeated Germans. It is rather Nerzhin's birthday party that is distinguished by the spirit of Christmas because its participants are truly united by toasts to friendship and love. Whereas the spirituality of this party is emphasized by its taking place under the altar vault, the spiritual poverty of the Order of Lenin party is symbolized by the "tobacco altar" where Makarygin takes his guests. It is there the Marxist Radovich pronounces *Fumo, ergo sum* because the Stalinist regime apparently leaves no room for *cogito*. On the other hand, this party surpasses the others in culinary richness. Finally, Stalin's own birthday, shown only in a flashback, is memorable because of the murder of a Communist leader on its eve, as if a birthday present to the tyrant.

While remaining parts of different stories, indeed of different worlds, the toasts by Captain Nerzhin and Captain Shchagov are in a contrapuntal relationship because they reinforce thoughts of immortality which cross the mind of the most powerful man, Stalin, and the most powerless, Innokenty. Stalin's comparison of mankind to a blind puppy looking for a bowl of milk is echoed in Sologdin's comparison of Rubin to a puppy on a chain. The scene in which Stalin endeavors to write his opus on linguistics reiterates the theme of language destruction in the labs of the sharashka. That Rubin still believes in Marr is especially ironic because he also believes in Stalin who is about to undo Marr. The purge of words of foreign derivation, described as a part of the campaign against "cosmopolitanism," finds its counterpoint in Sologdin's purge of the "bird words." Innokenty's return to such "old-Russian" words as Truth, Good, and Evil, is paralleled by Stalin's return to orderlies and shoulder boards.

The Dantean analogy is sustained throughout the novel, although the notion of the first circle is not invoked again until the very end. This is accomplished with the help of such seemingly unrelated scenes and episodes as the visits of the prisoners' wives, compared to the ancient Greek steles where "the living look fondly at the dead person, who looks toward Hades"; the episode of the hellish bathhouse in "Buddha's Smile"; Innokenty's induction into the hell of Lubyanka in the chapter entitled "Abandon Hope, All Ye Who Enter Here." The story "Buddha's Smile," incidentally, recapitulates such important themes of the novel as that of "never before" and that of the blindness of the West; in a sense, it forms a niche in the novel's "cathedral" into which a miniature model of the "cathedral" is placed.

Finally the image of the sharashka as a new Noah's Ark (chapter 48) forms a counterpoint to the image of the Lubyanka ministry as a "battleship" (*linkor*) that is about to destroy Innokenty's frail "sailboat" (*chelnok*). (Whitney omits this word in his translation in chapter 1 and thus undermines the impact of the recurrent "boat" image.) One cannot help thinking that once his sailboat is torpedoed, Innokenty may save his soul by boarding the unassailable ark of the netherworld. The importance of this image, developed into a chapter-long analogy between the sharashka and Noah's Ark (though, characteristically, Noah is never mentioned), is emphasized by the fact that it appears almost exactly in the middle of the novel. Seemingly unrelated to any of the four "arching" story lines it occurs at the point of nearest proximity to them all as if suspended from the apex of the dome where all arches conjoin.

From here, from the ark, confidently plowing its way through the darkness, the whole tortuous flow of accursed History could easily be surveyed, as from an enormous height, and yet at the same time one could see every detail, every pebble on the river bed, as if one were immersed in the stream.

In these Sunday evening hours solid matter and flesh no longer reminded people of their earthly existence. The spirit of male friendship and philosophy filled the sail-like arches overhead.

Perhaps this was, indeed, that bliss which all the philosophers of antiquity tried in vain to define and teach others. (48:340)

One of the high points of the entire novel, this passage belongs to the finest expressions of Solzhenitsyn's art, not only because it conveys his favorite themes of male friendship, blessing in misfortune, and blindness of mankind; or because it anticipates the heights from which Innokenty would see Epicurus' wisdom as the "babbling of a child"; or because it echoes the Dantean image of the first circle; or because it unites in itself the objective observations of a historian with the passion of one "immersed in the stream." This is true also because it achieves the unity of reality and symbol, of which Böll spoke (chapter VIII): the unity of the real arches of a former chapel turned sharashka with the sails of the ark of fancy. And it is true also because in the image of the ark Solzhenitsyn attains that unity of content and form, of image and message, of theme and structure which must be the ultimate goal of art.

Indeed, reading the novel is, in a sense, like going aboard this ark, moving from one deck to another, entering into dialogues with its passengers, stepping into their berths, and looking out of their individual portholes, symbolically called in Russia "illuminators." One may not see a new Mt. Ararat. But from this ark not only all the details of the novel but "the whole tortuous flow of accursed History" are likely to be seen much more clearly.

CHAPTER X

A Language of Dialogue and a Dialogue of Languages

TO INDICATE the most distinctive quality of Dostoevsky's style Bakhtin used the word *dialogic* as virtually on a par with the word *polyphonic*.

> Everything in Dostoevsky's novels turns around the pivot of dialogue and dialogic juxtaposition. Everything is a means to the end of dialogue. One voice does not determine anything and solves nothing. Two voices are the minimum for life, the minimum for existence.[1]

To be sure, Bakhtin is not applying these words in a narrow sense, for according to him,

> All relationships between external and internal parts and elements of [Dostoevsky's] novels have a dialogic character. He constructed his novels as a "great dialogue." The typographically distinguishable dialogues between his characters are just a part of that "macrodialogue" which they illuminated and intensified. Finally, the dialogue goes inside, penetrates each word of a novel and makes it bivocal, enters every gesture and every mimetic movement contorting and lacerating a character's face; and it is this "microdialogue" that determines the peculiarities of Dostoevsky's verbal style.[2]

Like Dostoevsky's novels, *The First Circle* is dialogic through and through. It is built as a macrodialogue; it abounds with dialogues and is distinguished by the bivocalism, or dialogism, of its narrative tone. As in Dostoevsky's novels, all the manifestations of dialogue are organically interconnected and help to achieve the effect of polyphony.

Centered around Stalinism, the macrodialogue of *The First*

Circle would not seem perhaps as "great" as Dostoevsky's macrodialogues on the ultimate issues of God, God's world, and the meaning of existence. One should not forget, however, that Solzhenitsyn makes the issue of Stalinism larger by treating it not as an isolated political event of Russian history but as a phenomenon rooted in the spiritual history of mankind. Moreover, there is a strong ideational continuity between the macrodialogue of *The First Circle* and that of Dostoevsky's novels, continuity that is most clearly evinced in Solzhenitsyn's portrayal of Stalinist rule as a fulfillment of Dostoevsky's prophecies of totalitarianism. (See chapter I.)

The novel's macrodialogue branches out into numerous ideological dialogues between characters. The most important of these are Rubin's analogy between the sharashka and Dante's first circle and Pryanchikov's reply to him (chapter 2: "Dante's Idea"); the dialogues between Rubin and Nerzhin about Stalinism and Hitlerism and about "cosmopolites" (4: "Boogie-Woogie"), on the nature of happiness and the meaning of *Faust* (7: "Oh, Moment, Stay!"), about Stalin's "greatness" and the style of his writings, about "metaphysics," skepticism, dogmatism, and the role of "technico-scientific" intelligentsia (8: "The Fifth Year in Harness"); the dialogue between Rostislav and Nerzhin in which the former describes Stalinism as a cyclical repetition of the Roman slavery and the latter insists on the necessity of faith and love (14: "Every Man Needs a Girl"); the seesaw "Socratic dialogues" between Sologdin and Nerzhin at the sawhorse under the open sky (24: "Sawing Wood"); the supervised conversation between Nerzhin and Nadya which culminated in his confession of faith in God (37: "The Visit"); the dialogue between the painter Kondrashev-Ivanov and Nerzhin in which the basic Marxist axiom, "The mode of existence determines the mode of consciousness," is countered by the painter's faith in the "image of perfection" (42: "The Castle of the Holy Grail"); the "Lyceum Feast" debate about socialist realism, women, and friendship (53: "The Banquet Table"); the "duel-debate" between Sologdin and Rubin in which the latter admits that Communist ethics are founded on the principle "Ends justify means" (60: "A Duel Not According to the Rules"; and 64: "Clenched Fists"); Nerzhin's "midwifery" in extracting Spiridon's adage "The Wolfhound is right, the Cannibal is not" (63: "Spiridon's Standards").

While these ideological, Socratic dialogues take place in the first circle among its "wise men," on the outside among "free" citizens there occur mostly dramatic dialogues which are relatively less important in the novel's strategy.[3] Among them are Innokenty's phone call (chapter 1), Abakumov's conversation and private dialogues with "The Troika of Liars" (15) and Stalin (20); Innokenty's taped phone call to his wife (55), and Colonel Klimentiev's conversation with Nadya in the Moscow subway (26). To the same category should also be referred conversations between prisoners and free citizens, such as Abakumov's private dialogues with Pryanchikov and Bobynin (16, 17) and Yakonov's dialogue with Sologdin (73).

This is not to say that all ideological life has ceased to exist among the "free." Rather, drowned by the official "monologue," it has turned into inner dialogues. When Roitman begins to feel "the whip of the persecutor of Israelites" on his own back he does not share his pain with his beloved wife but with his "inner self, his nighttime self." Similarly, Innokenty engages in philosophic dialogues not with his friends who call him epicurean but with Epicurus' books, with his dead mother's notes, and with himself. Whenever a conversation between "free" citizens embarks upon heterodox matters it is cut short by the fear of saying too much. Thus, when Radovich in his search for "Leninist purity" suggests to Makarygin that Stalinism is not the only way to socialism, he is quickly reminded that he transgresses the line "beyond which . . . Makarygin could be nothing but a prosecutor" (58:429).

That Solzhenitsyn attaches great importance to dialogue is

evident in the fact that the principal ideologists of *The First Circle* are characterized not only by what they say but also by their attitude toward the dialogic form of communication. Thus, Rubin "could never bear listening to others for long. In every conversation, he was the one to impart the treasures of inspiration he had unearthed" (8:38). A conversation for him is always a one-way street, a means to display his thoughts and feelings. He is, in this sense, a "monologist," whose form of communication exactly matches the content of his beliefs, that is, the "absolute truth" of Marxism. Sologdin, on the other hand, appears at first to advocate a dialogue for dialogue's sake. "We can't all have the same views and the same standards. What would happen? There would be no argument, no exchange of opinion. It would bore a dog!" he says (24:157). But in his "duel" with Rubin he proves himself primarily interested in his own personal triumph and the humiliation of his opponent. His dialogue for dialogue's sake appears then to be a cover for the advancement of his own "absolute truth." Only Nerzhin is portrayed as a true proponent and practitioner of dialogic communication. In this sense, he is a "polyphonist" willing to listen to, and capable of hearing, ideological "voices" other than his own. On the opposite pole stands Stalin: he is not only a "monologist" but tries to reduce the only permissible ideology of Marxism-Leninism to his own monologue. Believing that his only peers are Kant and Spinoza, he does not seek advice from specialists even when he is writing his treatise on linguistics. His monologue on the subject symbolically leades to "a dead end." [4]

The main function of Solzhenitsyn's use of dialogues in the novel is to ensure that each hero-ideologist speaks for himself. Although the narrative mode of *The First Circle* is somewhat reminiscent of the epic sweep of the Tolstoyan novel with its "omniscient narrator," it is important to note that its principal ideas are expressed not in the narrative but in dialogues, a stylistic feature that Solzhenitsyn shares with Dostoevsky rather than Tolstoy. As I have tried to demonstrate in the preceding analysis of individual heroes of ideas, each of them appears to be speaking for the author in one dialogue or another: Rubin, when he introduces the title image of the novel, or offers his interpretation of *Faust*, or orchestrates a mockery of the Stalinist justice with the help of the Prince Igor tale; Sologdin, when he reveals to Nerzhin his rules on how to face difficulties, or defeats Rubin in the field of Marxist dialectics, or talks about Dostoevsky, or indicts Stalinism's ethical motto; Nerzhin, when he extols the role of "technico-scientific" intelligentsia, or reminds Rostislav of the necessity of faith and love, or declares his faith in God; and Innokenty, when he reminds the writer Galakhov that "a greater writer is a second government," or renounces the materialist philosophy of Epicurus.

The integrity of each voice in the novel's dialogues is further ensured by the fact that most dialogues remain open-ended, that is, not concluded by any final word uttered by either the omniscient narrator or Nerzhin, whom we have identified as the author's hero. During the "Lyceum Feast" debate that ensues after his birthday party, Nerzhin recedes into the background, his ideological voice sounding no stronger than those of his guests. The debate ends with Nerzhin's opinion about art strongly rebuked by the old Bolshevik Adamson with whom even Sologdin joins forces. In another dialogue the painter Kondrashev-Ivanov, a rather episodic figure, appears to be speaking for the author while the author's hero plays the role of devil's advocate. Here is the conversation after Nerzhin argues that his experience in a labor camp taught him that "the mode of existence determines the mode of consciousness":

> "No!" Kondrashev stretched out his long arms, ready at this moment to do combat with the whole world. "No! No! No! That would be degrading. What is one to live for then? And tell me, why are people who love each other faithful when

they're separated? After all circumstances dictate that they betray one another! And how do you explain the *difference* in people who have fallen into the *same* conditions, even the same camp?

Nerzhin was confident of the advantage his experience gave him in comparison with the fantastic concepts of this ageless idealist. Yet one could not help but admire his objections.

"A human being," Kondrashev continued, "possesses from his birth a certain essence, the nucleus, as it were, of this human being. His 'I.' And it is still uncertain which forms which: whether life forms the man or man, with his strong spirit, forms life! Because—" Kondrashev-Ivanov suddenly lowered his voice and leaned toward Nerzhin, who was again sitting on the block—"because he has something to measure himself against, something he can *look to*. Because he has in him an image of perfection which in rare moments suddenly emerges before his spiritual gaze." (42:297)

The dialogue is terminated when the painter offers to illustrate his point with his painting "The Castle of the Holy Grail," after which the chapter is named. The narrator's only comment is "This is the way all arguments with artists end. They have their own logic." Thus, Solzhenitsyn leaves it up to the reader to decide whether he wants him to take the side of Nerzhin's life experience or the painter's "own logic." Despite the fact that Nerzhin is the author's hero, the author himself appears to question "the advantage of his experience" and endorses "the fantastic concepts" of the painter. Ironically, Nerzhin's own conduct is more in agreement with his opponent's argument than with his own. As he later admits to Simochka "the lower I sink into this inhumanely cruel world, the more I respond to those who, even in such a world, speak to my conscience" (81:600). The painter is undoubtedly one of "those." Paradoxically, while the painter's position in this dialogue reminds one of Dostoevsky's critique of the "theory of environment," Nerzhin argues with the help of the Marxist axiom justifying his theory.[5] By leaving the dialogue open,

Solzhenitsyn demonstrates his ability to retain distance even from the author's hero, to maintain a dialogue with him, and to ensure the integrity of ideological voices other than his own. The novelist's polyphonic strategy finds its expression not only in the typographically distinguishable dialogues but also in the narrative itself. This is especially evident when the narrator reports what the characters-ideologists think. The following excerpts from chapter 61, "Going to the People," may serve as an example.

> Rubin knew perfectly well that the concept of "the people" is artificial, a preposterous generalization, that every people is divided into *classes*, and that even classes change in time. To look for life's supreme understanding in the peasant class is a squalid and fruitless occupation, because only the proletariat remains consistent and revolutionary to the end, to it alone the future belonged, and the supreme understanding of life can only be found in the proletarian collectivism and unselfishness.
>
> And Sologdin knew equally well that "the people" is an over-all term for a totality of humans of slight interest, gray, crude, preoccupied in their unenlightened way with daily existence. The Colossus of Spirit does not rest on their multitudes. Only unique personalities, shining and separate, like singing stars strewn through the dark heaven of creation, carry within them the supreme understanding. (61:449)
>
> Having got over one more bout of enthusiasm, Nerzhin— whether definitely or not—understood the people in a new way, a way he had not read about anywhere: the people is not everyone who speaks our language, nor yet the elect marked by the fiery stamp of genius. Not by birth, not by the work of one's hands, not by the wings of education is one elected into the people.
>
> But by one's soul.
>
> Everyone forges his soul year after year.
>
> One must try to temper, to cut, to polish one's soul so as to become *a human being*.
>
> And thereby become a tiny particle of one's own people. (61:451)

Several aspects of this text are polyphonic. First, the novel's macrodialogue is expressed here through a dialogic juxtaposition of different viewpoints on one of the "great" questions of Russian literature. There are three such viewpoints: Rubin's based on the "absolute truth" of Marxism; Sologdin's, based on the "absolute truth" of an *Übermensch*; and Nerzhin's, founded on the notion of individual responsibility before humanity. All three differ sharply from each other. All three dialogically oppose each other. As to the author's opinion, it is not conveyed monologically, by an external guiding comment or a concluding remark, but dialogically, by an internal microdialogue with each viewpoint. This microdialogue is carried out by means of a certain bivocalism in the narrative tone.

For Rubin and Sologdin this effect is achieved through a mimicry of their patterns of thought and a parody of their language; in the case of Nerzhin, through a direct interruption of the narrative with the question "whether definitely or not?" The question, by the way, comes as a counterpoint to the "absolute truths" of his friends. Even though in the final analysis most critics would probably agree that only Nerzhin expresses Solzhenitsyn's own ideas about the people, this is not obvious at first reading. In fact, the narrative mimicry of Rubin and Sologdin is so smoothly introduced, the ironic voice of the narrator so well balanced with their feigned voices, that each of them is likely to seem the main hero at least for the moment. Thus some critics were able to designate Rubin as the main spokesman for the author on a par with Nerzhin (see above, chapter VII), and even such perceptive stylists as Leonid Rzhevsky have occasionally mistaken the voice of Sologdin for that of the author.[6]

Furthermore, although Nerzhin's voice in this case is most consonant with that of the narrator, Solzhenitsyn deliberately avoids presenting it as yet another "absolute truth" and, in fact, undercuts its finality by interrupting it with the question "whether definitely or not?" As a result, just as with Dostoevsky, readers and critics have had difficulties in discerning Solzhenitsyn's ideological voice not only in dialogues but in the narrative itself. *The First Circle*, like Dostoevsky's great novels, can hardly be fully appreciated unless the reader ceases to be a mere listener and becomes actively involved in the narrative.

As with other aspects of Solzhenitsyn's polyphonic strategy, Bakhtin's book on Dostoevsky provides a key for explaining the verbal structure of *The First Circle*. Noting that Dostoevsky's verbal mastery has stayed virtually out of reach for conventional stylistics because of a preponderance of the dialogic element in his novels, Bakhtin argues in favor of a new stylistic approach which

> should be based not only and *not so much* on linguistics, but rather *on metalinguistics* that studies the word not just in a language system, not within a "text" taken out of its dialogic context, but precisely in the sphere of dialogic communication, that is, in the sphere of the word's true life.[7]

In an effort to lay down foundations for such a metalinguistic approach Bakhtin offers a classification of all possible "words," or types of verbal expression. Here is an abstract thereof:

TYPE I

The direct word of the author or of a narrator who could be closely identified with the author;

TYPE II

The word-object of a character depicted,
    Subtype 1: Indicative of the character's social group or dialect (a clerk, a peasant, a student, a Northerner),
    Subtype 2: Indicative of his individual traits (manners of speech, speech defects);

TYPE III

The bivocal word (that is, a word in reference to another person's word),
    Subtype 1: The unidirectional bivocal word (all kinds of

stylization and the nonobjectivized word of the author's hero),
Subtype 2: The heterodirectional bivocal word (all kinds of parody and irony),
Subtype 3: The active bivocal word deflecting somebody else's word (remarks in a dialogue, internal polemic, and hidden dialogues).[8]

On the basis of this classification Bakhtin argues that while Dostoevsky's polyphonic novels are distinguished by a strong preponderance of the bivocal "word" (Type III), the homophonic novels of his contemporaries are dominated by univocal "words" (Types I and II). More specifically he points out Dostoevsky's predilection for the second and third subtypes of the bivocal "word."

Applying Bakhtin's classification to *The First Circle* one realizes that all varieties of the bivocal "word" play a prominent role in it. The passage quoted from chapter 42, "The Castle of the Holy Grail," may serve as an example of the active subtype of the bivocal "word" (Subtype 3). The painter's remarks there indeed actively deflect the Marxist axiom, "the mode of existence determines the mode of consciousness," advanced by the author's hero. The active subtype of the bivocal "word" is employed in numerous ideological dialogues of the novel.

In the narrative proper Solzhenitsyn most frequently employs the other two subtypes of the bivocal "word," the heterodirectional (Subtype 2) and unidirectional (Subtype 1). In the narrative quoted above, presenting three different views of the people, the paragraphs on Rubin and Sologdin belong to the heterodirectional subtype because the narrator mimics his characters' language for the sake of parody and creates irony from the direction of their thoughts. The passage involving Nerzhin, however, belongs to the unidirectional subtype because there is no irony implied and no parody of Nerzhin's language is discernible: the direction of the "word" of the author seems to coincide with that of the author's hero. However, the awareness that Nerzhin does not always speak for the author prevents one from taking this passage for the author's "direct word" (Type I).

Even though the use of the bivocal "word" types is most consistent with the polyphonic strategy of assuring a greater independence for each ideological voice, this does not mean that the univocal "word" plays no role in characterization. The univocal "word" of both types becomes especially prominent in the portrayal of Stalin as a historical personality. The "direct word" of the narrator can be best exemplified by such univocal, and unequivocal, statements as "Mistrust of people was Iosif Djugashvili's determining trait" (20:148).

Victor Erlich is, however, mistaken when he classifies the narrative discourse about Rubin, "He was all-in-all a tragic figure" (66:476), as an "unabashedly explicit authorial generalization" which makes Solzhenitsyn look "sturdily and expansively old-fashioned" when compared to "the post-modern sophistication of Nabokov and Borges, John Barth and Nathalie Sarraute."[9] I consider it, rather, an example of authorial mimicry of Rubin who, being a literary critic, *prefers* to view himself in those terms. When analyzed according to Bakhtin's metalinguistics, this authorial statement should be classified as belonging to the heterodirectional bivocal "word" type (III, Subtype 2) rather than to the "direct word" type (I).

The "word-object" is used in Stalin's dialogues with his subordinates. In them his strong Georgian accent comes to the fore. However, as soon as the author moves to an introspection of Stalin's cast of mind, he switches to the heterodirectional (parodistic) bivocal "word" that also predominates in the characterization of Rubin and, to a lesser extent, of Sologdin. Not unlike Dostoevsky, Solzhenitsyn "is not afraid of the most extreme activization of heterodirectional accents of the bivocal word."[10]

At least in one respect Solzhenitsyn's verbal style in *The First Circle* appears to be even more dialogic than that of Dostoevsky. This has to do with the duality of the language in which the novel is written. On the one hand, it reflects a return to the language of classical Russian literature; on the other, the novel can hardly be properly understood unless one is familiar with the Russian language of the Soviet period. The difference is not just between two historical phases of the same language, but between two languages belonging to different ethical value systems. Solzhenitsyn expresses this awareness when he reports the reactions of Innokenty to reading from the archive of his dead mother:

> The very words in which his mother and her women friends had expressed themselves were old-fashioned. They wrote, in dead seriousness, with capital letters: "Truth, Beauty, Good, Evil: ethical imperatives." In the language Innokenty and his friends used, words were more concrete, and therefore more comprehensible: moral intelligence, humaneness, loyalty, purposefulness. (55:397)

It is quite clear that what Innokenty discovered was not just a few "old-fashioned words" but a whole language of ethical values different from his own. This was the language of Dostoevsky and Tolstoy, Pushkin and Gogol, Turgenev and Chekhov—in short, the language of all Russian culture before 1917. As to the language of Innokenty and the people of his circle, it is no more than a Russian "Newspeak."

A crucial difference between the two languages consists in the fact that while the "old-fashioned" Russian was based on a more or less universal ethical value system, the Russian "Newspeak" has been designed to reflect the Party's Marxist jargon. The English translation illustrates the difference. While the translator has no trouble with the "old-fashioned" words" he stumbles on "the more concrete and therefore more comprehensible" words of the "Newspeak." That is because those words, though they were used even before the Revolution, have meaning for Innokenty defined by their concrete Soviet connotation rather than by their original denotation.

Thus, *ideinost* means for Innokenty not "moral intelligence" (as the translator has it), not even "being imbued with ideas" (its abstract denotation), but "being imbued with the immortal ideas of Marxism-Leninism." The word *gumannost'* meant for a Turgenev being humane to all humans but for Innokenty it exists only in its concrete Soviet connotation determined by the Marxist notion of class struggle. This is precisely the kind of *gumannost'* that he rejects when he decides to call Dobroumov's apartment. Similarly, *predannost'* is not just an abstract loyalty but the most concrete devotion to the Party and to whoever happens to be at its top; and *tseleustremlennost'* definitely implies only purposefulness in accord with the Party.

The ethical gap between the two languages is also evinced through Innokenty's reaction to the notion of "other opinions" that he finds in his mother's notes:

"Never consider yourself more in the right than others. Respect other opinions, even those opposed to yours."
That was rather old-fashioned, too. If my view of the world is correct, how can I respect those who disagree with me? (55:397)

This suggests yet another important distinction between the two languages. While the "old-fashioned" Russian, that is, Russian proper, is distinguished by an attitude of respect toward different opinions, and in this sense is a "dialogic" and a "polyphonic" language, Innokenty's "Newspeak," that is, Russian Sovietese, appears designed to serve a single "correct world view" and therefore is bascially a "monologic" or "homophonic" language.

Innokenty's transformation from a *homo soveticus* to a mere human being is accompanied by an increased use of "old-fashioned" words and notions both in the narrative and in his own vocabulary. His new attitude can hardly be characterized without such "old-fashioned" words as Good, Evil, Truth, and Conscience. Certainly, it is not Gorky's kind of pity that he feels toward Dr. Dobroumov when he decides to phone him. However, in spite of his return to the language of his Mother Russia, he remains acutely aware of his former "Newspeak." Even his new ethical imperative, "You also have only one conscience," is but a dialogic response to a Russian Sovietese cliché, an overused quotation from Nikolai Ostrovsky's novel *How the Steel Was Tempered*. In this sense, he does not switch completely from one "language" to another but instead becomes "bilingual." Solzhenitsyn underscores this when he quotes this ethical maxim as a title for the entire chapter dealing with Innokenty's spiritual transformation.[11]

Innokenty is by no means the only character in whose portrayal "bilingualism" plays an important role. Rubin is torn between the language of human sympathy and understanding (for that "brave man" who dared to think that "medicine does not ask a patient's nationality") and the Marxist jargon of "objectivity," "laws of history," and "progress." Nerzhin's descent into hell starts from the moment he feels an aversion to the style of Stalin's writings. Stalin himself is shown at the moment he becomes entangled in the web of his Marxist jargon, while he is quite comfortable with such "old-fashioned" words as orderly, shoulder boards, and supreme (*den'shchik, pogony,* and *verkhovny*).

The conflict between the two languages, Russian Sovietese and Russian proper, reaches symbolic dimensions when Sologdin creates his own private language, the Language of Ultimate Clarity, in a challenge to the official Language of Apparent Clarity. Although the author obviously has his tongue in his cheek with respect to Sologdin's creation, his irony is chiefly levelled against the Language of Apparent Clarity which is equated not only with the Marxist jargon of Stalin and Rubin but also with Russian Sovietese in general.

While writing the novel Solzhenitsyn was undoubtedly facing the same problem as his character. Like Sologdin, he had to create his own language because the available national language seemed inadequate for an expression of his ideas. Unlike Sologdin, however, he created his language not through a purge of words or an exclusion of the other language from his purview, but by letting the two languages enter into a dialogue with each other. Whether expressed through an exchange of verbal shots in a duel-debate, through a mimicry of his characters, or through an irony in the narrative, this dialogue of languages leaves its stylistic imprint on every page of the novel. In *The First Circle* Solzhenitsyn has demonstrated, among other things, his "polyphonic" ability to hear, comprehend, and imitate not only different ideological voices but different languages as well.

CHAPTER XI

The Question of Genre:

The First Circle as a Menippean Novel

WHAT IS the novel's genre and its relationship with polyphony? Bakhtin's study of Dostoevsky also points the direction in which the answer to this question should be sought. In the 1963 edition of his book Bakhtin complements his 1929 descriptive study of Dostoevsky's poetics with an excursus into the history of genres. He does so in an apparent effort to bring his work closer to his methodological ideal, in which the synchronic and the diachronic aspects of stylistics would be combined. Bakhtin begins his excursus by observing that the polyphonic strategy of Dostoevsky was incompatible with the prevailing prose genres of his time:

> Neither hero nor idea nor the principle of polyphonic structure fitted into such genre and plot-structure varieties as biographic, sociopsychological, everyday-life, and family novels; that is, into those forms which were predominant in the literature of the time and which were employed and developed by such writers as Turgenev, Goncharov, Lev Tolstoy. In comparison with them, the works of Dostoevsky clearly belong to a different genre type, alien to them.[1]

Dividing the novelistic genre into three main roots as the epic, the rhetorical, and the carnival, Bakhtin links Dostoevsky's polyphonic novels with the carnival. More specifically he links them with such seriocomic genres of antiquity as the Socratic dialogues and the Menippean satires which originated from the folklore of ancient carnivals. Even though the carnival as a social phenomenon later disintegrated, its world view has continued to be expressed through what Bakhtin calls the "carnivalization of literature," a process that has spanned hundreds of years and left its mark on such diverse writers as the authors of the early Christian literature, Dante, Cervantes, Shakespeare, the authors of picaresque and adventure novels, Poe, Balzac, Pushkin, and Gogol. In accordance with the common practice of using ancient terminology for modern words, Bakhtin suggests that the Dostoevskian polyphonic novel be called a Menippean satire to indicate its kinship with all carnivalized literature. He sees no contradiction between the terms "polyphonic" and "Menippean," and, in fact, qualifies them as mutually supportive:

> Having linked Dostoevsky with a certain tradition, we certainly have not in the least diminished the profound originality and individuality of his art. For he is the creator of *a true polyphony* which did not exist and could not have existed in Socratic dialogues, in the ancient Menippean satires, or in the medieval mystery plays, or in the art of Shakespeare and Cervantes, Voltaire and Diderot, Balzac and Hugo. But polyphony was *substantively* prepared by this line of European literature. This tradition, beginning with Socratic dialogues and Menippeas, was reborn and renovated by Dostoevsky in the innovative form of the polyphonic novel.[2]

For *The First Circle*, the results of the preceding analysis of its characterization, setting, structure, and verbal texture lead to the conclusion that, like Dostoevsky's polyphonic novels, it falls into the Menippean genre type. Of course, the word *Menippean* should be understood here as Bakhtin understands it, that is, as an indication of the essence of the genre and not in the ancient sense of a genre canon. Here is a brief review of some of the more specific qualities of *The First Circle* that are akin to carnivalized literature in general and to the Socratic dialogues and the Menippean satires in particular.

The carnival world view of *The First Circle* is most evident in that it shows not a normal life in a normal world but, as Bakhtin puts it, a life inside out in a world upside down.[3]

Characteristic of the novel is the same pathos of change and transformation, of death and resurrection, that forms the core of the carnival world view. Although the novel takes place at the summit of Stalin's power, a significant part of its effect is derived from the offstage death and subsequent "dethroning" of the man who aspired to immortality and to the crown of Emperor of the Planet. Such a view of history leaves the reader without pessimism after completing his tour of the vicious circle.

Among other carnival-inspired elements of the novel are the theme of descent into the nether world; the theme of relativity between the real and the illusory, between the prisoner and the free man, between hell and paradise; and the use of the setting (the sharashka) as a reshuffler of the "normal" hierarchic relations between people and values. Regarding this last element, one notes that the sharashka's boss, Yakonov, is a former prisoner; his deputy, Roitman, is likely to become one; the prisoner nicknamed "Iron Mask" is, on the other hand, a former boss; Rubin, a Communist, former Major, professor, and a Jew celebrates Christmas with the defeated Germans, discusses Marxist dialectics with a "reactionary priest-lover," and keeps company with illiterate peasants, deserters, and petty criminals. *The First Circle* is also distinguished by an extensive use of such carnival-inspired features as parody, especially the *parodia sacra* (chapter 49: "The Comedy Act"), and masquerade (chapter 54: "Buddha's Smile," and 87: "Meat").

In addition, *The First Circle* has a number of specific features of the Socratic dialogues, with which it shares, first of all, the belief in the dialogic nature of truth, a belief underlying the whole novel. Like the Socratic dialogues, the novel challenges the official ideology's claim to be in possession of the absolute truth and does so not with the help of another monological ideology, another absolute truth, but with a dialogic method of searching for truth. As in Plato's dialogues, the heroes of *The First Circle* are ideologists who reveal their ideas in situations of crisis, on the threshold between life and death, good and evil. Moreover, the novel appears to imitate directly such devices of the Socratic dialogues as syncrisis, that is, the juxtaposition of different viewpoints on a certain subject, and anacrisis, that is, the verbal provocation of a person to reveal his innermost thoughts and feelings. The former may be exemplified by the "duel-debate" between Rubin and Sologdin and the latter by Nerzhin's extracting from Spiridon his "homespun truths." In fact, Nerzhin is referred to in the novel as a "disciple of Socrates." Moreover, while the conversations under the open sky at the sawhorse seem to epitomize the seesaw tension of a Socratic dialogue, the "Lyceum Feast" debate may be seen as a symposium (an after-feast conversation), a device characteristic of seriocomic genres in general.

Finally, *The First Circle* has a number of characteristics in common with the genre of Menippean satires defined by Bakhtin as the "genre of ultimate questions." Although Menippus' own writings were lost, their principal features are well known, mainly through the works of his ancient followers such as Varro, Seneca, Lucian, Petronius, Apuleus, and Boethius. The genre's main innovation was to lower philosophic ideas from a heaven of speculative thought to the crucible of earth, to treat them, as Americans say, at the gut level. As compared with the Socratic dialogues the Menippeas are distinguished by a stronger emphasis on the latter part of their seriocomic duality, namely, on the element of laughter, mockery, and derision, and by the increased role of free imagination and fancy at the expense of historical authenticity. Among literary devices typical of Menippeas are the testing of men and their ideas through exceptional situations built into the plot; a *pro et contra* juxtaposition of different world views; a multilevel, contrastive setting including a king's palace, a slave's hut, a market, and a prison, and often encompassing Olympus,

Earth, and Hades; the themes of madness, split personality, and the abnormal in general; characters' eccentric behavior and speeches contrary to all norms; an extensive use of contrasts and oxymorons; a blend of symbolism, mystique, and fantasy with crude naturalism, profanity, and journalistic topicality; the inclusion of different genres, and a mixture of verse and prose in the same work; verbal innovations, colloquialisms, and stylistic experimentation.

Most of these elements are as strongly felt in *The First Circle* as they are in Dostoevsky's novels. However, in contrast to the ancient Menippeas, and to Dostoevsky, for that matter, Solzhenitsyn seems to have much less use for fantasy, eccentricities, and the abnormal. This is largely because the reality he depicts is of itself so unbelievable and abnormal that it often surpasses a fantasy of the mind and replaces it as a testing ground for men and their ideas. As Helen Muchnic puts it, "When a fantastic reality, more harrowing than even Dostoevsky's visions, cries out to be explained, when actualities have out-distanced the powers of fancy and forced the imagination to cope with their extravagance, speculative adventures cannot seem serious." [4]

Another major deviation of *The First Circle* from the ancient Menippeas may be seen in its antiutopian thrust, which replaces the element of social utopia frequently found in the Menippeas. This brings it closer to Dostoevsky and the antiutopian satires of Zamyatin, Orwell, and Aldous Huxley. Unlike them, however, Solzhenitsyn wrote from deep within a utopia turned into a reality in opposition to the one that the utopia intended. This circumstantial detail could not but affect his work in the direction of greater authenticity and realism. Therefore his authentic account of the Stalinist penal system is combined in the novel with a satire of the whole of Soviet society, with an ironic treatment of its official ideological premises, with a parody of its official language, and with a travesty made of its official literature.

CHAPTER XII

Polyphony of
Cancer Ward

IN THIS CHAPTER I shall attempt to demonstrate the polyphonic strategy of *Cancer Ward* by focusing on (1) the arrangement of characters, including the question of the author's hero; (2) genre peculiarities; and (3) symbolism of the novel.

The Arrangement of Characters

"It takes all sorts to make a world. We're all in the world together!" says Aunt Styofa, an orderly at the cancer ward, to Dyoma, a sixteen-year-old patient, when he has spoken harshly about the whorish ways of his mother. This sounds strange to Dyoma, because he did not expect Aunt Styofa, who has taken a motherly interest in him, to defend his "bad" mother. When he goes on to complain about injustice in fortune itself, which strikes down some with an incurable disease and lets others' lives "run smooth as silk from beginning to end," Aunt Styofa tries to soothe him by saying, "It all depends on God. God sees everything. You should submit to him, Dyomusha." But Dyoma, far from being ready to submit, persists in his rebellious thoughts: "Well, if it's from God it's even worse. If he can see everything, why does he load it all on one person? I think he ought to try to spread it about a bit" (10: 121, 122).[1]

Thus ends one of numerous ideological dialogues in the novel in which neither side is prepared to surrender any ground and upon which no final, authoritative comment is provided by the author. The reader is left free to choose a side or otherwise to make sense of the dialogues.

Before interpreting this particular dialogue, let me first observe that it is clearly reminiscent of the one between Alyosha and Ivan in *The Brothers Karamazov*, in which Ivan accuses God of cruelty and injustice especially toward innocent children and offers to return his "admission ticket" to this world of God. There can be no doubt that, in spite of his enormous compassion and understanding of Ivan, Dostoevsky was on the side of Alyosha when he adjudged Ivan's stance as rebellion. By the same token, I think that Solzhenitsyn, in spite of the fact that Dyoma eventually emerges as one of the positive heroes of the novel, is in this dialogue essentially on the side of Aunt Styofa. The meaning of the dialogue is then two-fold. First, Solzhenitsyn may well have charged Aunt Styofa with the task of giving a lesson in humility to the rebellious young generation of the Soviet Union as represented by Dyoma and Asya (the chapter is quite deliberately titled "The Children"). With Aunt Styofa—and with Alyosha and Dostoevsky—Solzhenitsyn seems to be saying a firm yes to this world in spite of the fact that he personally has been burdened with much more than his share of suffering. Second, this dialogue has a meaning which goes beyond mere thematic interpretation, for it may well indicate Solzhenitsyn's strategy of arranging his characters so he can gather together all sorts of people with all sorts of views on life. The name of that strategy is polyphony.

Of course, the setting of the novel, an oncological hospital, offers the author an excellent opportunity to gather together all sorts of people, a representative cross-section of all social layers of a multinational society: doctors and patients; members of the new class and common workers and peasants; Russians and ethnic minorities; Communists and non-Communists. But how can they be made believable and their views credible? How can the polyphony be made to work?

This Solzhenitsyn achieves through the technique of shifting viewpoints of narration, as if the novel were written not by himself but by each of his characters. As he himself described it, the polyphonic technique consists of letting "each character become the main hero as soon as the action reverts to him," or—one might say concerning *Cancer Ward*, where action is even less prominent than in *The First Circle*—as soon as the focus is on that character himself. Consequently, each character in the novel is shown not from the outside in (as is often the case with Lev Tolstoy) but rather from the inside out (as with Dostoevsky). And when occasionally a character is shown from the outside he is seen not so much from a single, fixed viewpoint of the omniscient narrator as through his reflection in other characters. The author successively assumes, as it were, the mask of his characters, and with this mask he borrows *their* personalities, mimics *their* patterns of thought and style of expression, and immerses the reader in *their* stream of consciousness. Through the use of this technique in *Cancer Ward*, Solzhenitsyn allows us to see the world through the eyes of both the patients and their doctors; of the former labor camp prisoners and of those who send them there; of the Communists, Christians, and atheists.

We enter the cancer ward with a new patient, Pavel Nikolayevich Rusanov, an important bureaucrat and Party hack with strong ties to the KGB. His viewpoint, and perception of the ward and the world, remains dominant in the two opening chapters. He recoils at the prospect of being a roommate to "the eight abject beings who were now his 'equals.'" He despises them as "either apathetic wrecks or non-Russians." Among the Russians he distinguishes a "bandaged devil" and "a villainous cutthroat's mug," whom he later calls "Bone-chewer." Although in chapter 2 we are introduced to their true names, Podduyev and Kostoglotov, we do not see the world through their eyes until much later, in chapters 8 and 6 respectively, when the author first assumes their masks. Meanwhile, in the intervening chapters, from the third to the fifth, the reader had already seen the patients through the eyes of Zoya, a practicing medical student, and Dr. Vera Gangart. Of the book's thirty-six chapters, Rusanov's and Kostoglotov's viewpoints are each predominant in nine, while another dozen or so characters—Zoya, Vera, Dr. Dontsova, Vadim Zatsyrko, Dyoma, Dr. Oreshchenkov, Shulubin, the orderly Elizaveta Anatolyevna—share the remaining eighteen. In spite of the preponderance of just two viewpoints, which are contrapuntal to each other, Solzhenitsyn uses the technique of shifting viewpoints so adroitly that he creates the impression of movement in an otherwise immobile world and makes the reader trust in his basic fairness to characters regardless of their ideological affiliation. But the polyphonic strategy that allows the characters greater independence and freedom to espouse their views does not imply any sort of moral relativism on the author's part. Bakhtin demonstrated this in respect to Dostoevsky, and the same must be said regarding Solzhenitsyn's novels, in which the author treats all characters fairly and lets the reader decide where his sympathies or antipathies lie.

Rusanov is certainly not an attractive character. No matter how much he suffers from cancer, he is unlikely to elicit much sympathy from the reader: he is almost as bad a person as Stalin in *The First Circle*. But even he may have a saving grace in his love of his family. Whereas he himself may be beyond salvation, there seems to be at least a possibility for his redemption in the next generation through his son Yuri, a lawyer who is about to take up a struggle for justice in Soviet courts. Most important is the fact that, like Stalin in *The First Circle*, Rusanov is condemned not because he is a Communist but because he is a scoundrel; not because of his former crimes, but because of his refusal even to admit those crimes. This is made especially clear through two portraits that form counterpoints to Rusanov.

One is Yefrem Podduyev. On the basis of his past record he is perhaps even more repulsive than Rusanov, more guilty of crimes against humanity: he admits having executed without trial seven members of the Constituent Assembly; he has made his many "wives" unhappy; he was cruel as a labor camp overseer. But from the moment Podduyev's conscience is reawakened the reader feels no antipathy toward him.

Another counterpoint to Rusanov may be seen in Vadim Zatsyrko, a young geologist and a dedicated Communist. Rusanov's entry to the ward is marked by his offering a bribe to secure favors from the doctors and staff; Vadim, by contrast, "could not bear string-pulling in any shape or form." Although he is mostly in political agreement with Rusanov, he is differently conceived. "Once a single passion got a grip on you it ousted all others" (19:252). That is what the reader hears about him while the author allows us to eavesdrop on Vadim's stream of consciousness. There is no irony implied in this statement: Vadim is indeed conceived as one of those "Russian boys" who dedicate themselves entirely to a single idea or a single passion. Dostoevsky made them famous in the past, and Solzhenitsyn has resurrected them in modern fiction and, in fact, used almost precisely the same phrase to describe his autobiographical hero Nerzhin in *The First Circle*. Vadim is an honest Communist who embraces the idea of serving his country—by finding a new method of prospecting for ore deposits—almost to the point of obsession.

Ironically, Vadim's extraordinary dedication to his country puts him in conflict with the prevailing inefficiency of the system.

It exasperated him at school and college when the students were always told to assemble for class, an excursion, a party, or a demonstration, an hour or two earlier than necessary, on the theory that they were bound to be late. Vadim could never stand the half-hour news bulletins on the radio. . . . It made him mad to think that whenever he went to a shop there was a

ten-to-one chance of finding it closed for stocktaking, stock
renewal or transfer of goods. (19:246)

To the extent that all this criticism could have been made by
Solzhenitsyn himself, Vadim is apparently an autobiographical
figure reflecting the author's own youth. After Vadim learned
of his terminal disease,

> He became like a moving body approaching the speed of
> light. His "time" and his "mass" were becoming different
> from those of other people. His time was increasing in capac-
> ity, his mass in penetration. His years were being compressed
> into weeks, his days into minutes. All his life he'd been in a
> hurry, but now he was really starting to run. (19:249)

Reading those lines one cannot help thinking of Solzhenitsyn
himself, now working feverishly on the completion of his life
project before sickness or age might overtake him.

Vadim apparently expresses Solzhenitsyn's idea in thinking,
apropos of his own mother, whose excessive love, he realizes,
was the real cause of his cancer, that "It was wrong to be too
pragmatic, to judge people solely by results; it was more humane to judge by intentions" (19:246). But the same sentence
seems to express Solzhenitsyn's own attitude to Vadim and his
characters generally. It could be inferred also that such an attitude is indispensable to a writer's ability to think or write poly-
phonically. Only when a Zatsyrko or a Rubin is judged by other
than the actual results of his ideological commitment does he
emerge as a decent and even heroic figure. Conversely, a
Rusanov and a Stalin appear villains to the reader precisely
because of their not having had or pursued unselfish intentions.

If Vadim Zatsyrko is best judged in terms of his unselfish
motivation and unwavering dedication to his country, Aleksei
Filippovich Shulubin, another Communist, should rather be
judged by the suffering he has undergone as a result of his
cowardice. His life has been a continuous surrendering of his
ideas, principles, and conscience for the sake of self-preservation. A graduate of the Timiryazev Academy in Moscow, a

specialist on Marxist dialectics and a former lecturer, he has been reduced to the position of a provincial librarian, not because he had opposed the Party line, but because he had failed to support it with sufficient enthusiasm. Described as a bird with clipped wings, he epitomizes the surrender of Soviet intelligentsia to the demands of the totalitarian state. Even now he dares to bare his soul to Kostoglotov only in secret and because he faces surgery with little chance of survival. Quoting Pushkin's verse about "our vile time" when man was "either tyrant or traitor or prisoner," he classifies himself as a traitor. But "Haven't I earned," he asks Kostoglotov, "the right to a few thoughts through my suffering, through my betrayal?" (31:444). Yet, he has, and that is why the author entrusts him with expressing what might appear at first sight as the social philosophy of the novel.

Shulubin seems to play the role of spiritual mentor to Kostoglotov, a relationship somewhat similar to that of Sologdin to Nerzhin in *The First Circle*. Not only does he expose Kostoglotov to Francis Bacon's doctrine of popular idols but he is the only man in the novel—and so far the only hero-ideologist in Solzhenitsyn's fiction in general—who seems to offer an alternative to the present form of socialism in the USSR. A more bookish person than Kostoglotov, Shulubin instructs him, "I should say that for Russia in particular, with our repentances, confessions and revolts, our Dostoevsky, Tolstoy and Kropotkin, there's only one true socialism, and that's ethical socialism. That is something completely realistic" (31: 440).

An interesting thing about Shulubin's "ethical socialism" is that it is presented in the novel only as a hypothesis in which the author himself might, but only might, believe but which he does not hallow with any conclusive authorial comment. In fact, he even refrains from an indirect comment through his autobiographical alter ego in the novel, Kostoglotov, who has "midwifed" Shulubin's "truth." Although sympathetic to

Shulubin and his ideas, Kostoglotov has his reservations, and at the end disagrees with Shulubin's rejection of happiness as a goal of social progress. The proposition of ethical socialism is made and well-received but not sanctioned; the dialogue remains open-ended; the reader has the choice to decide with whom to side. In this Solzhenitsyn proves himself a true polyphonist, knowing how to avoid interposing his authority between character and reader.[2]

There is no denying that Kostoglotov plays a special role in the novel. He is undoubtedly a strongly autobiographical figure. But is he the main hero of *Cancer Ward*? I think not—certainly not in the usual sense of being the author's mouthpiece. His special role consists in being the author's eyes and ears rather than mouth. He is the author's secret agent sent out among other characters to observe them, as it were, with two more than ordinary eyes, to eavesdrop on their private thoughts, and to make them speak. He is in the line of character development which in Russian literature has produced such heroes as Alyosha Karamazov and Gleb Nerzhin. Like them he is the embodiment of the idea of polyphony.

What are his special qualifications for such a special role? First, he is set apart from all other characters, and the readers, by being a rare survivor of both a neglected tumor and labor camps. He himself sees that experience in almost mystical terms. Introducing himself to Zoya, he says:

> This autumn I learned from experience that a man can cross the threshold of death even when his body is still not dead. Your blood still circulates and your stomach digests, while you yourself have gone through the whole psychological preparation for death—and lived through death itself. Everything around you, you see as if from the grave. And although you've never counted yourself a Christian, indeed the very opposite sometimes, all of a sudden you find you've forgiven all those who trespassed against you and bear no ill-will towards those who persecuted you. You're simply indifferent to everyone and everything. (3:31)

Compared with other characters, then, Kostoglotov is especially well-suited to function as the author's "eye": to observe
life in a detached and objective manner from a vantage point
outside of ordinary experience.

Second, Kostoglotov's mystical experience "beyond the
threshold" has taught him to understand human nature, its ill-
nesses and cures, better than even his doctors. "After all," he
argues with Dr. Dontsova, "man is a complicated being, why
should he be explainable by logic? Or for that matter by eco-
nomics? Or physiology?" (6:75). While this argument is
pointed against the Marxist assumptions of economic and
"scientific" determinism, it also echoes Sologdin's, and Solzhenitsyn's, praise of Dostoevsky for his ability to create characters "as complex and incomprehensible as people in real
life" (see chapter I), an ability that Bakhtin considered essential for Dostoevsky's polyphony.

Third, like Nerzhin in *The First Circle*, Kostoglotov is portrayed as an inveterate skeptic. At one point he calls on his
fellow patients to follow the advice of Descartes to "suspect
everything." When Rusanov tries to stop a debate by invoking
the authority of Lenin, Kostoglotov replies: "No one on this
earth ever says anything 'once and for all.' If they did life
would come to a stop and succeeding generations would have
nothing to say" (11:135).

As in the case of Nerzhin, Kostoglotov's unusual experience, understanding, and skepticism never turn into mere cyn-
icism, self-pity, or resignation. All his extraordinary qualities
are brought to bear after his initial attitude of indifference toward "everyone and everything" changes into an active concern for all. His compassion for the suffering of his fellow
patients brings him to the point where "he no longer set himself apart from free man, as he used to, but was joining them
in the common misfortune" (11:139). His former self-cen-
teredness gives way to the realization that other people might
have their own stories to tell. As he admits to Shulubin,

One's own troubles are always the worst. For instance, I might
conclude that I've led an extraordinarily unlucky life, but how
do I know? Maybe yours has been even harder. How can I
judge from outside? (31:432)

Throughout the novel Kostoglotov, and through him Solzhenitsyn, is engaged precisely in overcoming the natural limita-
tions of his outside viewpoint. When he becomes acquainted
with people he always tries to get inside them, underneath
their skin, to see the world with their eyes, and to hear out
their life stories. It is he who plunges Podduyev, and through
him the rest of the ward, into a soul search by suggesting that
he read Tolstoy's moral parables. From Shulubin, a man who
would talk to no one, he extracts his "ethical socialism"; from
Elizaveta Anatolyevna, an orderly to whom nobody talks, the
declaration that all "literary tragedies" of past world literature, including *Anna Karenina*, "are just laughable compared
with the ones we live through."

> "So why should I read *Anna Karenina* again? Maybe it's
> enough—what I have experienced. Where can people read
> about us? *Us?* Only in a hundred years' time?"
> She was almost shouting now, but her years of training by
> fear didn't desert her. It wasn't a real shout, she didn't cry out.
> *The only one who had heard her was Kostoglotov*. (34:479,
> emphasis added)

And, we might add, Solzhenitsyn, who made her audible by
his "polyphonic" ability to hear and amplify someone else's
voice. Even when Kostoglotov fails to befriend people, he is
anxious to find out how they feel, think, and express themselves. The following passage from the scene describing the
reactions of the patients to *Pravda's* failure to commemorate
Stalin's death perhaps best illustrates Kostoglotov's function
as the author's eavesdropping device:

> Kostoglotov had been awake all the time. Rusanov and
> Vadim had been rustling through the paper and whispering to

each other, and he had heard every word. He had deliberately
not opened his eyes. He wanted to hear what they would say
about it, what Vadim would say about it. (23:314)

Like Nerzhin and Alyosha, Kostoglotov has his firm convictions and principles but is reluctant to condemn other people. Upon hearing Shulubin's story of how he had become a
"traitor," Kostoglotov disagrees with his low opinion of himself. He especially disagrees with Pushkin's indictment of
people like Shulubin:

> Pushkin was too rash as well. A storm breaks trees, it only
> bends grass. Does this mean that the grass has betrayed the
> trees? Everyone has his own life. (31:435)

Kostoglotov's main opponents in the novel are not the people
of different opinions and convictions but those who would not
tolerate the difference. Among them are Rusanov and his
daughter Aviette, who was always upset "when people's ideas
failed to fall into one of two clear-cut categories: the soundly
argued and the unsoundly argued. She hated it when they
ranged vaguely through all the shades of the spectrum" (21:
286). Kostoglotov struggles to preserve the richness of that
spectrum, and Solzhenitsyn converts that richness into one of
ideological polyphony.

In all this, Kostoglotov's function is essentially similar to
Nerzhin's in *The First Circle* and, for that matter, to Alyosha's
in *The Brothers Karamazov*—not so much rhetorical as structural. He is a spokesman less for the author than for polyphony. Most importantly, he is a practitioner of polyphony and
a catalyst making polyphony possible.

Menippean Genre Features of the Novel

As with *The First Circle*, the polyphonic strategy of *Cancer
Ward* is implemented with the help of an extensive use of char-

acteristic elements of the Menippean genre, with, first of all, a
reliance on a number of these elements that are common to
every variety of the genre, including Socratic dialogues and
Menippean satire proper. Unified by the general atmosphere of
a "carnival world view," these elements encompass the theme
of change and transformation, of death and resurrection; the
theme of the "dethroning" of a "king" and the expulsion of
the gods from Olympus; the theme of relativity between what
is real and what is not; and the use of setting as a reshuffler of
the usual hierarchy of men and values.

As in *The First Circle*, the general atmosphere of the "carnival" pervades *Cancer Ward* and is rooted most strongly in
the fact that it shows not a normal life in a normal country but
a life inside out in a country upside down. For most of the
characters, life is turned inside out simply because strange
things happen when one finds oneself, as they do, on the
threshold of death. However, a few of them realize that the
sickness itself is a consequence of the country's being turned
upside down. For them life is, Kostoglotov says, like the river
Chu "that ends its life in the sands, a river flowing nowhere,
shedding the best of its water and strength haphazardly along
its path" (22:295). For Shulubin life has changed because of
the country's indulgence in the idolatry of the market place,
"And over all idols there is the sky of fear, the sky of fear
overhung with grey clouds. . . . Darkness and gloom descend
before their proper time. The whole world makes you feel ill
at ease" (31:436). Whereas Shulubin describes the country
in nearly cosmic terms, Elizaveta Anatolyevna singles it out
on historical grounds: she tries to escape from her life into
books because all the tragedies of other countries and of former times "are just laughable compared with the ones we live
through." Finally, even for Rusanov the country appears upside down, albeit for a different reason. When he becomes
upset with his fellow patients because they are reading Tol-

stoy's "priest-ridden booklet" he is about to accuse them of "playing into the hands of the enemy." But he stops short of doing so because "in ordinary life [in the USSR] there was always some enemy to point to, but who could be the enemy here, in a hospital bed?" (15:201). He could not go on with his denunciations not only because he was in a hospital but because the Soviet Union of 1955 was clearly in an "abnormal" state for the Stalinists who felt at that time surrounded by "Absurdities" (the title of chapter 16) and haunted by specters (chapter 17).

Whereas in *The First Circle* the carnivallike effect largely depends on the reader's awareness of the offstage death and subsequent defamation of the man who had aspired to immortality and the crown of Emperor of the Earth, in *Cancer Ward* we are made witness to the first official steps in the ritual of the "dethronement" of the "idol-king." Since Stalin had died in 1953 the ritual is enacted by proxy—Rusanov, who stands for everything for which his idol-king stood. The ritual is replete with three official announcements: first, that the entire Supreme Court is replaced; second, that the Stalinist premier is ousted; and third—through *Pravda*'s failure to commemorate Stalin's death by carrying his image and assuring its readers that he is "alive and will live forever"—that the idol-king himself is overthrown and banished from the Marxian Olympus.

Solzhenitsyn's portrayal of the historical event as a carnivallike ritual is reinforced by the fact that each of the three official announcements is accompanied by theatrical gestures pertaining to Rusanov, a stooge for Stalin: the first two by the injections which are administered by his doctors and of which he is tearfully afraid, and the last, by his own vodka toasts—"to swill the despair out of his soul"—in the company of the "capitalist speculator" Chaly, a gesture showing his ultimate degradation. In a contrapuntal development of the ritualistic scene, Solzhenitsyn lets the reader peer into the mind of Kostoglotov, Rusanov's antagonist and Stalin's former "slave" now witnessing his demise. In Kostoglotov's mind the first two announcements are accompanied by the sound of Beethoven's "four muffled chords of fate" and the third, by the memory of the labor camp's reaction to the news that "the old cannibal has kicked the bucket": "Bring out your guitars, strum your balalaikas!" (23:314).

The ritual of "dethronement" is also linked with Rusanov's learning privately, during his wife's visit, that Rodichev, the man whom he had long ago sent down all the circles of the nether world, is rehabilitated and may have returned to town. This makes Rusanov fear retribution as much as he fears the cancer in his neck.

> His fate lay there, between his chin and his collarbone.
> There justice was being done.
> And in answer to this justice he could summon no influential friend, no past services, no defense. (14:196)

Thus, Rusanov's cancer itself is portrayed as a reminder, if not a direct expression, of retributive justice, a motif often found in carnival-inspired literature. Even though the novel ends with Rusanov's temporary escape from the grip of his fateful cancer, even though the specters that once haunted him seem to go their way too (chapter 21), the reader is assured that justice is not only possible but inevitable.

Like the goddess Themis' scales of justice, the theme of retribution is balanced in the novel by the theme of rebirth and resurrection. Not only is Rodichev's name (from the Russian word-root *rod-*, birth) suggestive of a rebirth but his very rehabilitation is described as an "inconceivable resurrection of the dead." The phrase is certainly not accidental. It had been used more than once in *The First Circle*, and it reverberates through *Cancer Ward* as well. Kostoglotov's own miraculous recovery, although inconclusive in its ambivalence, may be seen in the last two chapters as the beginning of a new world of spiritual resurrection.

Even the fact that the novel's temporal setting is confined to a few weeks in January, February, and March of 1955 cannot be attributed solely to autobiographical authenticity.[3] Just as *The First Circle* takes place in three days around Christmas A.D. 1949 in order to symbolize the mystery of the birth of light in the midst of darkness, it cannot be overlooked that *Cancer Ward*'s taking place in 1955, with an emphasis on the spring, is pregnant with the suggestion of a rebirth of both nature and the nation, as if the Dionysian festivals or the Eleusinian mysteries of ancient Greece were being reenacted in a provincial Asian town of the USSR in A.D. 1955.

Besides its similarities to all carnival-inspired genres, *Cancer Ward*, like *The First Circle*, also shares a number of specific features with both the Socratic dialogues and the genre of the Menippean satire proper.

With the Socratic dialogues it shares, first of all, the belief in the dialogic nature of truth, a belief as essential to the total strategy of *Cancer Ward* as it is to that of *The First Circle*. "No one on this earth ever says anything 'once and for all,'" Kostoglotov replies to Rusanov who tried to squash all debate by reference to the "once and for all" authoritative utterances of the "classics" of Communism. "If they did," he explains, "life would come to a stop and succeeding generations would have nothing to say" (11:135). Notice the universality of Kostoglotov's frame of reference and his near equation of life with an incessant dialogue. For him, and for Solzhenitsyn, the budding rebirth of the nation is unthinkable without a rebirth of ideological dialogues. Thus the whole novel is one huge macrodialogue with the ideology that is essentially monologic and intolerant of any form of ideological dissent.

The prime challenge is not to the political trappings of Communism but to its ethical and epistemological assumptions.

As in *The First Circle*, Solzhenitsyn often invokes in *Cancer Ward* Nikolai Ostrovsky's slogan "We Have But One Life" which was elevated by Soviet propaganda to the level of unquestionable wisdom. When Rusanov tries to sway Podduyev from Tolstoy to Ostrovsky, Kostoglotov rebukes him with bitter sarcasm:

> "Why stop a man from thinking? After all, what does our philosophy of life boil down to? 'Oh, life is so good! . . . Life, I love you. Life is for happiness!' What profound sentiments. Any animal can say as much without our help, any hen, cat, or dog." (11:137)

There can be no better setting for the challenge than the oncological hospital where the materialist philosophy is tested on the threshold of life and death, and found untenable. Like Nerzhin in *The First Circle*, Kostoglotov plays the role of initiating dialogues, keeping them going, and midwifing the birth of truth. It is he who palms off on Podduyev "the blue book with the gold signature" of Lev Tolstoy. That book's provocative question, "What Do Men Live By?" serves in the novel as a principal test of the characters' world view. Kostoglotov also plays the role of a homegrown Socrates when he addresses the cancer ward with his speech about the possibility of self-induced healing (chapter 11, "Cancer of the Birch Tree"). In this speech and in the "blue book" litmus test, as well as in several private conversations of Kostoglotov with other characters, Solzhenitsyn deftly employs a combination of two principal devices of the Socratic dialectical method, the anacrisis, that is, a verbal provocation of a person to reveal his views, and syncrisis, a juxtaposition of different views.

True to the Socratic belief that truth can be born only through dialogues, *Cancer Ward*, like *The First Circle*, relentlessly challenges the Communist claim to the absolute truth, not by expounding another absolute truth, but by insisting that mankind, lest it descend to the level of hens, cats, and dogs, should practice what comes to it most naturally, that is, a say-and-listen, dialogic communication. Thus, while polyphony in general and ideological dialogues in particular are Solzhenitsyn's predominant artistic media, they also are his principal message.

The novel also contains a number of features characteristic of the genre of Menippean satires as preserved in the writings of Menippus' latter followers, including Varro, Seneca, Lucian, Petronius, Apuleus, and Boethius. Not only does it share with the genre a concern for the ultimate questions of life and death, and of the meaning and the value of life, but it treats them in a characteristically Menippean fashion, that is, on a mundane, popular, and universal level. What could be a better test for the speculative philosophies of life than the crucible of a cancer ward, where death lives next door to everyone, regardless of age, nationality, sex, ideology, or politics? What could be a better place to upset the usual hierarchy of men and values than a second-rate hospital in a second-rate town of a second-rate Asiatic province of the Soviet Union? The cancer ward represents not only a cross-section of Soviet society but also a microcosm of modern mankind that sooner or later, whether it becomes Communist or not, will have to face the ultimate question of life and death.

Although it lacks the multilevel, contrastive setting of most Menippeas, *Cancer Ward* abounds in description of such favorite Menippean locales as a slave's hut (Kostoglotov's hut in Ush-Terek), a market (actually a Soviet *univermag*, that is, "universal store") a prison (in Kostoglotov's flashbacks), and a zoo.

The theme of relativity between the free man and the prisoner which played an important role in *The First Circle* is superseded here by the relativity between the sick man and the healer. Dr. Dontsova fails to detect her own cancer. Zoya, a practicing medical student, fails to administer sex-inhibiting hormone injections to Kostoglotov because she is interested in him as a man. Kostoglotov, on the other hand, "a specialist in being ill" and a returnee from beyond the threshold, is portrayed as having an unusual ability to cure himself and others. His arguments against Dr. Friedlander's materialistic view of sex have an encouraging if not a healing effect on Dr. Gangart. He also convinces his fellow patients of the value of Dr. Maslennikov's "chaga" extract, which has no seal of official approval, and, moreover, of the idea of self-induced healing, which is in direct conflict with everything their doctors say. The patients, educated and uneducated alike, listen to him because

> They all longed to find some miracle-doctor, or some medicine the doctors here didn't know about. Whether they admitted as much or denied it, they all without exception in the depth of their hearts believed there was a doctor, or a herbalist, or some old witch of a woman somewhere, whom you only had to find and get that medicine from to be saved. (11:140)

Throughout the novel the reader feels that its numerous references to the miraculous and mysterious—"Which of us from childhood has not shuddered at the mysterious?"—are not present by chance but form a theme as relevant to the whole as in any Menippea.

The novel also shares with other seriocomic genres of antiquity such carnival-inspired formal features as the mixture of prose and verse (the latter is interspersed almost as prominently as in Dostoevsky's *The Devils*, which Bakhtin considered a modern Menippea), of the elevated and the profane and even obscene (the quotations from Pushkin, Yesenin, and Herwegh are used side by side with the bombastic lines of Shulubin's daughter and the graffiti limericks of Chaly, whose buffoonery calls to mind that of Captain Lebyadkin in *The Devils*); the use of anecdotes, popular songs, and the vernacular in general; the use of animal allegories (especially in the last two chapters where Kostoglotov's visit to the zoo harks

back to the anecdote at the end of chapter 2 about Allah granting man a shorter span of time); the use of irony, sarcasm, and
parody including *parodia sacra* (e.g., the ritual of "dethronement"); the use of masquerade (the scene at the House of Culture when Zoya bursts into tears because her "gorgeous"
monkey tail was stolen, 12:154); a combination of social satire and a social utopia (in Shulubin's "ethical socialism"); the
inclusion of letters and tales (e.g., the medieval Christian tale
of Kitovras); and a blend of naturalistic descriptions and journalistic topicality on the one hand with mystery and symbolism
on the other.

Symbolism in *Cancer Ward*

There is a strong tendency among critics to see Solzhenitsyn as
a realist whose strength lies primarily in his ability to describe
authentically his actual experiences. However, the "overarch-
ing impression . . . of relentless veracity" (Erlich) often
causes critics to underestimate the importance of his realism's
symbolic implications.

Everything in *Cancer Ward* is symbolic. The names of characters—Zoya, Vera, Vega, Rodichev, Rusanov, Kostoglotov
—not only all lend themselves easily to symbolic interpretations, but the author himself called attention to the fact. Here
is the scene in which Oleg Kostoglotov and Zoya discuss her
name.

> "Zo-ya," said Oleg liltingly, "Zo-ya! Do you know what
> your name means?"
> "Zoya means life," she replied crisply, as though reciting
> a slogan. She liked explaining it. She stood there, resting her
> hands on the window-sill behind her back, leaning a little to
> one side, her weight on one leg.
> "And what about the 'zo-' in it? Don't you sometimes feel
> close to those 'zo-ological' ancestors of ours?"
> She laughed in the same mood as he had spoken.

"We're all a little like them. We provide food, feed our
young. . . . Is there anything wrong in that?" (12:170)

No, there is nothing wrong in that, but throughout the novel
Zoya is portrayed so as to justify her name as a symbol of the
animal in human nature, of the instinct for self-preservation
and physical procreation. As the reader watches her through
the window, he realizes that she is "leaning a little to one side,
her weight on one leg."

But what about the other, no less important "leg" of human
nature? This, the spiritual aspect is best embodied in Dr. Gangart, through her first name, Vera, and her nickname, Vega.
Vera in Russian means "faith." It is about her we read:
"There is great satisfaction in remaining faithful, perhaps it is
the greatest satisfaction of all. Even if no one knows about
your faithfulness, even if no one values it" (25:346). Eventually Vera's faithfulness to her loved one is elevated into
faithfulness to an ideal. In the eyes of Kostoglotov she becomes, as she had been to her friend killed during the war,
Vega, an unattainable but eternally attractive star of idealism.

Among other names one can mention the narrow political
and strictly Soviet implications of the name that Rusanov gave
to one of his sons, Lavrenty, after Lavrenty Beria, a former
head of the secret police. As mentioned before, the name of
the "rehabilitated" Rodichev suggests a rebirth. Rusanov's
own name, because of its *rus-* root, may be read as indicative
of its bearer's belief that he most fully represents Russian patriotism, when in fact he is portrayed as a *partyot* rather than
patriot. Kostoglotov is apparently the one whose lot it has
been, despite his genuine Russianness, to swallow nothing
but bones from the table of the Rusanovs who currently rule
Russia.

The numbers that enter the lives of the characters are also
symbolic. Although Rusanov as a Party man is not supposed
to believe in superstition, the first thing he reacts against upon

entering the cancer ward is the fact that it bears the unlucky number thirteen, or "the devil's dozen" in a popular Russian definition. Kostoglotov, on the other hand, on learning that the medicine prescribed by the doctors cost fifty-eight roubles, reflects that "at every stage of his life he was pursued by the figure 58" (35:495), an allusion to the fact that he had been convicted under Article 58 of the Soviet Code.

The frequent associations of characters with animals are symbolic. Zoya is associated with, nicknamed after, and best remembered as a bee (unfortunately translated as "teddy-bear"), an essentially positive creature, diligent, useful, and harmless unless disturbed. Vivacious and dynamic, she allows Kostoglotov to drink the honey of her kisses in a confirmation of his physical convalescence. But his spiritual regeneration has to wait until he sees "a miracle of spirituality": "the Nilgai antelope, light brown, on fine, light legs, her head keen and alert but not in the least afraid." In the eyes of the antelope, "big, trustful, and gentle," Kostoglotov recognizes the gaze of Vera. And "the likeness was so true it was unbearable," as if it were "witchcraft" or a "transmigration of souls" (35:508). Shulubin, with his big and transfixed round eyes, is often referred to as a "night owl," perhaps suggesting not only an owl's proverbial wisdom but also the fact that during all his Soviet career he was true to himself only at night.

The physical setting of the novel is symbolic: Soviet Asia, the capital of Uzbekistan, an oncological hospital, cancer ward no. 13. Tashkent and Central Asia are places where unfortunate human remnants of the once proud Communist vision of the International are brought together into a forced conglomerate composed of natives and their Russian overseers as well as other national minorities and political deviants, often delivered here via camps and exile: Germans and Koreans, Tatars and Kazakhs, Russians and Ukrainians. In the hospital—symbolically presided over by an incompetent Uzbek, a token of the official myth of national liberation—both doctors and pa-

tients are brought to the threshold of death, where their philosophies of life are tested and found untenable regardless of the
age, sex, nationality, or political loyalty of their exponents.
The setting in time is also symbolic: the first part of the novel, in which the principal characters are brought to the ward,
occurs during winter; the second, in which they seem to con-
valesce, takes place at the time of spring blossoms. The process of Kostoglotov's seeming recovery is paralleled by the
beginning of the country's recovery from the vestiges of Stalinism. Neither recovery is conclusive. Both give rise to a
pause between hope and doubt.

Symbolic too are the various forms of cancer that afflict the
patients in a certain pattern. A philosophy lecturer who had
abused his vocal cords by "clouding people's brains" with his
Marxist-Leninist agitprop is stricken with cancer of the throat,
a fact which Kostoglotov ponders with tongue in cheek: "But
what a coincidence—in the throat, of all places!" (11:149).
Rusanov, who had pulled the rope around many a neck, suffers
from cancer of the neck and feels that "his fate lay there, between his chin and his collarbone." Podduyev, who had lied
all his life, is afflicted in his tongue. Among the least sinful,
Asya, whose name incidentally counterpoints that of Turgenev's classical heroine, apparently represents that substantial
part of the Soviet young generation which, Soviet propaganda
notwithstanding, indulges heavily in promiscuous sex. Not unexpectedly she is stricken with cancer of the breast. Dyoma's
affliction seems to suggest the state-sponsored overindulgence
in sports. He has contracted his tumor after injuring his leg in
a soccer game. Finally, Kostoglotov suffers from cancer of
the stomach because he has apparently swallowed too many
"bones," the bones of labor camps and injustice. Also full of
irony and symbolism is the fact that Dr. Dontsova, an essentially benevolent and decent person and a competent practitioner of modern Soviet methods of curing cancer, is stricken

with cancer herself. She will not stay in her own hospital for treatment but will go to Moscow.

Everything in *Cancer Ward* is symbolic and, at the same time, real—down-to-earth, genuine, authentic. None of the symbols seems contrived or invented. The names are common, the dates set according to the perpetual calendar 1955; many other facts are verifiable, and the whole story is based squarely on the author's all-too-real suffering and miraculous recovery from cancer of the stomach. Then what kind of symbolism is this, and what does it have to do with either polyphony or the Menippean genre?

The author himself has offered two hints as to how these questions may be answered. The first one is found in the transcripts of the 22 September 1967 meeting of the Moscow section of the Soviet Writers' Union, during which suitability of the novel for publication in the USSR was discussed. Solzhenitsyn replied to his detractors:

> They reproach me even for the title, saying that cancer and the cancer ward are not a medical subject but some kind of symbol. Let me reply to this: What an easy-to-get symbol if to obtain it one had to go through cancer and all stages of dying. My writing is too solid for a symbol, and it has too many medical details for being symbolic.[4]

Invoking the authority of medical specialists who all concurred that the novel contains a bona fide description of cancer, Solzhenitsyn concludes: "This is cancer exactly the way it is."

Whether or not Solzhenitsyn was completely candid in making the statement one can only surmise. However, as I read it, he does not deny symbolism as such but only its "easy-to-get," artificial variety. Still, the statement may have discouraged those critics who have refused to read *Cancer Ward* as merely a realistic novel. "A Western critic, mindful of the larger thrust of Solzhenitsyn's fiction and conditioned to symbol-hunting," Victor Erlich has intoned, "may be tempted to

construe *Cancer Ward* as a parable for a deadly disease which
had eaten its way into the Soviet body politic." Insisting that
Cancer Ward is "a sturdily realistic novel rather than al-
legory," he has advised that the temptation "ought to be
resisted." [5]

In spite of both the advice and Solzhenitsyn's own remark,
a number of outstanding Western critics have succumbed to
the temptation of "symbol-hunting." George Nivat has found
in *Cancer Ward* "an immense network of apparently subordinate signs" and skillfully interconnected some of them in
his illuminating article "On Solzhenitsyn's Symbolism." In
fact, in his search for symbols he went as far as to state—correctly, I think—that the very architecture of Solzhenitsyn's
novels "is not a matter of chance, but of Symbol." [6] Nor did
Michel Aucouturier fail to notice in Solzhenitsyn "a network
of symbols and new meanings" pertaining not just to the Soviet
Union but to "the whole reality and the problems of existence."
However, he hardly answered the question of Solzhenitsyn's
symbolism by saying that "Every great novel, every great
work of art is symbolic." [7] In fact, he may have obscured the
issue by calling Solzhenitsyn's symbolism "the symbolism of
the realists," among whom he indiscriminately included Flaubert and Maupassant, Tolstoy and Dostoevsky. Neither Solzhenitsyn nor, for that matter, Dostoevsky belong to that
illustrious company.

As to the nature of Solzhenitsyn's symbolism another hint,
dropped during his 15 November 1966 interview with Mr.
Komoto of Japan, may provide the clue. Although it was his
first interview with a foreign reporter, its content remained
largely unknown until the publication of *Bodalsia telenok s
dubom* (The calf butted the oak) in 1975. In it Solzhenitsyn
said that *Cancer Ward*

> is not just about a hospital because, *if one uses an artistic ap-
> proach*, every particular phenomenon becomes, to use a math-

ematical analogy, a *bundle of planes*, that is, a multitude of life planes intersecting with each other at a chosen point.[8] (emphasis added)

This statement is highly revealing. It implies that life and the world are themselves inherently polysemous, that is, endowed with several meanings or several ways of having their meanings read. But even if they were not, they would become so in an artist's hand. This view is undoubtedly closer to Plato's doctrine of ideas and to all those who were inspired by it—from St. Augustine, the medieval mystics, Dante, and Dostoevsky, down to the European and Russian symbolists—than to either the Russian or French "naturalist schools" or to any other realists insofar as their "symbolism" was limited by an absence of polysemy of their positivist, rationalist, and materialist assumptions. But if one were to point out a particular literary school among Solzhenitsyn's predecessors in the usage of symbols, it would have to be the Russian Acmeists, Gumilyov, Mandelshtam, and Akhmatova.[9] Like their symbols, Solzhenitsyn's are never overly nebulous, obscure, or private, never overly conspicuous, but always well-balanced, full-blooded, life-affirming, courageous, and firmly rooted in reality.

While Solzhenitsyn has apparently challenged us to view each of his works as "a bundle of planes," he has also made it clear why the form of the polyphonic novel appeals to him most: not only does it allow him to illuminate a larger number of planes in the light of the consciousness of different characters but it also affords him an opportunity to make their intersection "at a chosen point" a vital one. "The multitude of life planes" confirms here Solzhenitsyn's adherence to what Bakhtin considered one of the cornerstones of Dostoevsky's "form-determining ideology" and of polyphony itself: a belief in a plurality of worlds or, at least, in a plurality of "systems of measurement" of the world.

In his interview with Mr. Komoto the writer asserts, incidentally, what he would later reassert in the interview with Ličko—his preference for the form of the polyphonic novel, with virtually the same explanation:

> The literary form that appeals to me most is the "polyphonic" novel (without a main hero but where the most important character is the one who in a given chapter is "caught" in the narrative) with exact indicators of time and space.[10]

Thus, the author extrinsically confirms what his novel suggests intrinsically: there are several ways of reading it and there are several levels or planes on which it can be understood. But no matter how many planes one might discover in it, they must all meet in the "bundle" with the parameters of time and space precisely indicated. Therefore, the novel can and should be read, first of all but not exclusively, as "a sturdily realistic novel." As such, it makes good reading: it captures the reader's attention with a popular and universal topic and maintains it to the end through fine characterization and a wealth of authentic details about both cancer and the "true" life of the USSR in the post-Stalin years. Few would disagree that the novel drives the point home: "This is cancer exactly the way it is." Few would fail to extend this judgment to the country at large. The novel can and has been rightly appreciated as one of the truly great works of realism. But this is only a part of Solzhenitsyn's artistic design.

We should not forget that the authenticity, truthfulness and —in Erlich's words—"sturdiness" of the novel's realism is but a foundation for an edifice of ideas without which the foundation would seem perfectly complete, concrete, and replete but lacking in one thing, its *raison d'être*. To be sure, the edifice is less solid than the foundation—but should it not be so? It also might appear to different viewers in different lights, shapes, and even sizes, but then, I think, the author wanted it so. Thus, the foundation of the novel is realistic; its edifice is symbolic. Each serves its particular purpose, each complements the other and reflects on the other. To return to Solzhenitsyn's mathematical analogy, the various contours of the symbolic superstructure of the novel correspond to different "planes of life," their realistic foundation corresponds to the "chosen point" where these planes intersect, and the whole structure of the novel corresponds to the "bundle of life planes."

It is perhaps in this sense that Solzhenitsyn spoke of the title image of *Cancer Ward* as too solid to be merely a symbol. It is certainly solid enough to be the foundation for a number of symbolic interpretations of the novel's different planes of life.

On one of them, the novel might be interpreted as a story of spiritual enlightenment in the face of death, in the manner of Lev Tolstoy's "The Death of Ivan Ilyich," as several critics have suggested. This interpretation can be accepted, however, only if we keep in mind the crucial difference between the two authors: whereas Tolstoy presents Ivan Ilyich's plane of life and, especially, his mode of enlightenment as one and only one, which shows Tolstoy again to have been an essentially monological writer, Solzhenitsyn suggests this option as merely one of many.

On another plane, *Cancer Ward* may be read as a story of the incipient political convalescence of the USSR from the cancer of the Soviet body politic as manifested in the labor camps and exiles of Stalin's era. Kostoglotov makes the connection by asking the question: "A man dies from a tumor, so how can a country survive with growths like labor camps and exiles?" (36:520). Kostoglotov's own incomplete and costly physical recovery is paralleled by the limited and half-hearted nature of the official Soviet de-Stalinization, as it is portrayed in the novel.

On yet another plane—the one that I recognize most acutely —the cancer itself, whether as individual affliction or social malignancy, is but one manifestation of a much more pervasive and deep-seated national malaise of Russia that has long been tormenting not only her body (the *korpus* of the Russian title) but also her soul. When Rusanov asks Kostoglotov what could be worse than cancer, the latter knows the answer: "Leprosy." And he goes on to explain: "It is worse because they banish you from the world while you are still alive. They tear you from your family and put you behind barbed wire. You think that's any easier to take than a tumor?" (11:147). Reading this, one is jolted into an awareness that the allegorical equation of the title image with the entire Soviet Union may not be the worst thing Solzhenitsyn could have implied. In fact, this equation gives much credit to the Soviet Union and is valid only insofar as it is applied to some of the best years of Soviet history, those in which the novel's events were being enacted and in which the official taboo against the theme of social ills was lifted just long enough to give the writer hope that his novel might be published in his homeland.

On this plane of interpretation, *Cancer Ward* becomes a full-fledged modern myth, that of Russia as a sick nation of the world, afflicted with a potentially fatal illness. The origin of her illness may predate the Revolution but it assumed its present dangerous character when the Communists took it upon themselves to play the role of diagnostician and performed Marxist-Leninist "surgery" on her in 1917.[11] Since then Russia has been continually shuttled from leper houses to cancer wards to psychiatric asylums, that is, "rescued" from flames to frying pan.

The novel confronts the reader with the questions: Can Russia be cured? If so, how can it be done? At what cost? From whom to expect a rescue? The answers are imbedded in the depth of its symbolism and wrapped in the enigma of the mysterious and miraculous, but are still perceptible and command our attention. Yes, Russia can and should be saved. But she cannot rely on outside help, certainly not on the services of the political "doctors" in the Kremlin who, even when they have good intentions, are all too ready to use evil means. Certainly she cannot expect a rescue from her medical doctors as long as they are subservient to the political ones and guided by Marxist-Leninist "science." If Russia is to be saved, the cure is more likely to come from the "old-school" doctors like Oreshchenkov, Maslennikov, and Kadmin, as well as from their young Soviet disciples like Dr. Gangart. Perhaps modern injections, x-rays, or blood transfusions can help, but Russia surely needs a transfusion of faith similar to the one Kostoglotov receives from Vera Gangart. Perhaps, Russia can be helped by Shulubin's "ethical socialism," but she surely needs the bravery of Kostoglotov (who at the end manages to pacify one of the "possessed" common criminals harassing Russian people) and the idealism of the young Dyoma whom Kostoglotov advises to live like the spiral-horned goat, "like the continuation of the rock itself."

All this means that ultimately Russia can expect a cure from no one but herself. The cure must come from within, from "the light that is within you." Kostoglotov suggests this to his brethren-in-misfortune by telling them the "miraculous fairytale" of the so-called self-induced healing. Characteristically, even this "miraculous" plane of the novel is introduced in such a way that it intersects with other planes at a point of authenticity. Just as Nerzhin of *The First Circle* seeks to corroborate his incipient religious faith in mathematical scholarship, Kostoglotov introduces the "fantastic" idea by stating, with a quote from Abrikosov's and Stryukov's *Pathological Anatomy*, a Soviet medical textbook, that there might be a connection between the development of tumors and the central nervous system. The idea not only sinks into the mind of his listeners; they also begin to realize that the healing cannot be induced by the sheer will to live. As Podduyev says, "I suppose for that you need to have . . . a clear conscience" (11: 133). He is right, of course. And Russia herself cannot be healed until and unless she repents, and both her sinners and her victims come to realize that need. The miracle of self-healing and resurrection can take place only when Russia clears her conscience by telling the truth about the past, including the truth of *The Gulag Archipelago*; by confessing her sins and crimes against her own citizens and other nations; and by restoring her faith in her ideals, herself, and the world. Having gone through all nine circles of hell, she managed to preserve the "unspoiled, undisturbed and undistorted image of eternity" of which the novel itself is a prime witness. But she must also endure her purgation, not through an Aristotelian tragic catharsis by pity and fear, but through the catharsis of a spiritual, indeed religious, regeneration.

The novel makes it clear that while treating Russia's malaise one should not forget that it is not a peculiarly Russian malaise but rather an extreme, Marxist-Leninist case of the universal epidemic of secular materialism. Through the symbolic figure of the "old-school" doctor Oreshchenkov the writer states the central theme of the novel, "that modern man is helpless when confronted with death, that he has no weapon to meet it with" (32:448). But by having been, with Kostoglotov, beyond the threshold of death and by being now, like him, "a specialist in being ill," Russia may well hold the key to healing not only herself but the world at large. Just as "the whole tortuous flow of accursed History" was seen much more clearly from the new ark of *The First Circle*, so the future of Russia, and of mankind, looks much brighter in the light of Kostoglotov's, and Solzhenitsyn's, first day of creation.

CHAPTER XIII

The Unperceived Signal

or

August 1914 as an Anti-Tolstoyan Poem

Solzhenitsyn is the first *modern* Russian novelist, original and great. His books, and among them especially *August 1914*, exhibit the unprecedented creative alloy of a cosmic epopee with tragic catharsis and latent homily.   Roman Jacobson

SINCE 1971 when *August 1914* was first published, there have been few critics who continue to insist on Solzhenitsyn's "Tolstoy connection" as far as his world view is concerned. But there are still many who continue to insist on Tolstoy's allegedly predominant *artistic* influence on Solzhenitsyn. Ironically, as a final proof of that, they point to the very work, *August 1914*, that put an end to their former insistence on Tolstoy's philosophical influence. (In so doing, they evidently do not bother to ask the inevitable question: Is there any interdependence between Solzhenitsyn's world view and his artistic expression?) More specifically, the pro-Tolstoyan critics of Solzhenitsyn maintain that Tolstoy's *War and Peace* was used as a model for *August 1914*. Not surprisingly, their usual verdict is that Solzhenitsyn is no match for Tolstoy and that his novel is inferior to its model.[1]

Nothing could, however, be farther from the truth. More than other works of Solzhenitsyn, *August 1914* shows not only that its author rejects Tolstoy's philosophy of history as expounded in *War and Peace* and his moral doctrine as preached in later years, but that he also overwhelmingly rejects Tolstoy's philosophy of art as practiced both in *War and Peace* and after his conversion. In fact, Solzhenitsyn's rejection of Tolstoy the philosopher and moral teacher is most profoundly manifested precisely in his artistic practice, which differs so radically from Tolstoy's that it would be more appropriate to speak of *War and Peace* as an antimodel for *August 1914*.

In this chapter an attempt will be made to demonstrate that the difference in the two novels stems from the difference in two contrasting conceptions of art—Tolstoy's monological one versus Solzhenitsyn's and Dostoevsky's polyphonic one. The connection with Dostoevsky here is especially important, for although Solzhenitsyn does not imitate him—putting aside the fact that Dostoevsky never wrote a novel on a similar subject —the artistic strategy of *August 1914* is rooted in a vision of the world profoundly akin to that "form-determining ideology" from which, according to Bakhtin, the polyphonic strategy and technique of *The Devils* and *The Brothers Karamazov* originated.

As if in anticipation of the inevitable reading and interpretation of *August 1914* in the light of Tolstoy's *War and Peace*, Solzhenitsyn appears to have deliberately given readers and critics a signal not to do so. Because it has remained largely unperceived or ignored by critics, it is important to explicate it here.

The signal is quite appropriately given at the very beginning of the "knot," in chapter 2, through a flashback dialogue between Tolstoy the "Prophet" and "Seboath," as he is called there, and his unworthy disciple and humble worshipper, Sanya Lazhenitsyn. The dialogue occurs in the forest near Tolstoy's estate in Yasnaya Polyana, where the young Sanya has sought out the sage in an effort to solve the contradictions he has felt rising between his heart and mind. He asks only three questions. The first is "What is the aim of man's life on earth?" The reply comes as expected, "To serve good and

thereby to build the Kingdom of God on earth," with which
Sanya seems to have no quarrel. As to the second question,
"How do I serve good?" he is much less satisfied with the answer, "Only through love," even though he knows it to be the
main principle of the Tolstoyan doctrine. When Sanya ven-
tures his opinion, "Shouldn't one envisage a kind of intermediate stage with some less exacting demands and use that to
awaken people to the need for universal good will?" the sage
replies "Only through love! Nothing else. No one will ever
discover anything better." Discouraged by the lack of reci-
procity on the part of his idol, but "still hoping for a crumb
of comfort," Sanya brings himself to ask the third and final
question:

> "But there's one other thing, Lev Nikolaevich. I very much
> want to write poetry, I do write poetry, in fact. Tell me, is that
> all right, or does it absolutely contradict what you believe?"

Since this is just the question that has received least attention from the pro-Tolstoyan critics of *August 1914*, Tolstoy's
lengthy answer deserves to be quoted in full:

> "How can you enjoy lining up words in ranks like soldiers
> according to their sounds? That's like children's trinkets.
> That's unnatural. The job of words is to express *thoughts*! You
> don't find much thought in poetry, do you? If you read twenty
> poems and then try to recall what they were all about, you'll
> get all confused. It's like a joke that is heard today, forgotten
> tomorrow." Tolstoy's forehead darkened. Looking past Sanya,
> he added: "There's a lot of poetry written nowadays, but
> there's not a bit of good in any of it." (2:24/19)[2]

The answer amounts of course to a rejection not only of
poetry, especially the symbolist poetry of Tolstoy's contemporaries, but also of all aesthetics founded on principles other
than the belief that "the job of words is to express thoughts."
It particularly clashes with Dostoevsky's—and Solzhenitsyn's,

as his Nobel Prize lecture makes it abundantly clear—belief
in the triunity of truth, goodness, and beauty. Tolstoy's judg-
ing poetry in terms of goodness without regard to its beauty,
reflects his actual pronouncement, in his programmatic essay
What Is Art?, that "the notion of beauty not only does not
coincide with goodness, but rather is contrary to it; for the
good most often coincides with victory over the passions while
beauty is at the root of our passions." [3] Finally, Tolstoy's answer implicitly conflicts with the polyphonic poetics of Dostoevsky and Solzhenitsyn which is always cognizant of the
polysemy of verbal expression and of the dialogic nature of
truth. Throughout his conversation with Sanya, Tolstoy is portrayed as a monological dogmatist utterly incapable of the dialogic form of communication. He shows no interest in his
admirer's opinion because he is convinced that "no one will
ever discover anything better" than his "truth." Characteristically, the conversation ends with Tolstoy's final word on art,
after which he continues his solitary walk along a "rectangu-
lar" path.

Although the narrator offers no comment on the merits of
Tolstoy's answer, he makes it clear that the dilemma with
which Sanya came to the sage—the contradiction between his
heart and mind—remains unresolved.

> Sanya had expected Tolstoy to say that about poetry; that
> was clear enough. But nevertheless he secretly remained at-
> tracted to writing verse and rimes. He sometimes used to write
> things in girls' albums, just for fun. However, by restraining
> himself in his poetry he had not saved much time, nor had he
> discovered the surest way of serving the Kingdom of God on
> earth.
>
> As with poetry, he also felt torn by contradictions in his
> attitude toward women. (2:24/19)

If anything, the encounter with Tolstoy makes Sanya realize
that the "best thoughts and best faith" of his Tolstoyan creed

"were not founded on a rock of granite." We do not know whether in future volumes Sanya would have his own say on the matter of art and poetry. But we do know that at the outbreak of war four years later he takes a big step away from his idol. In spite of the Tolstoyan pacifist convictions of his *mind*, he follows the dictates of his *heart*, which "felt sorry for Russia," and volunteers for the war. This is precisely Solzhenitsyn's way of debating Tolstoy the "historiosoph" and moral preacher: not by adding to his novel "historiosophic" chapters in which he could debunk Tolstoy monologically, as Tolstoy did his opponents, not by sermonizing to his readers, but by creating characters who would debate Tolstoy with their words, actions, and lives.

The only time the narrator of *August 1914* enters the debate in his own "voice" is to be found in chapter 40:

> (We might want to console ourselves with the Tolstoyan conviction that it is not generals who lead armies, not captains who command ships or infantry companies, not presidents or leaders who run states and political parties—were it not that all too often the twentieth century has proven to us that it is *they*.) (40:350/441)

The passage is remarkable for two things, its brevity and the fact that the author felt it necessary to set it apart from the rest of the chapter parenthetically. It is as if Solzhenitsyn wanted to indicate that he personally has no desire to debate something so obviously wrong. As a chronicler of the time, he misses no occasion to let the events and characters of his novel debate Tolstoy. But, since the content of this particular debate is less relevant to our thesis we shall not go into it in detail; instead, we shall concentrate on the question that is most relevant: Did Solzhenitsyn let Tolstoy's utterance on art and poetry stand unchallenged?

I think not. However, one would look in vain for the author's own comment on that matter, for there is none in the whole novel, not even of the brief, parenthetical kind that he allowed himself in regard to Tolstoy's "historiosophy." This is simply not Solzhenitsyn's way to argue, for he apparently feels that what is allowed a historian or literary critic is impermissible for an artist. It is especially on the issue of art that he refuses to debate Tolstoy by delivering his own monological diatribe. Had he done so, had he succumbed to the temptation of repudiating Tolstoy's aesthetics in his own narrative, one could indeed say that he had been influenced by his opponent. No, Solzhenitsyn debates Tolstoy in a different way, by writing a novel that is founded precisely on those aesthetic principles which Tolstoy had denounced. More than anything else *August 1914* is Solzhenitsyn's answer to Tolstoy's aesthetics in general and to his artistic practice in *War and Peace* in particular. Specifically, the novel is Solzhenitsyn's answer to Tolstoy's pronouncements on poetry.

Tolstoy's negation of poetry is countered by Solzhenitsyn's extensive use of poetry in the novel. *August 1914* is saturated with all kinds of poetry: limericks and soldiers' songs (in the montage chapters and at the end of many others); the poetry of the period (also in the montage chapters and in characterization); and, most of all, folklore poetry in the form of proverbs, sayings, and riddles. There can be little doubt that Varsonofiev the "Stargazer" speaks for the author when he says that "the best poetry of all is in riddles." The novel is literally riddled with riddles, proverbs, and sayings that are frequently used by characters and in the narrative. And it is riddled with them figuratively because the novel breathes the air of the Churchillian dictum that Russia is a mystery wrapped in an enigma.

But if the best poetry of all is in riddles, the next best must be the symbolist poetry, of which Tolstoy so strongly disapproved because he had found no "goodness" in it. It is precisely this kind of poetry that Solzhenitsyn quotes in the novel on more than one occasion, and there are reasons to believe that he does so not simply to illustrate the cultural ambience of the period. Most notable are the two stanzas quoted in the middle and at the end of chapter 57, here presented in sequence:

> Созидающий башню — сорвется,
> Будет страшен стремительный лёт.
> И на дне мирового колодца
> Он безумье свое проклянёт.

> Разрушающий — будет раздавлен,
> Опрокинут обломками плит,
> И, всевидящим Богом оставлен,
> Он о смерти своей возопит.

> The builder of the tower will fall,
> Dreadful will be his flight,
> From the bottom of the well of the world
> This madman shall curse his plight.

> The destroyer will perish in peril,
> Overturned by the crushing stones,
> And, forsaken by all-seeing God,
> He will beg for his death with moans.[4]

They are quoted in the context of the chapter written, as it were, from the narrative viewpoint of Agnessa Martynovna Lenartovich, the widowed mother of Sasha Lenartovich, and her sister Adalia. This is a family of revolutionary populist (*narodnik*) background, to whom the portrait of Uncle Alexander, executed for an act of terrorism, is as sacred as an icon. Using the terminology introduced by Bakhtin for a metalinguistic analysis of Dostoevsky's polyphonic narrative style, the chapter is an example of Solzhenitsyn's use of the "bivocal word" (see chapter X). The second, heterodirectional variety of the "bivocal word" predominates in the chapter because the views of the "progressive" sisters are parodied. These views are expressed, as it were, in an inner dialogue with the views of Mrs. Lenartovich's beautiful but "nonprogressive" daughter Veronika and her school friend Yelya (or Likonya). Therefore, when the two stanzas are introduced as examples of the apolitical "backwardness" of the young girls, especially

of Yelya, who is said to recite them constantly, and then are
referred to as "symbolist rubbish," "obscure gibberish," and
"sacrilegious," the reader is bound to suspect that the opposite is true, that they are neither nonsensical nor rubbish nor
sacrilegious.

But are they symbolist? What do they mean? What do they
have to do with the rest of the novel? These questions ought to
be asked because Solzhenitsyn, like every great artist, never
includes in his work anything accidental. Certainly, he would
not casually include a piece of poetry of the sort that his Tolstoy so intensely dislikes.

Strictly speaking, the two stanzas are not symbolist. Un-
attributed in the novel, they actually belong to a poet better
known as the founder of Acmeism, Nikolai Gumilyov. In fact,
in his article "The Legacy of Symbolism and Acmeism," published prior to the action of the novel, Gumilyov "retired"
the term symbolism in favor of its successor Acmeism. That
the elderly sisters consider Gumilyov's poetry "symbolist
rubbish" thus reveals more about them than the poet. Their
failure to recognize the verse as Acmeist rather than symbolist
indicates their cultural backwardness. But there is more to it
than that.

The two quoted stanzas are from the poem "The Choice,"
which was written around 1910, that is, before Acmeism became a household word among the Russian reading public.
Since at that time Gumilyov considered himself an apprentice
to Valerii Bryusov, a leading symbolist, the poem may con-
ceivably be classified as symbolist, so much so that even later,
with the emergence of Acmeism, Gumilyov aspired not to destroy symbolism but to put it to better use. Still, many an
admirer of the symbolists would find it shocking that Solzhenitsyn chose, of all poets, the Acmeist Gumilyov to illustrate
the symbolist indulgence of the young girls, and there must be
reasons for the choice of the two stanzas other than merely an
ironic comment on the "progressive" ignorance of the elderly

sisters. Those reasons ought to be sought in the quoted stanzas themselves, and in how they are made to function in the novel.

In the first stanza, the tower is undoubtedly a symbol, immediately suggesting the Biblical story of the Tower of Babel: Noah's descendants tried to build a tower "whose top may reach unto heaven" high above "the old city"; the Lord punished them for that presumption by confounding their language and thus preventing them from communicating with each other and completing the construction. He also scattered the builders, with their language confused, "abroad upon the face of all the earth" (Gen. 11:1–9). Like the Tower of Babel in the Biblical story, the tower of the poem symbolizes the futility of human efforts to surpass in creativity the Creator Himself. Furthermore, in a more specifically Russian frame of reference, the stanza suggests the tower of Dostoevsky's "The Grand Inquisitor," which stands for, and falls with, the efforts of the socialist atheists to build a new form of society not only without but also against God. (See chapter I.)

The second stanza initially appears to be antithetical to the first, especially because Glenny translated the "destroyer" in it as "the destroyer of the tower" of the first stanza (the Russian original has no mention of the tower here). It is more likely, however, that the destroyer destroys not the tower but rather the "old city," doing so, as it were, to clear a place for the new tower. In that case, the builder and the destroyer of the poem are not opposites but rather allies in their equally godless ambition. The destroyer, however, will be forsaken by the "all-seeing God" even in his agony: crushed by the debris of his own destruction he will beg for death.

Thus, the two quoted stanzas contain the veiled reply of the young girls (Veronika shares Yelya's attitude to poetry) to the elderly ladies who had been nagging at them for not taking part in the destruction of imperial Russia so that a place could be cleared for the future socialist Tower of Babel. (As such they belong to the third variety of the "bivocal word," name-

ly, to the active bivocal word deflecting someone else's word.)
Although the elderly ladies cannot completely understand all
the implications of their "symbolist gibberish," they sense
correctly their "sacrilege" against the religion of atheist socialism that they preach.

But if Gumilyov's two stanzas speak for the two girls, who
would otherwise have remained speechless in the novel, do
they not also speak for its self-effacing author? I believe that
they do, however indirectly. By incorporating them into the
body of his work, Solzhenitsyn dramatically enhances their
latent political implications and thus may be suggesting what
is likely to become the main ideational thrust of the whole
book cycle: a sacrilege against, and prophecy of doom for,
the entire Soviet enterprise in constructing the Tower of Communism in place of the "old world" to be destroyed in the
fire of wars and revolutions. Although *August 1914*, as the first
"knot" of this cycle, is mostly concerned with how the stage
was set for that destruction, that is, with the doom of the old
world rather than the one to come, Solzhenitsyn has the two
stanzas remind us of two deeper perspectives from which the
cycle is being written: the historical perspective of an already
fulfilled prophecy, and the prophetic perspective of a not yet
fulfilled history. The historical perspective tells us, through
the evidence of *The Gulag Archipelago* (among much other
evidence), that there were indeed thousands upon thousands of
the most ruthless destroyers of the old regime as well as of the
most zealous builders of the new one who from the depth of
the Gulag were begging for their own deaths. The prophetic
perspective is a reminder that even though the Tower of Communism appears today stronger than ever, it is not the one originally intended, and even if it were, it is bound to fall because
the Communists, who have been scattered "abroad upon the
face of all the earth," at least since the Third International,
no longer speak the same language.

While Solzhenitsyn apparently chose Gumilyov's two stan-

zas for the suitability of their content to the "knot," the choice
also seems to reflect his preference for the Acmeist kind of
symbolism: less nebulous, less private, less morbid, but more
earthly, more universal, and more life-affirming. These Acmeist features are already evident in the poem "The Choice,"
from which the two stanzas are quoted. Here are the remaining
two:

> А ушедший в ночные пещеры
> Или к заводям тихой реки
> Повстречает свирепой пантеры
> Наводящие ужас зрачки.
>
> Не спасешься от доли кровавой,
> Что земным предназначила твердь.
> Но молчи: несравненное право —
> Самому выбирать свою смерть.[5]

> But the one who flees to the darkness of caves
> Or seeks his refuge in the backwaters of a quiet stream
> Shall end his days frozen in horror
> In the face of a vicious panther.
>
> You cannot escape the bloody fate
> That the heavens decreed for mortals.
> Don't protest in vain: you're assured the right
> To choose your own path to death.

The poem apparently reflects Gumilyov's tragic view of
life, for all three choices inevitably lead to a tragic death. Still,
the prerogative of the heavens to issue fatal decrees to mortals
is not challenged but stoically accepted and, one might say,
acmeistically reaffirmed. In fact, the tone of the poem is typical of Gumilyov's work: it is so demonstratively manly and
heroic, so defiantly Nietzschean and superhuman, that critics
often accused Gumilyov of striking the pose of a hero. He
proved them wrong. When the war broke out in 1914 he, alone
among the established poets, volunteered for front-line duty.
He served with distinction throughout the war and twice earned
the Cross of St. George, the highest award for bravery. When

Lenin's Bolsheviks took power in October of 1917, Gumilyov was abroad having been commissioned by the provisional government as a liaison officer to the Western allies. And again he made a courageous choice: he went back to Russia reportedly saying that he had hunted lions in Africa and the Bolsheviks could not be more dangerous than the beasts. But they were. In the summer of 1921 Gumilyov was executed for allegedly participating in an anti-Communist plot.

Although the charges were probably trumped up, one thing is undisputed: Gumilyov knew how to make a courageous choice and stick to it to the end. Still, his was not one of the three choices he had portrayed in the poem (though he did not suggest that they exhaust the range of choices): he did not seek his refuge in the backwaters of the Revolution, neither was he with the destroyers of the old regime nor with the builders of the new one. But he was in their midst by his own volition. Among other things, he was teaching the young "Proletarian" poets how to write poetry, reminding them perhaps of the wisdom of the "old city" and of the fate of the Tower of Babel. Gumilyov's tragic death, the heroic aura of this Russian Kipling, and the fact that he still remains "unrehabilitated" in the USSR, all these undoubtedly contributed to Solzhenitsyn's selection of his poetry to be an integral and essential theme of *August 1914*. One might even say that the poet himself was the kind of hero who would fit perfectly in the novel. But the decisive factor for the selection of his poetry must have been Solzhenitsyn's affinity with Acmeist symbolism.

By incorporating the verse into the body of the novel Solzhenitsyn has demonstrated that, contrary to Tolstoy's opinion, there is no uncrossable line between the art of a novelist and that of the poet—that poetry in general, and especially the variety that Tolstoy disliked most, can and does have a meaning or several meanings. However, in contrast to Tolstoy's novelistic technique, especially to his "historiosophic" chapters, that meaning is not to be handed to the reader on a platter but only to be suggested in a manner that engages his intellect and imagination.

The use of "symbolist" poetry in *August 1914* is, however, only a small part of Solzhenitsyn's answer to Sanya's third question or, rather, to Tolstoy's reply to it. The rest of the answer is to be found in the poetics of the novel itself, especially in the symbolism of its setting, structure, characterization, themes and images, all of them functioning within a polyphonic conception of art. While *August 1914* is as strongly imbued with symbolism as any of Dostoevsky's novels, it is also more authentically realistic than any of the so-called critical realist novels, including those of Tolstoy. This is because Solzhenitsyn's symbolism is deliberately based on an earthly realism, and in this respect it is indeed akin to the symbolism of the Acmeists.

Invested with symbolism in the novel are its historical setting and the events it describes; its characters, both fictional and historical, with their thoughts, dreams, and images; the objects that come into their lives; the action and final outcome. Compressed into just twelve days in August, the narrated time is characterized as *die höchste Zeit* of Russia's destiny, of her fateful trial in the crucible of the battle of Tannenberg. While Solzhenitsyn the chronicler offers to the reader as authentic an account of that battle as can be found, Solzhenitsyn the poet makes us aware that even from the German *Realpolitik* viewpoint the battle has symbolic significance as a reenactment of the battle of Tannenberg of 1410 when an alliance of Poles, Lithuanians, and Russians put a stop to the Teutonic *Drang nach Osten*. Even though in 1914 the Russians did not quite reach the town of Tannenberg, the victorious Germans chose the name for the battle as if to confirm the hand of Providence (*Vorsehung*) and historical retribution (*Strafgericht*). On the Russian side General Samsonov is acutely aware of the fact that the defeat is falling on the Day of Assumption and the Day of the Miraculous Image of Christ. Realizing also that the latter has been the battle standard of the Russians since the beginnings of the nation, he cannot help thinking "It was as though Christ and the Mother of God had rejected Russia" (44:389/490).

And then again, while Solzhenitsyn the realist documents all the particulars of the ill-prepared advance of Samsonov's army into East Prussia, down to the map mileage between its constantly vacillating lines of march, the poet in him observes: "The clock of fate was suspended above the whole of East Prussia, and its six-mile-long pendulum was ticking audibly as it swung from the German side to the Russian and back again" (11:98/115). He writes "audibly" because the German artillery managed to harass the misled Russian troops. However, for the toy lion, which figures more prominently in the novel than it would seem to deserve from an ordinary realist point of view, the clock of fate swung only once: from the Russian trenches, where it was first found, to the radiator of General von François's car, where it was triumphantly fastened by the Germans, in spite of the fact that the lion had fought with the Russian soldiers and survived with them the "giant flails" of German artillery that "threshed their souls out of their bodies like little grains to be used for some unknown purpose" (25: 226/281). For the time being, the tempered "souls" of the Russian soldiers were used for the purpose of the retreat ordered by their incompetent commander.

Solzhenitsyn's use of the network of symbols as a unifying element of the novel's structure may be exemplified by the recurrent image of a wheel. It occurs for the first time in one of the "rear" chapters: it is the image of the red engine wheel of the train that takes Lenin further away from Russia at the outbreak of war. We see the wheel through the eyes of Lenin who thinks of it in terms of a revolutionary momentum he hopes to derive from the war that he considers a "gift of history." Immersed in Lenin's stream of consciousness, we read: "The wheel turns, gathering speed—like the red wheel of the engine—and you must keep up with its mighty rush. He who had never yet stood before the crowd, directing the movement of the masses, how was he to harness them to that wheel, to his own racing heart, how to check their impetus and put them into reverse?" (22:28/28).[6]

The answer to this "rear" chapter question seems to be provided in the "front-line" chapters where the destruction of war is symbolized by the dramatic visual image of fiery wheels. In the screen section of chapter 25 it is the wheel of a burning windmill. "With no wind," the narrator says, "the ribs of the red-gold blades are turning mysteriously. LIKE A CATHERINE WHEEL. And the wheel crashes to the ground in a shower of blazing fragments" (25:228/283). In the screen chapter 30 it is the wheel of a horse-drawn ambulance. In the madness of the retreat under enemy fire, the wheel comes off, "rolls on ahead and overtakes the ambulance." In its wild run the wheel grows bigger "until it fills the whole screen":

> THE WHEEL rolls on, lit up by fire—
> Alone, unstoppable,
> Crushing everything—
> THE WHEEL!!!   (30:287/359)

Finally, in chapter 39, when Samsonov is offered by his staff officers "a sensible plan of the 'sliding shield,'" he thinks, "This too was something that revolved, repeating revolutions of the sky" (39:348/438). But in vain he seeks his support in this kind of revolving wheellike movement, as if during the incompetently conducted war the wheel of history refused to serve its former masters. But in the present volume Lenin has barely begun putting it into reverse.

The outcome of the novel—the historical defeat of Samsonov's army, the fictionalized death of its commander, and the fictional breakthrough of Colonel Vorotyntsev from behind the German lines to the Imperial High Command headquarters—also invites symbolic interpretations. Is not the defeat portrayed in a way that suggests that the Russian army was sacrificed by the leaders of Russia in the name of their alliance with Western democracies? From the very beginning Samsonov considers the whole operation not only ill-planned by the general staff but also ill-conceived by the Russian diplomats. Vorotyntsev seems to corroborate that view when he accuses General Zhi-linsky of making the "fatal decision" to begin war operations at one-third readiness of the Russian army. When Zhilinsky objects that this has been done according to the convention with France, Vorotyntsev retorts: "According to that convention Russia promised 'decisive help,' not suicide!" (64:570/713). Moreover, while there are several unfavorable references to the Western allies and especially to France in the novel, the reader is pointedly reminded that Vorotyntsev and the "Young Turks" of the general staff would have preferred to keep an "eternal alliance" with Germany "as Dostoevsky fervently advised us to do" (12:111/132).

However, the emphasis of the novel is not on how the tragedy could have been averted but on how it could have been endured. Samsonov cannot bear to live with it. He contemplates and prepares his suicide knowing full well that "suicide is considered a sin" (48:429/541). We hear the click when he cocks his revolver but we never hear the shot. Did he commit suicide or was he cut down by a stray bullet? We shall probably never know, and it hardly matters, in the novel at least. What matters is that he is ready for suicide. Symbolically, he loses his orientation and prays neither to an icon nor to the East as he should have, but to a star. His last words, however, ask forgiveness of the Lord. This end is at once symbolic and ambivalent in its symbolism.[7] Does Samsonov offer a sacrifice-in-person in the manner of Christ (Vorotyntsev sees him, for instance, as "a 230 pound sacrificial lamb")? Or does he aggravate his misdeeds as commander by the personal sin of suicide? Did not Russia of old, together with Samsonov, take the path of suicide that finally ended her existence in 1917? Or was she, like Samsonov and his army, a victim of her foreign and domestic enemies (who had in fact conspired against her; Solzhenitsyn brings that conspiracy into focus in *Lenin in Zurich*) as well as her Western allies who failed to reciprocate for her sacrifice?

If the figure of Samsonov symbolizes a Russian knight rendered powerless partly from circumstances but mostly by his passivity, the figure of Colonel Vorotyntsev embodies a volitional element of the composite Russian national character. Vorotyntsev's sense of mission is akin to the religious zeal of Avvakum, to the fervor of Dostoevsky's heroes of ideas, and, for that matter, to Lenin's political fanaticism. We learn of his awareness that he probably is a descendant of the famed warrior Mikhailo Vorotynsky, executed on the order of Ivan the Terrible who saw in him a rival for the throne. Like his name's saint, St. George, Vorotyntsev is ever ready to do battle against Russia's dragons wherever he can find them: in the field of battle, in the Party dissension of Lenartoviches, and even in the Imperial High Command. Battle is his *höchste Zeit*. He believes the fortune teller who predicted he would die a solder's death in 1945. Would it be in the ranks of the Russian Liberation Army that fought against Stalin? We cannot know it yet. But one should not be surprised if in the following volumes Vorotyntsev does witness Russia's final hour as the death of that Biblical grain which falls to the ground only to be reborn manifold. His favorite author, Dostoevsky, had reminded the Russians of that possibility, and if it occurs Solzhenitsyn apparently wants Russia to be reborn in the image of men like Vorotyntsev.

Although both Samsonov and Vorotyntsev are most prominent in the "front-line" chapters of the novel, they can hardly be called the novel's main heroes in the sense of being the author's chief ideological spokesmen, as, for instance, Pierre

Bezukhov and André Bolkonsky were for Tolstoy in *War and Peace*, that is, when the author did not speak for himself.[8] Consider, for instance, a dozen quotations from *August 1914* which may or may not contain a key to the novel's ideological orientation:

1

Certain notions of Oriental religions beautifully complement the truth of Christianity, don't they? The soul accepts them all together, and without feeling contradictions, as different manifestations of beauty.

2

It was almost impossible to find another such church anywhere in Russia. This coincidence could not be mere chance! It was a mystical sign.

3

"If you ask me, it's a great pity that Napoleon didn't beat us in 1812. His rule wouldn't have lasted long, and then we would have been free."

4

And like Tolstoy's Kutuzov he realized that one should never issue decisive and resolute orders; that NOTHING BUT CONFUSION COULD RESULT FROM A BATTLE STARTED AGAINST ONE'S WILL.

5

"Russia, my dear man, needs to be looked at from far, far away—almost from the moon! . . . Russia's center of gravity will shift to the northeast: that's a prophecy that's bound to come true. Incidentally, Dostoevsky came to the same conclusion toward the end of his life; he gave up his ideas about Constantinople—read his last essay in *Diary of a Writer*."

6

Germany! What power! What weapons! And what determination she had shown in striking through Belgium. . . . If fight they must, then fight they would. How resolute were the orders of their High Command! Not a hint of Russian vacillation there.

7

For Russia the monarchy has been not a set of shackles but a clamp: it has not fettered the country but preserved it from disaster by binding it together.

8

"Living in this country, one must make up one's mind once and for all and stick to one's decision. Do I really belong to it heart and soul?"

9

"History is *irrational*. . . . It has its own, and to us perhaps incomprehensible, organic structure. . . . History grows like a living tree. And as far as that tree is concerned, reason is an ax: you'll never make it grow better by applying reason to it."

10

"The stuff of history is not *opinions* but *sources*."

11

"Life was brought to us by some unknown force; we don't know where it came from or why . . ."

12

"The people who get things done around here are not the rebels but the doers. They go about it discreetly and they don't make a lot of fuss, but they get things done." [9]

Perhaps the most remarkable thing about this bundle of quotations is that none of them "belongs" to the author or even to the two most prominent characters, Samsonov and Vorotyntsev (whose roles appear to be primarily structural and symbolic). They belong, in fact, to as many different characters, including such obvious villains as Lenin and Lenartovich. Each quotation so personifies a character that he or she indeed appears to be the "main hero" and chief spokesman for the author for as long as it takes to be uttered. Moreover, each quotation is either a remark in an actual ideological dialogue, with which the novel abounds, or is taken out of a character's inner dialogue with another person or idea. Thus, all of them belong to one or another variety of the "bivocal word" and therefore present the reader with the challenge of deciding to what extent, if at all, they express the author's viewpoint or the novel's ideological message.

Each of the twelve quotations either introduces, counterpoints, or echoes these major themes of the novel: the mystical-religious theme; the theme of history and (mostly anti-Tolstoyan) "historiosophy"; the theme of Russia's uniqueness and her destiny; the theme of her adversary Germany; the theme of patriotism and national identity; and the theme of "doers versus rebels." Of course, the purpose of my gathering the quotations together here is not to exhaust the novel's thematic range but rather to indicate how the themes are developed. And while it is not the task of this chapter to discuss themes, a few comments might be in order.

The first quotation, from Irina Tomchak's stream of consciousness, introduces the mystical-religious theme. Irina is superstitious and believes, among other things, in the transmigration of souls. Does she speak now for the author? She may, because she is generally portrayed with great sympathy, because, like Solzhenitsyn, she stresses the importance of beauty, and because the theme of transmigration has occurred elsewhere in his work (cf. *Cancer Ward*). In that case, Solzhenitsyn's relationship to the Russian church and Christianity in general may be much less orthodox than is usually assumed. The second quotation counterpoints the first: it belongs to Grand-Duke Nikolai Nikolaevich, the commander-in-chief of the Russian army, and his seeing a positive mystical sign in the fact that his headquarters are located near the church of St. Nicholas is deliberately ironic, in view of the impending Russian defeat.

The third and fourth belong to the would-be deserter Lenartovich and to General Blagoveshchensky, one of the principal architects of the defeat. They are but two of numerous instances in the novel where Tolstoy's "historiosophic" views are parodied. (Incidentally, Lenartovich's sympathetic speculation about Napoleon's attempted conquest of Russia echoes not only Bezukhov's initial lack of patriotism, but also the opinion of Smerdyakov in *The Brothers Karamazov*.)

The fifth opinion, on the importance of the northeast for the future of Russia, is voiced by the engineer and former anarchist Obodovsky. It apparently reflects the views of Solzhenitsyn (see his *Letter to the Soviet Leaders*), who seems to take very seriously not only the religious and artistic ideas of Dostoevsky but also his geopolitical projections. While the reference to the moon seems to underscore Solzhenitsyn's own scientific-mathematical bent, it is also suggestive of Russia's unique stature among the nations of the world and her special destiny. Perhaps one has to look at Russia from the moon to see not only her geographical but also her spiritual map.

In the sixth quotation, Germany is praised neither by Vorotyntsev nor any of his friends in the general staff, but by Lenin. His admiration for the ruthlessness of the German invasion of a third country serves as a counterpoint to those in the novel who admire Germany for her economic efficiency and superior military organization but never for her ruthlessness.

The seventh belongs to Major General Nechvolodov, a historical figure, portrayed as one of the ablest and most dutiful Russian generals. His stance in favor of the monarchy has added weight because he is shown to be no favorite of the imperial court. Nechvolodov's patriotic devotion to Russia is echoed, in the eighth quotation, by an unlikely bedfellow, Arkhangorodsky, an engineer and Jew who leads a progovernment demonstration by patriotic Jews in spite of his daughter's argument that the Jews have no reason to support the war.

Although the ninth and tenth are uttered by two different persons in two different dialogues—by Varsonofiev the "Stargazer" in his conversation with the two "Russian boys," the "Tolstoyan" Sanya and his "Hegelian" friend Kotya, and by professor Andozerskaya in her talk with girl students—they illustrate Solzhenitsyn's technique of the ideological juxtaposition of views which at first seem mutually exclusive and yet are presented with equal persuasiveness. While Varsonofiev asserts the irrationality of history (his argument is, by the way, reminiscent of Edmund Burke), Andozerskaya stresses the need for the scholarly and rational study of it. Solzhenitsyn seems to endorse both views.

The last two quotations also illustrate a dichotomy, this time between things esoteric and practical. Cosmological ideas expressed in the eleventh quotation seem to echo the mystical-religious ideas of such characters as Irina Tomchak and Varsonofiev. However, this time they come from the rather secular viewpoint of Colonel Smyslovsky in his dialogue with Nechvolodov. The twelfth quotation expresses, however, a very different attitude, elaborating on one of the most prominent themes in the novel, that of "doers versus rebels," engineers versus lawyers, practical action versus an endemic Russian indolence and wistfulness. One does not have to guess on which side the author's sympathies lie, but one must beware of Solzhenitsyn's bivocalism: the last quotation is uttered by one of the "Young Turks," Colonel Svechin, in a reproach to none other than Vorotyntsev.

Thus in *August 1914* Solzhenitsyn implements a true polyphony of ideological voices, diverse, articulate and virtually independent from his own. He also proves himself a deft practitioner of, to use a musical metaphor, the laws of counterpoint, which he applies to the development of each of his major themes as well as to their mutual arrangement. By compressing the narrated time to a dozen days of trial by war, he enables himself to array a variety of views on the same subject as well as to elicit a more genuine response from each of his characters.

While writing the novel Solzhenitsyn apparently was acutely aware of the fact that, as a rule, "military life, consisting of a series of unequivocal commands, allowed no room for ambiguities," as the soldier-writer Nechvolodov puts it. If Solzhenitsyn managed, as I think he did, to overcome this handicap in a novel three-fourths of which is "front-line" chapters, it is largely due to the fact that, together with Nechvolodov, he believes in "two planes of existence." From this, Nechvolodov thinks, "the marvels of Russian history stemmed" (21:189/231). One might add: "and of Russian literature." By being a bundle, a "knot," of perhaps more than two planes of existence, *August 1914* is one such marvel.

We cannot know, at least until we have future "knots," whether Sanya Lazhenitsyn followed Tolstoy's advice to restrain his poetic flights. If he did, it was unfortunate. What we do know, however—and this is extremely fortunate—is that his highly nonfictional "son," Aleksandr Solzhenitsyn, did not heed the advice. His *August 1914* is monumental proof of that. In fact, the "knot" is, as it were, a single poem. Not only its words but also its sentences and paragraphs, chapters and themes, images and characters are lined up "in ranks like soldiers according to their sounds." Although the main job of these "soldiers" might not be to express thoughts—there are philosophers, historians, and literary critics for that—they still somehow manage to convey to the reader many thoughts. Solzhenitsyn's word-soldiers always seem to go beyond the call of duty by engaging in combat with the thoughts of their readers. Bitter and unrelenting as it often is, this combat is never as lopsided in favor of the commander-in-chief as it is in the case of Tolstoy the "historiosoph." After all, one might hope that the twentieth century has shown to us more than just the ineptitude of Tolstoy's historiosophy.

August 1914 is indeed a modern novel, exhibiting as it does "the unprecedented creative alloy of a cosmic epopee with tragic catharsis and latent homily." Conceived on a scale comparable to that of *War of Peace*, it is more profoundly cosmic. Its tragic catharsis evolves along the lines of Dostoevsky's rendition of the parable of the Gadarene swine in *The Devils*.

Its homily never turns into Tolstoy's sermonizing, and by being less explicit and more latent than the homily of *The Brothers Karamazov*, it may prove even more powerful.

Ultimately, the difference in the artistic strategies of *War and Peace* and *August 1914* originates in the difference of their authors' world views. In his Nobel Prize lecture Solzhenitsyn described this difference thus:

> One artist imagines himself the creator of an autonomous spiritual world; he hoists upon his shoulders the act of creating this world and of populating it, together with the total responsibility for it. But he collapses under the load, for no mortal genius can bear up under it, just as, in general, the man who declares himself the center of existence is unable to create a balanced spiritual system. And, if a failure befalls such a man, the blame is promptly laid on the chronic disharmony of the world, to the complexity of modern man's divided soul, or to the public's lack of understanding.
>
> Another artist recognizes above himself a higher power and joyfully works as a humble apprentice under God's heaven, though graver and more demanding still is his responsibility for all he writes or paints—and for the souls which apprehend it. However, it was not he who created this world, nor does he control it; there can be no doubts about its foundations. It is merely given to the artist to sense more keenly than others the harmony of the world, the beauty and ugliness of man's role in it—and to vividly communicate this to mankind. Even amid failure and at the lower depth of existence—in poverty, in prison, and in illness, a sense of enduring harmony cannot abandon him.[10]

In the former artist, one recognizes Tolstoy with his endeavors to create an autonomous and homophonic spiritual world (even though Solzhenitsyn probably did not aim this remark primarily at him). One cannot help agreeing with those critics who, like George Steiner, have argued that "Tolstoy's relation to his characters arose out of his rivalry with God and out of his philosophy of the creative act," and thus his extraordinary artistic talents were "impoverished by the thinness of (his) metaphysics."[11] In the latter artist, however, Dostoevsky and Solzhenitsyn are clearly seen. Tempered by the enormous amount of suffering through which both authors had gone, their keen sense of the harmony of the world infused their work with the unity that is most compatible with the polyphonic diversity of world views of their characters. Still, as Solzhenitsyn himself admits in the same address, the workings of art are "too magical to be wholly accounted for by the artist's view of the world, by his intention, or by the work of his unworthy fingers." Or by a literary critic.

Spiritual Realism

or

Solzhenitsyn as a Synthesizer

> It has the sweep of Tolstoy and the spirit of Dostoevsky, thus
> synthesizing the two minds which were thought to be antitheti-
> cal both in the nineteenth century and on into present-day
> literary criticism, and it *is* unmistakably Solzhenitsyn.
>
> Heinrich Böll

IN HIS BRILLIANT ESSAY *On Socialist Realism*, written at the
end of the fifties, Andrey Sinyavsky asked an important question that ought to be reiterated in regard to all modern Russian
writers who have refused to follow the official Soviet literary
doctrine. Referring to the unique historical and cultural experience of Russia after the Revolution, Sinyavsky wondered on
behalf of all present and future nonofficial Russian writers,
"Is it possible that all the lessons that we received were taught
in vain and that, in the best of cases, all we wish is to return
to the naturalist school and the critical tendency?" He expressed a strong hope that "this is not so and that our need
for truth will not interfere with the work of thought and
imagination." [1]

As regards Solzhenitsyn, Sinyavsky's question has a special
pungency. Ever since Yevtushenko had praised him as "our
only living classic," his art has been routinely seen in terms of
the nineteenth-century tradition. But is it a mere return to "the
naturalist school and the critical tendency?" Does Solzhenitsyn's "need for truth" somehow interfere with his "thought
and imagination?" Have we been, even "in the best of cases,"

frustrated in our hope for a new art that would go beyond what our forefathers bequeathed to us?

In spite of the worldwide recognition of Solzhenitsyn's work, there has been a tendency, even among his most sincere admirers, to compare him with nineteenth-century writers, not in order to discover his vital roots but to bury him among them.

I strongly disagree with such a tendency. I think that Solzhenitsyn's art is innovative in the best sense of the word, particularly in its synthesis of the two prevailing trends of classical Russian literature previously thought to be mutually exclusive, the Tolstoyan and the Dostoevskian. However, unlike most scholars, I think that it is the latter that provides the basis for this synthesis.

While I am convinced that the affinity of Solzhenitsyn's art with that of Dostoevsky is of singular importance for determining his place in Russian literature, it is not my intention to deprecate Tolstoy or to suggest that there are no other sources of inspiration for his art. On the contrary, I find myself in agreement with those who, like Deming Brown, define his art as a synthesis of several trends of the Russian literary tradition. Noting that among the sources for his art there have been mentioned such diverse models as Tolstoy and Dostoevsky, Leskov and Turgenev, Saltykov-Shchedrin and Chekhov, Pilniak and Babel, Melnikov-Pechersky and Bunin, Remizov and Klychkov (one must add to this list the Russian symbolists and especially the Acmeists),[2] Professor Brown called Solzhenitsyn "a synthesizer, who partakes of many influences and adds much that is his own." As, on the other side of the Atlantic, Heinrich Böll described this synthesis, "It has the sweep of Tolstoy and the spirit of Dostoevsky." However, differing from Professor Brown and many others who insist on "the predominant influence"[3] of Lev Tolstoy, I think that Solzhenitsyn's assimilation of Dostoevsky's polyphony into his art not only provides the most essential component of this synthesis, but also serves as a catalyst that makes such a synthesis possible. Just as in his fiction, Solzhenitsyn demonstrates his ability to hear, understand, and imitate the voices of his characters, so in actual life he has proved himself an artist capable of absorbing different artistic "voices," and recreating them in a new synthesis.

Among the "voices" he has assimilated, an important one belongs to what Mochulsky generalized under the name of descriptive art. Although apparently unfamiliar with the work of Bakhtin, Mochulsky came to the same conclusion, that Dostoevsky's art was distinctly different from that of his great contemporaries Tolstoy, Turgenev, and Goncharov. Following in the footsteps of Merezhkovsky and Vyacheslav Ivanov, Mochulsky called Dostoevsky's art expressive in contradistinction to the descriptive art of his contemporaries:

> His art is contrary to the poetics of Tolstoy, Turgenev, Goncharov: against the *statics* of descriptions and history he advances the *dynamics* of events—movement, action, struggle.

> To the principle of descriptiveness he opposed the principle of expressiveness (that which he called poetry); to the epic—the drama, to contemplation—inspiration. Descriptive art reproduces a natural given: it is directed to the sense of measure and harmony, to the Apollonian principle in men; its summit lies in impassionate, aesthetic contemplation; expressive art tears itself away from nature and creates a myth about man: it calls upon our will and questions our liberty; it is Dionysian and its summit is tragic inspiration. The first is passive and natural, the second active and personal; we admire one, participate in the other. One glorifies necessity, the other affirms freedom; one is static, the other dynamic.[4]

In his three polyphonic novels, Solzhenitsyn has fused together the expressive and the descriptive principles, the dynamic and the static, the Dionysian and Apollonian, the dramatic and the epic, the Dostoevskian and the Tolstoyan; in short, the two kinds of art that have been, since the nineteenth century, considered mutually exclusive. The polyphonic novel as well as the characteristics of the Menippean genre afforded Solzhenitsyn the form in which such a fusion, such a synthesis, could best succeed.

As George Steiner observes in his brilliant book pointedly entitled *Tolstoy or Dostoevsky*, the two writers "exercise upon our minds pressures and compulsions of such obvious force, they engage values so obviously germane to the major politics of our time, that we cannot, even if we should wish to do so, respond on purely literary grounds."[5] This must be even more true of Solzhenitsyn who has been, and inevitably will continue to be, considered in relationship to his two great predecessors. As to the nature of their contrarieties, Steiner noted that the Russian symbolist poet, novelist, and literary critic Dmitry Merezhkovsky (1865–1941), who "was probably the first to consider Tolstoy and Dostoevsky in contrast to each other," did not consider them irreconcilable. Indeed, Merezhkovsky hoped that—in Steiner's words—"there would come a time when Tolstoyans and Dostoevskyans would join forces." Merezhkovsky himself expressed this hope:

> There is a handful of Russians—certainly no more—hungering and thirsting after the fulfillment of their new religious Idea: who believe that in a fusion between the thought of Tolstoy and that of Dostoevski will be found the Symbol—the Union—to lead and revive.[6]

Although Steiner remained rather skeptical about the likelihood of such a fusion, and concluded his book by saying that Tolstoy and Dostoevsky are "irremediably at odds," both as thinkers and as artists,[7] we may well be witnessing that fusion, that synthesis, taking place before our eyes, in the art of Solzhenitsyn.

As to a name for this synthesis, if great art needs any special name at all, I think it may be called *spiritual realism*. While the noun *realism* here implies a commitment to a truthful depiction of all the visible, tangible, rational, and material reality surrounding an artist, the adjective *spiritual* implies a recognition of, a concern for, and a will to express artistically, a spiritual reality—immaterial, invisible, intangible, perhaps irrational, and yet just as real. One emphasizes the topical, social, changeable, and temporal; the other emphasizes the constant, all-human, immutable, and eternal. One describes current human affairs; the other interprets them *sub specie aeternitatis* and turns them into myths. One finds facts; the other looks for their symbolic significance. One grows with the growth of the world; the other opens new vistas through insight, imagination, fantasy, and hypotheses. One provides firm ground under a writer's feet; the other allows him to fly weightlessly and at will. One informs; the other offers guidance. One is based on knowledge; the other on faith. One is rooted in a particular time, and appeals to a nation, to a generation; the other is addressed to each man and to mankind, future, past, and present. More specifically, while *realism* suggests a continuation of the tradition of social criticism, *spiritual* suggests a rebirth of Dostoevsky's concern for a "higher reality." Joined together, the words *spiritual realism* mean a recognition of different ways of measuring the same world; they also mean the artistic affirmation of such a coexistence. Such a synthesis has been attempted by many, achieved by few. Solzhenitsyn is among the few.

Coming back to the question raised by Sinyavsky, the answer is no, Solzhenitsyn's dedication to truth has not interfered with his thought and imagination but rather stimulated them, and his art is not a mere return to so-called critical realism but represents a significant step beyond the achievements of the nineteenth century.

Notes

Introduction

1. See, for example, the articles by Milton Ehre, Kathryn Feuer, Mary McCarthy, and Philip Rahv in *Aleksandr Solzhenitsyn: Critical Essays and Documentary Materials*, ed. John B. Dunlop, Richard Haugh, and Alexis Klimoff (Belmont, Mass.: Nordland, 1973) (hereafter cited as Dunlop, *Solzhenitsyn: Critical Essays*); and Kathryn Feuer's introduction to her *Solzhenitsyn: A Collection of Critical Essays* (Englewood Cliffs, N.J.: Prentice-Hall, 1976) (hereafter cited as Feuer, *Solzhenitsyn: Collection*).

2. Gustaw Herling-Grudziński, "Realism rosyjski," *Kultura* (Paris), no. 10/252 (October 1968), pp. 131–42, esp. 133; Ludmila Koehler, "Eternal Themes in Solzhenitsyn's 'The Cancer Ward,'" *Russian Review* 28, no. 1 (1969): 53–65, esp. 55; Dorothy G. Atkinson, "Solzhenitsyn's Heroes as Russian Historical Types," *Russian Review* 30, no. 1 (1971): 1–16, esp. 9; Edward J. Brown, "Solzhenitsyn's Cast of Characters," *Slavic and East European Journal* 15, no. 2 (Summer 1971): 153–66, esp. 158; Leonid Rzhevsky, *Tvorets i podvig*, p. 76; Abraham Rothberg, *Solzhenitsyn: Major Novels*, p. 133; David Burg and George Feifer, *Solzhenitsyn*, pp. 240–41; Henning Falkenstein, *Solschenizyn*, passim; Christopher Moody, *Solzhenitsyn*, passim.

3. An exception is the article "Solzhenitsyn and Dostoevsky" by James M. Curtis, in *Modern Fiction Studies* 23, no. 1 (Spring 1977): 133–51, which was brought to my attention after this study had been completed. Curtis offers a very perceptive reading of Solzhenitsyn. I like his treatment of the writer in the light of T. S. Eliot's observation that "the most contemporary artist is at once the most traditional," and I agree with his unorthodox conclusion that "while Solzhenitsyn learned much from Tolstoy, Dostoevsky's themes and compositional structures proved more useful to him." I am also pleased to discover that his article is full of minute observations which coincide with my own. However, Curtis treats polyphony as merely an instance of the affinity between the two writers rather than

as its ideational basis, my assertion in this study. See also V. Seduro, "Solzhenitsyn and the Traditions of Dostoevski's Polyphonic Novel," *Sovremennik*, nos. 32–34 (1976–77).

4. This is noticeable even among critics who have applied the term "polyphonic" to Solzhenitsyn's work. Thus Herling-Grudziński seems unaware of its origin; Edward Brown, on the other hand, while noting that Solzhenitsyn may have been suggesting his affinity with Dostoevsky, does not explain why, and erroneously calls the interviewer a Yugoslav journalist.

5. See the extracts from Ličko's interview in *Solzhenitsyn: A Documentary Record*, ed. Leopold Labedz, pp. 10–15.

6. Pavel Ličko, "Jedného dňa u Alexandra Isajeviča Solženicyna: Literarna tvorba a umelecké názory," *Kultúrny život* (Bratislava), 31 March 1967. Significantly, although Solzhenitsyn himself did not include his interview with Ličko among the documents published in *Bodalsia telenok s dubom* (The calf butted the oak) because Ličko had apparently violated the writer's confidence on some other occasion (see Labedz, p. 10n), he offers there his earlier interview with Mr. Komoto of Japan, in which he also described his favorite genre as polyphonic (*Bodalsia*, p. 484).

7. M. Bakhtin, *Problemy tvorchestva Dostoevskogo*, (Leningrad: Priboi, 1929); 2d ed., rev. and enl. as *Problemy poètiki Dostoevskogo* (Moscow: "Sovetskii pisatel'," 1963); trans. R. W. Rotsel as *Problems of Dostoevsky's Poetics*, (Ann Arbor, Mich.: Ardis, 1973); V. N. Voloshinov, *Marxism and the Philosophy of Language*, trans. L. Mateika and I. R. Titunik (New York: Academic Press, 1973); idem, *Freudianism: A Marxist Critique*, trans. I. R. Titunik (New York: Academic Press, 1976); P. N. Medvedev and M. M. Bakhtin, *The Formal Method in Literary Scholarship: A Critical Introduction to Sociological Poetics*, trans. Albert J. Wehrle (John Hopkins University Press, 1978).

8. Most of the biographical information in this paragraph was provided to me by Dr. Michael Holquist of the University of Texas at Austin who generously let me use the notes for his forthcoming book on Bakhtin. He is inclined to believe that Bakhtin himself was the author of the aforementioned books of the "Bakhtin school."

9. A. V. Lunacharsky, "O mnogogolosnosti Dostoevskogo" [About Dostoevsky's polyphony], *Novyi mir* 10 (1929); reprinted in his *Stat'i o literature* (Moscow, 1957).

10. Bakhtin was neither the first nor the only one to have applied

the musical term "polyphonic" to the study of literature. The French symbolists had done so before him, and Roman Ingarden used it at about the same time (in *Das literarische Kunstwerk*, 1932). Bakhtin himself acknowledged borrowing it from V. Komarovich. He warned, however, that the term should be understood only "as a figurative analogy" serving "to indicate the new problems that arise when the structure of a novel goes beyond the limits of ordinary monological unity" (Bakhtin, *Problemy poètiki*, p. 29).

11. Victor Erlich, *Russian Formalism: History and Doctrine*, 2d ed. (London, The Hague, Paris: Mouton, 1965), p. 251. According to Krystyna Pomorska, Bakhtin's book on Dostoevsky "clearly belongs to the second phase in the development of the Russian Formalist school, the Structuralist phase," and "he actually treats a literary work structurally, definitely in accordance with Tynianov's and Jacobson's procedure" (see her foreword to Bakhtin's *Rabelais*, pp. iv, ix).

12. Bakhtin, *Problemy tvorchestva*, p. 3.

13. As to how these notions are used by Bakhtin see, for example, pp. 41, 43, and 50 of *Problemy tvorchestva*.

14. According to the entry on personalism in *Bol'shaia Sovetskaia Entsiklopediia* [Great Soviet encyclopedia], it is "a modern reactionary and idealist philosophy [designed to reduce] the class struggle and the national liberation efforts to a spiritual conflict inherent, as it were, in each man's soul." In the entry on pluralism we find that it is an "antiscientific point of view" opposed to the "scientific materialist world view," and espoused by such "ideologists of American imperialism" as B. P. Bowne (1847–1910), William James (1842–1910), and John Dewey (1859–1952).

15. Bakhtin, *Problemy tvorchestva*, p. 242.

16. Solzhenitsyn includes "the outstanding literary scholar M. M. Bakhtin" among the Soviet intellectuals arrested in 1929 in *The Gulag Archipelago* (New York: Harper and Row, 1974), p. 51.

17. See n. 7.

18. Bakhtin, *Problemy poètiki*, p. 108.

19. Ibid., p. 361.

20. Mihajlo Mihajlov, *Moscow Summer (1964)* (New York: Farrar, Straus and Giroux, 1965), pp. 26–27.

21. *Literaturnaia gazeta*, 11 July 1964.

22. Ibid., 6 August 1964.

23. Significantly, Yurii Mal'tsev in his *Vol'naia russkaia litera-tura, 1955–1975* [Free Russian literature] (Frankfurt am Main: Possev, 1976) points out a polyphonic quality in Andrey Platonov's novels and acknowledges a polyphonic tendency in Vladimir Maximov's *Seven Days of Creation*. An earlier trend toward polyphony may be also seen in Yevgeny Zamyatin's *We* and Mikhail Bulgakov's *Master and Margarita* (with its strong Menippean characteristics), and in the conception of Andrey Sinyavsky's *Golos iz khora* (in trans. as Abram Terts [Andrei Sini'avskii], *A Voice from the Chorus*, [New York: Farrar, Straus and Giroux, 1976]).

24. I am fully aware of the later, ninety-six-chapter, version of this novel which the author prefers. However, since he did not dis-avow the earlier version, with which most of the book's readers are familiar and which helped him to win the Nobel Prize, I feel free to base my research on it. Besides, significant as they are, those additional chapters that have appeared in the Russian émigré magazines, *Kontinent*, no. 1, and *Vestnik*, nos. 111–14, do not necessitate any revision or alteration of my thesis.

Chapter I

1. The numbers indicate the chapter and page number in the Bantam edition of the Whitney translation. Slight emendations in translation are occasionally made by the present author.

2. Bakhtin, *Problemy poètiki*, p. 7.

3. Ibid., p. 79.

4. The word "ideologist" should be understood as indicating a person committed to a certain attitude toward the world, not to a historically defined ideology.

5. Bakhtin, *Problemy poètiki*, p. 112.

6. Stalin is the only character in whose portrayal ethnic background plays a role. Yet, even there the emphasis is less on his being a Georgian than an oriental despot.

7. Fyodor Dostoyevsky, *The Brothers Karamazov*, trans. David Magarshack (Baltimore: Penguin, 1958), 1:295.

8. In his interview with Ličko (see Introduction, no. 6).

9. As Ivan Karamazov explains to Alyosha during their meeting at a tavern in book 5, *Pro and Contra*, "the Russian boys" are bound to talk only "about eternal questions: Is there a God, is there

immortality? And those who do not believe in God? Well, those will talk about socialism and anarchism and the transformation of the whole mankind in accordance with some new order." And once they conceive of an idea, they will believe in it as passionately as a Shatov, "so their whole lives pass afterward as though in the last agonies beneath a stone that had fallen on them and already half-crushed them."

10. Bakhtin, *Problemy poètiki*, p. 124.

11. Fyodor Dostoevsky, *The Possessed*, Signet Classics, p. 385.

12. Ibid., p. 384.

13. See Introduction, n. 15.

Chapter II

1. Fyodor Dostoyevsky, *The Brothers Karamazov*, trans. David Magarshack (Baltimore: Penguin, 1958), 1:297.

2. Ibid., 1:305.

3. The Cathedral of Christ the Savior in Moscow was, in fact, blown up on Stalin's order in 1929. The Palace of Soviets was planned to be erected in its place. However, the construction was delayed and eventually, after the dictator's death, an open-air swimming pool was built in the pit.

4. Dostoyevsky, *Brothers Karamazov*, 1:297.

5. Ibid., 1:306.

6. Edward J. Brown, "Solženicyn's Cast of Characters," *Slavic and East European Journal* 15, no. 2 (Summer 1971): 164, 165, 161, 162–63.

7. Alexander Schmemann, "O Solzhenitsyne," *Vestnik* 4, no. 98 (1971): 81.

8. Dorothy G. Atkinson, "Solzhenitsyn's Heroes as Russian Historical Types," *Russian Review* 30, no. 1 (1971): 9.

Chapter III

1. Dostoyevsky, *The Brothers Karamazov*, trans. David Magarshack (Baltimore: Penguin, 1958), 1:309.

2. Rubin's real, nonliterary model was Lev Kopelev, a Soviet literary critic, who had served his sentence together with Solzheni-

tsyn. Throughout the years he has retained his affection for Solzhenitsyn in spite of their ideological differences. According to David Burg and George Feifer, in the sixties Kopelev played "a substantial role in Solzhenitsyn's career" (*Solzhenitsyn*, p. 75), helping, for instance, with the publication of *One Day*. His memoirs of imprisonment, *Khranit' vechno*, were published in Russian in the U.S. and translated as *To Be Preserved Forever* (New York and Philadelphia: Lippincott, 1977).

3. Cf. Stalin's view of men as "blind puppies" looking for a bowl of "milk" in chapter II.

4. See, for example, the opinion of the *Times Literary Supplement* reviewer in chapter VII.

Chapter IV

1. As such he belongs squarely to the world of fiction in spite of the fact that Dmitry Panin, on whom Sologdin was modeled, has accepted the portrayal as his own and even has published a book entitled *Zapiski Sologdina* (Frankfurt am Main: Possev, 1973), translated as *The Notebooks of Sologdin* (New York: Harcourt Brace Jovanovich, 1976). My comparison of Sologdin with Stavrogin is certainly not meant to reflect on the integrity of his model.

2. In actual life Dmitry Panin, who served his sentence at the sharashka concurrently with Solzhenitsyn, was released and partially "rehabilitated" at about the same time. Because of his outspokenness and ideological heterodoxy, he was allowed to leave the USSR in 1972. Residing now in France, Panin has not ceased to oppose the Communist dictatorship, and came out with a series of books extremely critical of the regime. He has retained a deep attachment to Solzhenitsyn and was one of the first Russians to welcome him in exile.

3. Bakhtin, *Problemy poètiki*, p. 78. See also his subsequent discussion of what he calls the literary incompleteness (*literaturnaia nezavershennost'*) of Dostoevsky's characters.

Chapter V

1. All these details make Nerzhin the most autobiographical figure in Solzhenitsyn's fiction.

2. The engineer Sologdin rather calculatingly engineers his deal with Yakonov, and the philologist Rubin, his indulgence in poetry notwithstanding, conducts himself very "unpoetically" in the phonoscopy affair.

3. However, the same striving for knowledge that made Faust enter into his contract with the devil has kept Nerzhin from signing his. He wants to escape "the tentacles of cryptography" because he is afraid they would render his brain dead, his soul dried out: "What would be left then to think with? What would be left for learning about life?" (9:49)

4. Kathryn Feuer noticed that "the departing zeks are compared to Christ at Gethsemane, and Nerzhin's birthday is December 25," but failed to see "sustained Christian symbolism" in the novel. See her article "Solzhenitsyn and the Legacy of Tolstoy," in *California Slavic Studies* 6 (1971): 120n.

5. In Russian, the chapter's title is *Litseiskii stol*, an obvious allusion to Pushkin's celebrated poem of friendship at the lyceum where he studied. In Whitney's translation this allusion is lost.

6. One can only speculate as to whether there is any significance in the fact that just as Dante became "the sixth of the great company of intellect" assembled in the first circle of his *Inferno* (canto 4) when he was introduced by Virgil to Homer, Horace, Ovid, and Lucan, so Nerzhin/Solzhenitsyn became the seventh.

7. Bakhtin, *Problemy poètiki*, p. 130.

8. As such Nerzhin falls into the category of Russian "meek characters" (*smirnye*), distinguished by Apollon Grigor'ev from the "predatory" type (*khishchnye*), which he considered to be inspired by the West and "alien to us" (see *Sochineniia Apollona Grigor'eva* [St. Petersburg, 1876], vol. I, chap. 6).

Chapter VI

1. Gorky's notorious phrase, "Pity degrades men" ("Zhalost' unizhaet cheloveka"), is obviously alluded to here.

2. The quotation is from Ostrovsky's novel *How The Steel Was Tempered*.

3. Whitney mistakenly translates the Russian *nevestka* (daughter-in-law) as "his bride."

4. It cannot be overlooked that besides Innokenty, another man who is entirely innocent is arrested and going to meet the same fate.

Chapter VII

1. V. S. Pritchett, "Hell on Earth," *New York Review of Books*, 19 December 1968, pp. 3–5; Harrison E. Salisbury, "The World As A Prison," *New York Times Book Review*, 15 September 1968, pp. 37–41; Jeri Laber, "Indictment of Soviet Terror," *New Republic*, 19 October 1968, pp. 32–33; Donald Fanger, "Solzhenitsyn: Ring of Truth," *Nation*, 7 October 1968, pp. 341–42.

2. Maurice Friedberg, "The Party Imposes Its Will," *Saturday Review*, 14 September 1968, pp. 36–37, 116; C. J. McNaspy, review, *America*, 5 October 1968, p. 295; Mary Ellmann, review, *Yale Review* 59 (October 1969): 119–21.

3. Bakhtin, *Problemy poètiki*, p. 5.

4. "Infernal Machinery" (unsigned review), *Times Literary Supplement*, 21 November 1968, p. 1301.

5. Helen Muchnic, *Russian Writers: Notes and Essays* (New York: Random House, 1971), pp. 422, 426.

6. Solzhenitsyn is not alone in defining a polyphonic novel as a novel without a main hero. The Soviet *Kratkaia literaturnaia entsiklopediia* [Concise literary encyclopedia] (Moscow, 1968) lists "polyphonic novel without a main hero" among contemporary subgenres of the novelistic genre. See the entry on *Poetika*, vol. 5, p. 941.

7. Victor Erlich, for instance, considers it "a tribute to Solzhenitsyn's powers of characterization" that both Nerzhin and his ideological adversary Rubin "should be so thoroughly convincing, so richly credible. . . . If Nerzhin is a triumph of objectified introspection, Lev Rubin is a feat of empathy for the 'Other.'" "The Writer as Witness: The Achievement of Aleksandr Solzhenitsyn," in Dunlop, *Solzhenitsyn: Critical Essays*, p. 25.

8. Burg and Feifer, *Solzhenitsyn*, p. 75 and illustrations following p. 214.

9. In actual life Sologdin's prototype Panin has distinguished himself precisely by the "warrior" stance. According to a reviewer of his book *Zapiski Sologdina*, "Among numerous volumes of the memoirs about camps and jails this is the only book written not from the position of a victim, but from that of a *warrior*" (S. Goryanov, "S pozitsii bortsa," *Possev*, no. 4 [1974]).

10. One might perhaps expand the analogy to include Stalin as Fyodor Karamazov. Like him, Stalin is, in a sense, a "father" to

NOTES 211

the other characters. Quite in agreement with actual Soviet practice, he is referred to either as the Father of Eastern and Western Peoples or as *Pakhan*, a slang word meaning "damn old man" but mistranslated as "Plowman." Also like Fyodor, he vies with his "sons" in wooing the heart of Mother Russia. Perhaps at this point the analogy must end, for unlike *The Brothers Karamazov*, the novel is concerned not with a case of patricide but rather with the father's infanticidal drive.

11. Deming Brown, "*Cancer Ward* and *The First Circle*," *Slavic Review* 28, no. 2 (June 1969): 311; Georg Lukács, *Solschenizyn*, (Neuwied und Berlin: Luchterhand, [1970]), pp. 31, 36, 46, 72; Earl Rovit, "In the Center Ring," *American Scholar* 39 (Winter 1969): 170; Miroslav Drozda, "Románové umení Alexandra Solženicyna" [Solzhenitsyn's Novelistic Technique], in *Plamen* (Prague, 1969), 11, iv, p. 80.

12. Bakhtin, *Problemy poètiki*, p. 7.

Chapter VIII

1. Bakhtin, *Problemy poètiki*, p. 237.
2. Ibid., p. 21.
3. Ibid., p. 36.
4. Konstantin Mochulsky, *Dostoevsky: His Life and Work*, (Princeton, N.J.: Princeton University Press, 1967), p. 185. According to Mochulsky, Dostoevsky was hailed as a new Dante who had descended into a hell existing "not in a poet's imagination, but in reality."
5. Bakhtin, *Problemy poètiki*, p. 38.
6. Whitney's translation, however, conflates the two remarks and omits the reference to St. John, thus weakening the impression.
7. According to Burg and Feifer, the real setting was Marfino, "roughly ten miles north of the present Sheremetyevo International Airport" (*Solzhenitsyn*, p. 76n). In that case, Solzhenitsyn's shift to "Mavrino"—from Greek "mauros," a darkened one—is remarkable in symbolizing the sinister nature of the locale.
8. Bakhtin, *Problemy poètiki*, p. 42.
9. Pasternak, *Doctor Zhivago*, chap. 16, sec. 4.
10. Heinrich Böll, "The Imprisoned World of Solzhenitsyn's *The First Circle*," in Dunlop, *Solzhenitsyn: Critical Essays*, p. 225.

Chapter IX

1. Heinrich Böll, "Die verhaftete Welt," *Merkur* (Stuttgart) 23 (May 1969): 474–83. For an English translation, see Dunlop, *Solzhenitsyn: Critical Essays*.

2. Bakhtin also resorts to the Dantean image of a "mystical rose" to describe the structure of Dostoevsky's polyphonic novels: *Problemy poètiki*, p. 35.

3. Edward Brown, "Solzhenitsyn's Cast of Characters," *Slavic and East European Journal* 15, no. 2 (1971): 154.

4. Besides the four "novels" one can easily discern a *Bildungsroman* substratum, or a young generation novel, built into the book: the story of Rostislav Doronin and his love for Clara, his MGB supervisor and daughter of the prosecutor Makarygin. Traceable to at least nine chapters and interspersed throughout the book, this story gives added depth to the novel. However, since its protagonist is not among the five characters that I have analyzed individually, it has not been treated in the present study.

5. Robert Belknap, *The Structure of The Brothers Karamazov* (The Hague: Mouton, 1967), p. 57. On the use of the devices and especially on the significance of chapter titles, see James Curtis, "Solzhenitsyn and Dostoevsky," *Modern Fiction Studies*, 23, no. 1 (Spring 77): 133–51.

Chapter X

1. Bakhtin, *Problemy poètiki*, p. 339.

2. Ibid., p. 57.

3. There is, of course, no absolute division between ideological and dramatic dialogues. In the novel, ideological dialogues do sometimes have a certain dramatic function. Thus, the duel-debate between Sologdin and Rubin sets the former on a course of action by which he hopes to prove both his engineering talent and his ability to obtain freedom without having "to crawl on his belly," and it prompts the latter to review his past from an ethical viewpoint. Also Nerzhin's dialogue with the painter serves to strengthen his idealism and help him cut short his affair with Simochka.

4. Cf. Shigalyov's utterly monological approach. "I have become entangled in my own data," this socialist theoretician admits to his fellow revolutionaries, only to warn them that "any solution

of the social problem other than mine is impossible." Dostoevsky, *The Possessed*, trans. Andrew R. MacAndrew (New York: New American Library [Signet Classic], 1962), p. 384.

5. This Marxist axiom occurs in the novel on two other occasions, in chapters 39 and 58. Each time it boomerangs against the system allegedly founded on it: Rostislav uses it to explain his "criminal" record; his girl friend Clara, contrapuntally, to reproach her father, who claims to represent the "proletariat," for not having even "a hammer in the house." However, Whitney translates the Russian *bytie opredeliaet soznanie* differently each time and thus weakens the impact of repetition.

6. Rzhevsky quotes, for example, Sologdin's thoughts about the people as if they were Solzhenitsyn's own and finds them in agreement with the ideas of Pasternak as expressed by Vedenyapin in *Doctor Zhivago* (*Tvorets i podvig*, p. 28).

7. Bakhtin, *Problemy poètiki*, p. 270.

8. Ibid., p. 266. Bakhtin uses the Russian *slovo* (translated here as the "word" but also meaning a "discourse") in contradistinction to *rech'* (speech). One should keep in mind that he does not suggest that the division between different "word" types is absolute, and he stipulates that a verbal expression can belong to different "word" types simultaneously.

9. Victor Erlich, "The Writer as Witness: The Achievement of Aleksandr Solzhenitsyn," in Dunlop, *Solzhenitsyn: Critical Essays*, p. 17.

10. Bakhtin, *Problemy poètiki*, p. 273.

11. Whitney's translation of the chapter title, "You Have Only One Conscience," fails to communicate the dialogic character of the original because it omits the word "also" which refers back to the Ostrovsky quotation. Therefore, the translation sounds didactic and moralistic rather than dialogic.

Chapter XI

1. Bakhtin, *Problemy poètiki*, p. 135.
2. Ibid., p. 241.
3. Ibid., p. 164.
4. Helen Muchnic, "Cancer Ward: Of Fate and Guilt," in Dunlop, *Solzhenitsyn: Critical Essays*, p. 292.

Chapter XII

1. The chapter and page numbers refer to the Bethell and Burg translation in the Bantam edition. Occasional emendations of the translation are made by the present author.

2. During a press conference in Stockholm after he had received the Nobel Prize in December 1974, Solzhenitsyn reproached Western literary critics for wanting to identify him with socialist ideas. He pointed out, for instance, that contrary to their opinion even Shulubin, with his ethical socialism, "is entirely opposite to the author" (see Yury Mal'tsev, *Vol'naia russkaia literatura, 1955–1975* [Free Russian literature, Frankfurt am Main: Possev, 1976], p. 361).

3. As Solzhenitsyn explained in an interview with Nikita Struve, he had to expand the time limits of the novel to several weeks because the process of illness could not have been shown in a matter of three days (see *Vestnik*, no. 120 [1977], p. 135).

4. Solzhenitsyn, *Sobranie sochinenii*, 6:52–53.

5. Victor Erlich, "The Writer as Witness," in Dunlop, *Solzhenitsyn: Critical Essays*, p. 20.

6. George Nivat, "On Solzhenitsyn's Symbolism," in Feuer, *Solzhenitsyn: Collection*, p. 49.

7. Michel Aucouturier, "Solzhenitsyn's Art," ibid., p. 26.

8. Solzhenitsyn, *Bodalsia telenok s dubom*, p. 484.

9. It is no accident that in his interview with Struve (see n. 2 above) Solzhenitsyn praised Akhmatova for the laconism and density of her poetic expression.

10. Solzhenitsyn, *Bodalsia*, p. 484.

11. In *The First Circle* Solzhenitsyn makes Nerzhin ask apropos of Stalin, "Why should a butcher try to be a therapist?" (5:26). (See also chapter V of this study.)

Chapter XIII

1. See, for example, the articles by Ehre, Feuer, McCarthy, and Rahv in Dunlop, *Solzhenitsyn: Critical Essays*; Kathryn Feuer's introduction to her *Solzhenitsyn: Collection*; and Sidney Monas, "Fourteen Years of Aleksandr Isaevich," *Slavic Review* 35, no. 3 (September 1976).

2. The two page numbers, separated by a solidus, refer respec-

tively to the original Russian edition and the Bantam edition of Michael Glenny's translation (see Bibliography). References to the Russian original are necessitated because Glenny's translation has often been emended by the present author.

3. Lev Tolstoy, *What is Art?* (London: Oxford University Press, 1962), p. 141. See also Richard Haugh, "The Philosophical Foundations of Solzhenitsyn's Vision of Art," in Dunlop, *Solzhenitsyn: Critical Essays*, pp. 168–84.

4. Present author's translation.

5. N. Gumilyov, *Sobranie sochinenii v chetyrekh tomakh* [Collected works in four volumes], ed. Gleb Struve and Boris Filippov (Washington, D.C.: Victor Kamkin Bookstore, 1962), 1:55.

6. Although chapter 22 was omitted by Solzhenitsyn from the original edition and later published in *Lenin in Zurich*, it is considered here as an integral part of *August 1914*. The numbers refer to the chapter and pages of the original, *Lenin v Tsiurikhe*, and of its English translation (see Bibliography).

7. The ambivalence of Solzhenitsyn's attitude toward Samsonov is now documented in his memoirs, *Bodalsia telenok s dubom* (The calf butted the oak), where he draws a remarkable parallel between Samsonov and his friend, the late Soviet poet A. T. Tvardovsky, erstwhile editor of the "liberal" magazine *Novyi mir*. In a footnote to his account of Tvardovsky's forced resignation from the magazine, he writes: "I was told about the scene [of his departure] at the time when I was about to describe Samsonov's farewell to his troops. Suddenly I realized both the likeness of the two scenes and a strong similarity between the two characters: the same psychological and national type, the same inner grandeur, 'bigness,' and purity—but also the same practical helplessness and lagging behind their time; and the same aristocratic deportment, natural to Samsonov, but contradictory in Tvardovsky. Then I began to explain Samsonov to myself through Tvardovsky and vice versa—and understood each of them better" (*Bodalsia*, p. 303n).

8. Although in his interview with Nikita Struve the writer refrained from using the word "polyphony," he described his novelistic strategy in the same terms he had used in his interviews with Ličko and Komoto. Apropos of *August 1914* and the rest of the cycle he said: "Certainly there will be no single hero. That's my principle: a single person, with his views and attitudes, cannot reflect the totality of events and their meaning. There must be a dozen heroes, the favorite and leading ones; but the total number of characters is in the

hundreds while Russia herself is the chief heroine [of the cycle]"
(see *Vestnik*, no. 120 [1977], p. 143).

9. (1) 9:71/80; (2) 63:541/675; (3) 15:137/166; (4) 53:463/
581; (5) 61:528/659; (6) 22:30/30 (*Lenin in Zurich*); (7) 53:467/
586; (8) 62:577/670; (9) 42:376/474; (10) 58:503/630; (11)
21:189/231; (12) 64:553/691.

10. Dunlop, *Solzhenitsyn: Critical Essays*, p. 480.

11. George Steiner, *Tolstoy or Dostoevsky: An Essay in the Old
Criticism* (New York: Vintage, 1961), pp. 276, 274.

Conclusion

1. Abram Terts [Andrei Siniavskii], *On Socialist Realism* (New
York: Pantheon, 1960), p. 94.

2. In the interview with Nikita Struve, Solzhenitsyn said that
among all Russian classics he felt "closest" to Pushkin whom he
called a "guiding star." Among his modern "teachers" he named
the poet Marina Tsvetaeva (1892–1941) and the novelist Yevgeny
Zamyatin (1884–1937), both of whom he praised for creating works
of "high artistic density." I feel that these artistic preferences in no
way invalidate or detract from my basic thesis of Solzhenitsyn's
affinity with Dostoevsky. Quite to the contrary, his admiration for
Pushkin echoes that of Dostoevsky, and his interest in the two pio-
neers of modern Russian poetry and prose corroborates my conten-
tion that he is a much more innovative artist than is usually assumed.
Although he named neither Tolstoy nor Dostoevsky among his
"teachers," it was the latter whom he praised for the ability to treat
spiritual and ethical problems in a "sharper, deeper, more modern
and more providential way." As I have contended all along, Solzhenitsyn's relationship to Dostoevsky is a case of affinity rather than
of influence or conscious imitation (*Vestnik*, no. 120 [1977], pp.
155–56; see chapter XIII, n. 9).

3. According to Deming Brown, "Solzhenitsyn, like Tolstoy, is
sparing in his use of figurative language; he gives things their exact
right names and lets them stand for themselves. His occasional sim-
iles and metaphors are precise, clear, and disciplined, and only rarely
is there a full-fledged symbol. Like Tolstoy he is amazingly alert to
the relevance of the objects that surround daily life. . . . Tolstoyan
stylistic devices abound—long, one-sentence paragraphs . . . with
carefully balanced series of dependent clauses, word repetitions, and

strings of parallel prepositional phrases and verb forms. Similarly, Solzhenitsyn does not shy away from involved syntax and parenthetical interpolations" (see his article "Cancer Ward and The First Circle," *Slavic Review* 28, no. 2 [June 1969]: 304–5). Even if all of the above were true, it is hardly enough to call Tolstoy "the predominant influence."

4. Konstantin Mochulsky, *Dostoevsky: His Life and Work*, trans. Michael A. Minihan (Princeton: Princeton University Press, 1967), pp. 433–34.

5. George Steiner, *Tolstoy or Dostoevsky: An Essay in the Old Criticism* (New York: Vintage, 1961), p. 321.

6. D. S. Merezhkovsky, *Tolstoi as Man and Artist, with an Essay on Dostoevski* (London, 1902): cited in Steiner, p. 322.

7. Steiner, p. 322.

Select Bibliography

I. Works by Solzhenitsyn

In Russian

Avgust chetyrnadtsatogo (10–21 avgusta st. st.), Uzel 1. Paris: YMCA-Press, 1971.

Bodalsia telenok s dubom. Paris: YMCA-Press, 1975.

Interv'iu na literaturnye temy s N. A. Struve. *Vestnik Russkogo Khristianskogo Dvizheniia*. Paris, New York, Moscow, no. 120, (1977), pp. 130–58.

Lenin v Tsiurikhe. Paris: YMCA-Press, 1975.

"Nobelevskaia lektsiia 1970 goda po literature." *Grani*, no. 85 (October 1972), pp. 156–75.

Sobranie sochinenii, 6 vols. Frankfurt am Main: Possev, 1970. Additional chapters to *The First Circle* are to be found in *Kontinent*, Paris, no. 1 (1974) and in *Vestnik* (cited above), nos. 111–14.

In English

August 1914. Trans. Michael Glenny. New York: Farrar, Straus and Giroux, 1972; New York: Bantam, 1972.

Cancer Ward. Trans. Nicholas Bethell and David Burg. New York: Farrar, Straus and Giroux, 1969; New York: Bantam, 1969.

The First Circle. Trans. Thomas P. Whitney. New York and Evanston: Harper and Row, 1968; New York: Bantam, 1968.

Lenin in Zurich. Trans. H. T. Willetts. New York: Farrar, Straus and Giroux, 1976; New York: Bantam, 1976.

II. Works by and about Mikhail Bakhtin

Bakhtin, Mikhail. *Problemy tvorchestva Dostoevskogo*. Leningrad: Priboi, 1929. 2d ed., rev. and enl. as *Problemy poètiki Dostoevskogo*. Moscow, 1963. 3rd ed., 1972. Trans. R. W. Rotsel as

Problems of Dostoevsky's Poetics. Ann Arbor, Mich.: Ardis,
1973.
―――. *Tvorchestvo Fransua Rable i narodnaia kul'tura sredneve-
kov' ia i Renessansa.* Trans. Helene Iswolsky as *Rabelais and his
World.* Cambridge, Mass.: MIT Press, 1968.
―――. *Voprosy literatury i estetiki.* Moscow, 1975.
Seduro, Vladimir. *Dostoyevski in Russian Literary Criticism, 1846–
1956.* New York: Columbia University Press, 1957.

III. Books about Solzhenitsyn and His Art
(for articles, see chapter notes)

Barker, Francis. *Solzhenitsyn: Politics and Form.* New York: Barnes
and Noble, 1977.
Burg, David, and Feifer, George. *Solzhenitsyn.* New York: Stein
and Day, 1972.
Clement, Olivier. *The Spirit of Solzhenitsyn.* Trans. Paul Burns.
New York: Barnes and Noble, 1977.
Dunlop, John B.; Haugh, Richard; and Klimoff, Alexis, eds. *Alek-
sandr Solzhenitsyn: Critical Essays and Documentary Materials.*
Belmont, Mass.: Nordland, 1973: 2d ed., enl. New York and Lon-
don: Collier, 1975.
Falkenstein, Henning. *Alexander Solschenizyn.* Berlin: Colloquium,
1975.
Feuer, Kathryn, ed. *Solzhenitsyn: A Collection of Critical Essays.*
Englewood Cliffs, N.J.: Prentice-Hall, 1976.
Fiene, Donald M., comp. *Alexander Solzhenitsyn: An International
Bibliography of Writings by and about Him.* Ann Arbor, Mich.:
Ardis, 1973.
Labedz, Leopold, ed. *Solzhenitsyn: A Documentary Record.* New
York: Harper and Row, 1971.
Lopukhina-Rodzianko, T. *Dukhovnye osnovy tvorchestva Solzhe-
nitsyna* [Spiritual foundations of Solzhenitsyn's art]. Frankfurt
am Main: Possev, 1974.
Lukács, Georg. *Solzhenitsyn.* Trans. W. D. Graf. Cambridge,
Mass.: MIT Press, 1971.
Moody, Christopher. *Solzhenitsyn.* Rev. ed. New York: Harper and
Row, 1975.
Nielsen, Niels C., Jr. *Solzhenitsyn's Religion.* Nashville: Nelson,
1975.

Pletnev, R. *A. I. Solzhenitsyn*. Paris: YMCA-Press, 1973.

Rothberg, Abraham. *Aleksandr Solzhenitsyn: The Major Novels*. Ithaca, N.Y.: Cornell University Press, 1971.

Rzhevsky, Leonid D. *Solzhenitsyn: Creator and Heroic Deed*. Trans. Sonja Miller. University: University of Alabama Press, 1978.

Index

Abakumov, 26, 112, 113, 125
Acmeists, 167, 180; symbolism of,
 183, 184. *See also* Gumilyov,
 Nikolai
Akhmatova, Anna, 167
Anacrisis, 141, 158
Antichrist, 28
Antiformalism, 10
Anti-Semitism, 72
Apuleus, 141, 159
Avvakum (archpriest), 189

Babel, Isaak, 199
Bacon, Francis, 149
Bakhtin, Mikhail, 3–11 passim, 14,
 23, 52, 64, 79, 81, 83, 85, 87,
 95, 97, 109, 123, 138, 139, 146;
 biography of, 3–4; classification
 of "words," 131–32; and formal-
 ism, 4, 5, 6, 9–10, 205; rehabili-
 tation of work, 4, 7, 9; reviewed
 by Lunacharsky, 4, 9. Works on
 Dostoevsky: *Problemy poètiki
 Dostoevskogo*, 7–9; *Problemy
 tvorchestva Dostoevskogo*, 4–7.
 See also Bivocal "word," Dosto-
 evsky, Metalinguistics, Poly-
 phonic novel, Polyphony,
 Solzhenitsyn
Balzac, Honoré de, 8, 139
Bely, Andrei, 21
Bildungsroman, 212
Bivocal "word," 131–33, 179,
 181–82
Boethius, 141, 159
Bryusov, Valery, 180
Bulgakov, Mikhail, 21; *Master*

and Margarita, 206
Bunin, Ivan, 199
Burke, Edmund, 194

Caesarean plan, 27, 30
"Carnivalization of literature." *See*
 "Carnival world view"
"Carnival world view," 8, 138–39;
 elements of in *The First Circle*,
 139–40, 155; elements of in
 Cancer Ward, 154–57, 160–61
Cervantes, 8, 139
Chekhov, Anton, 134
Christ, Jesus, 25, 26, 28, 29, 56,
 57, 58, 60, 63, 83, 99, 100, 186
Christ figure, 55, 58, 60, 63, 66,
 117, 188
Christianity, 27, 62, 81, 99

Dante, *Divine Comedy*, 21, 31, 55,
 97, 103, 120, 121, 139,
 167, 209, 212; parallels with
 Solzhenitsyn's symbolism, 31,
 55, 76, 105–6; polyphony of,
 106; and title image of *The
 First Circle*, 103–7
De-Stalinization, 169
Don Quixote, 55
Donskoy, Dmitry, 52
Dostoevsky, Fyodor, 1–12 passim, 14, 18–20, 24–33 passim,
 50, 52, 62, 66, 79, 81, 84, 89,
 111, 115, 123, 127, 146, 149,
 151, 175, 188, 199; approach
 to characterization, 14–16; and
 "carnivalized literature," 8,
 138–39; creator of polyphonic

novel, 4–5, 6, 8, 139; "form-determining ideology" of, 6, 8, 167; relationship to Solzhenitsyn, 216. Works: *The Brothers Karamazov*, 83, 87, 88, 98, 119, 144, 153, 174, 193, 196, 210, 212; *The Devils*, 98, 160, 174, 195; *Diary of a Writer*, 190; "The Grand Inquisitor," 181; *The Idiot*, 98; *Notes from the House of the Dead*, 23, 98, 102; *Notes from the Underground*, 15. *See also* Bakhtin, Ideologists, Menippean satires, Polyphonic novel, Polyphony, Solzhenitsyn

Einstein, Albert, 9, 18, 19, 58, 61, 96
Enlightenment, 8, 9
Epicurus, 73–74, 75, 121, 127
Esenin, Sergei, 68, 160

Fedin, Konstantin, 10
Flaubert, Gustave, 166
Formalism, 4, 5, 6, 9–10, 205

Goethe, Johann Wolfgang von, 14, 21; *Faust*, 31, 39, 40, 55, 127
Gogol, Nikolai, 8, 21, 134
Goncharov, Ivan, 8, 107, 138, 200; *Oblomov*, 84
Gorky, Maxim, 135, 209
Grand Inquisitor, 11, 14, 21, 22, 24–32 passim, 83, 88
Grigor'ev, Apollon, 209
Gumilyov, Nikolai, 167, 180, 182–84; "The Legacy of Symbolism and Acmeism," 180

Homophonic novel, 4, 5, 7, 94–95
Huxley, Aldous, 142

Ideologists, 15, 16, 17, 21, 91, 129; definition of, 206
Ingarden, Roman, 205

Jews, 17, 61, 63, 89, 92, 113, 119, 140, 193

Kant, Immanuel, 126
Karamazov, Alyosha, 12, 19, 42, 60, 64–65, 66, 67, 83, 85, 87, 88, 91
Karamazov, Dmitry, 88, 91
Karamazov, Ivan, 12, 14, 18, 19, 35–36, 39, 42, 43, 77, 83, 87, 88, 91
Kipling, Rudyard, 184
Kirillov, 13, 19, 77, 92
Koestler, Arthur, 80
Komoto (interviewer), 166, 168, 204, 215
Kopelev, Lev, 89, 207, 208
Kropotkin, Prince Peter, 149

Lenin, Nikolai, 69, 112, 186–87, 189, 193
Lermontov, Mikhail, 21
Ličko, Pavel, 2, 10, 93, 204, 215
Lucian, 141, 159
Lunacharsky, Anatoly, 4, 9

Mandelshtam, Osip, 167
Marr, Nikolai, 120
Marxism, 32, 43, 61, 73
Marxism-Leninism, 37, 62, 135
Marxism-Leninism-Stalinism, 71, 136
Marya Timofeevna, 49, 50
Maupassant, Guy de, 166
Maximov, Vladimir, 206
Melnikov-Pechersky, 199
Menippean satires, 138–39, 141, 142, 154, 157, 160
Menippus, 141
Mephistopheles, 40
Metalinguistics, 131, 133, 179.

See also Bakhtin
Montaigne, Michel de, 62
Myshkin, Prince, 14

Napoleon Bonaparte, 27, 30, 33,
  34, 36, 113, 190, 193
Nevsky, Aleksandr, 49, 52
"Newspeak," 134–36
Newton, Isaac, 58, 61

Orwell, George, 115, 142
Ostrovsky, Nikolai, 71, 158;
  How the Steel Was Tempered,
  136, 209

Panin, Dmitry, 89, 208, 210
Parodia sacra, 140, 161
Pascal, Blaise, 58, 61
Pasternak, Boris, 21; *Dr. Zhivago*,
  82, 83, 85–87, 107
Personalism, 6, 8, 14, 205
Petronius, 141, 159
Pilniak, Boris, 199
Plato, 140, 167
Pluralism, 6, 8, 205
Poe, Edgar Allan, 8, 139
Polyphonic novel: coexistence in,
  6, 10; created by Dostoevsky,
  1, 4–5, 6–7, 8, 138–39; de-
  fined by Bakhtin, 4–5; defined
  by Solzhenitsyn, 2–3; dialogic
  nature of, 123–33; link with
  "carnivalized" literature, 8,
  138–42, 153–61. *See also*
  Homophonic novel, Menippean satires, Polyphony
Polyphony: as artistic innovation, 8;
  basic concepts of, 6; borrowed
  from music, 204–5; future of,
  6–7, 9–10; in other authors,
  206. *See also* Bakhtin, Dostoevsky, Personalism, Pluralism,
  Polyphonic novel, Solzhenitsyn
Porfiry, 78
Poskrebyshev, Aleksandr, 26

Pushkin, Aleksandr, 8, 21, 134,
  149, 153, 160
Pyrrho, 62

Rakitin, 30
Raskolnikov, Rodion, 14, 30, 77,
  78, 82
Robespierre, 36

Saltykov-Shchedrin, 199
Samizdat, 11
Sankhya, 54
Seneca, 141, 159
Sextus Empiricus, 62
Shakespeare, William, 8, 139
Shatov, 19, 77, 92
Shigalyov, 21, 22, 29, 212
Sholokhov, Mikhail, 84
Sinyavsky, Andrey, 97, 202; *A
  Voice from the Chorus*, 206;
  On Socialist Realism, 198
Socrates, 63, 141, 158; dialectical
  method, 158; dialogical technique, 140–41. *See also* Socratic dialogues
Socratic dialogues, 124, 125,
  138–39, 140–41, 154, 157,
  158. *See also* Anacrisis, Syncrisis
Solovyov, Vladimir, 21
Solzhenitsyn, Aleksandr: affinity
  with Acmeists, 167, 180,
  183, 184; attitude toward religion, 192; ethical socialism,
  149–50, 152, 171, 214; influence of other Russian writers,
  216–17; interviews with, 2–3,
  166–67, 168, 215–16; linked
  with Tolstoy, 1, 173–74, 203,
  216–17; on polyphony, 2–3,
  168; relationship to Dostoevsky, 216; on symbolism, 165;
  and spiritual realism, 201–2;
  as synthesizer, 199–202.
  Works: *Bodalsia telenok s*

dubom, 166, 204, 215; *The Gulag Archipelago*, 172, 182, 205; *Lenin in Zurich*, 189, 215; *Letter to the Soviet Leaders*, 193; "Nobel Prize Lecture" (epigraph), 87, 176, 196; *One Day in the Life of Ivan Denisovich*, 11, 19. *See also* Acmeists, Dostoevsky, Gumilyov, Komoto, Ličko, Pushkin, Struve, Tolstoy, Turgenev
Spinoza, 126
Stavrogin, Nikolai, 12, 13, 14, 45–52 passim, 92
Structuralist linguistics, 5, 205
Struve, Nikita, 215–16
Symbolists, 167, 199. *See also* Acmeists
Syncrisis, 141, 158

Tao, 62
Thinker (Rodin), 75
Tolstoy, Lev, 1, 8, 62, 81, 82, 85, 98, 107, 109, 119, 127, 134, 138, 145, 149, 199; aesthetic principle, 175; artistic strategy of, 184, 196–97; "histori-

osophy" of, 177–78, 195; as homophonic novelist, 7, 196; influence on Solzhenitsyn, 173–76, 203, 216–17; and sermonizing, 177, 196. Works: *Anna Karenina*, 84, 98, 152; "Death of Ivan Ilyich," 169; *Resurrection*, 84; *War and Peace*, 84, 98, 173, 174, 178, 190, 195, 196; "What Do Men Live By?" 158; "What Is Art?" 176
Tower of Babel, 76, 181, 184
Tsvetaeva, Marina, 216
Turgenev, Ivan, 4, 7, 8, 13, 107, 134, 138, 164, 200; "Asya," 164; *Fathers and Sons*, 84; *On the Eve*, 84
Tvardovsky, Aleksandr, 21, 215

Varro, 141, 159
Vedanta, 54
Verkhovensky, Peter, 30

Yevtushenko, Yevgeny, 198

Zamyatin, Yevgeny, 115, 142, 216
Zossima, Father, 83